Gods or Aliens?
Vimana and other wonders

Parama Karuna Devi

Jagannatha Vallabha Vedic Research Center

ISBN-13: 978-1720885047

ISBN-10: 1720885044

published by:

Jagannatha Vallabha Vedic Research Center

Website: www.jagannathavallabha.com

Anyone wishing to submit questions, observations,
objections or further information,
useful in improving the contents of this book,
is welcome to contact the author:

E-mail: jagannathavallabhavedic@gmail.com

phone: +91 (India) 94373 00906

Table of contents

Introduction

First of all we need to clarify that we have no objections against the idea that some ancient civilizations, and particularly Vedic India, had some form of advanced technology, or contacts with non-human species or species from other worlds. In fact there are numerous genuine texts from the Indian tradition that contain data on this subject: the problem is that such texts are often incorrectly or inaccurately quoted by some authors to support theories that are opposite to the teachings explicitly presented in those same original texts. Our book is meant to correct such misconceptions, and to present the perspective that we could call "orthodox", in the sense that it strictly respects the correctness of the original Hindu texts (from the Greek *orthos*, "correct").

Vedic manuscripts, traditionally written on palm leaves, had a rather short shelf life, and for the most ancient periods we must simply rely on the information handed down by tradition and reference quotes in more recent texts. Fortunately the Vedic system favored individualism in the transmission of knowledge, and therefore each one of the millions of qualifed *brahmanas* along the various ages was entitled to possess copies of all the original manuscripts: in this way a great number of texts have survived destruction, and books from very distant geographical locations can confirm each other about the accuracy of the text through cross verification. The versions of the Sanskrit texts published on internet are usually precise and reliable, but English translations are much more difficult to use because the existing versions were produced mostly by colonial indologists or by Indian scholars who studied in Christian missionary schools, where academic education was effected through English language with a strong anti-Hindu bias.

It is always better to prefer editions that include the original *devanagari* text, the transliteration (which could be laborious and sometimes difficult because of the *sandhi* rules), the dictionary meanings of each word, and a clear and simple literary translation with the possible different interpretations and levels of meaning. This is the format that we prefer to use in our own work. With the support of such books, even a reader who is not very expert in Sanskrit will be able to check the meaning of the words on some of the more efficient on line dictionaries, for example spokensanskrit.org, that has a triple search engine and approximation lists.

To determine the authenticity of a text, the Vedic system does not focus on the archeological and historical analysis, but on the consistency of the contents with the vast expanse of literature that has already been universally accepted by Vedic authorities, and especially on the consistency with the ethical and scientific principles (*dharma* and *vidya*) that constitute the life force of the entire ideological system. This is why the correct understanding of Vedic scriptures (which in our dissertation covers all the ancient Indian sacred literature, including the *Tantra*) can be taught only by a *realized* teacher, that is to say a person who has studied a sufficient quantity of original texts and has sincerely applied their teachings, thus attaining a direct vision (*darshana*) of the reality described by the texts. This paradigm shift is normally called illumination or realization, and it is the only true qualification of a *guru* (*tattva-vit*, "who knows the *tattva*") and a *rishi* (literally, "one who sees"). For a wider elaboration on these concepts and definitions, we invite our readers to peruse our publications on the subject of Hinduism and Vedic knowledge, and especially our ample work on *Bhagavad gita*, enriched with non-sectarian explanations.

Vedic scriptures and traditions deserve a serious and attentive study that presents them in a competent way, without trying to drag them down to a level of cheap denigratory science fiction for commercial or sensationalistic purposes. The result of presentations that are incompetent and approximative, if not downright biased, ends up being counter-productive for a serious research, and could discredit even the valid and legitimate points of those who question the old "politically correct" dogma of conventional history, that is based on the eurocentric colonialist approach conditioned by abrahamic ideologies. Of course we must protect the freedom of thought and expression, but this does not mean that all opinions should be considered equally valid irrespective of their contents and truth of the information on which they are built, because even "non-conventional" historians have the duty to engage in rigorous verification work.

This certainly does not mean that we cannot propose alternative theories to the official positions of mainstream academia that ignores "uncomfortable" archeological finds. On the contrary, it is important to circulate information and considerations that may be non-conventional but can help to shape a wider and deeper understanding of the antiquity of mankind, of the universe and of the very meaning of the search for knowledge - and of the original perspective of the civilizations that expressed it in accordance to the values they taught. In fact we believe that a truly scientific mentality must take into consideration all the existing data and objects and all possible explanations, and especially verify the contents of the ancient traditions of knowledge with the appropriate experiments, conducted correctly by following the procedures and modalities established by that tradition itself. This is the only method that can really work, as we can easily see if we apply a bit of common sense and we overcome intellectual dishonesty and cultural attachments.

We want to clarify that we have no objections also against science fiction as a literary genre that honestly presents itself as fiction. For the purpose of our dissertation we have defined the category of "science fiction" as including all the various branches that imaginatively construct alternative scenarios for history or politics, as well as all fantasy novels, both as books and in the form of films, videogames and so on. Just like the old folk stories, fairy tales and parables, modern story telling has a value that is proportionate to the level of wisdom and knowledge of the people who created them, and convey a view of both the inner and outer worlds that can be extremely useful as a metaphor of reality to facilitate individual and collective evolution. However, if the ideological foundations of a story are negative and degrading, the effect on the individual and on society will cause damage or even disaster to a degree that could appear dis-proportionate to those who underestimate the influence of these apparently innocent forms of entertainment especially on young and naive minds.

This is why the "mythological" figures of ancient civilizations (not just from India but from any other ancient culture) should be presented in fictional stories only by truly qualified persons or under the expert guidance of truly qualified persons, to avoid the risk of distorting their real meaning as religious symbols and thus further weakening the moral and spiritual fabric of society in general. Fooling around with the individual and collective subconscious through the propagation of negative or distorted myths has a deeply de-stabilizing effect, whether it is done simply out of ignorance, or out of greed for monetary or political profits, or even with more sinister intentions. In this regard, as an example, we can quote the explicit statements of the famous Giorgio A Tsoukalos, who on several occasions both in his TV show *Ancien Aliens* and elsewhere has emphatically declared "*the Gods do not exist*", which summarizes the logic behind his reasoning and the motivation of his work.

Many stories produced in the field of science fiction are fascinating, realistic or believable, brilliant, and sometimes they carry very valuable messages about ethical values, philosophy and society. They can help people widen their mental horizon, to see the "different" and unexpected with sympathy, to reflect on what could happen in the future at the individual and collective levels as a consequence of our actions today. Some particularly inspired science fiction work can come very close to a mythological vision - a symbolic story as a journey of inner transformation similar to the mysteric tradition - especially when it taps into genuine knowledge and wisdom, and develops a consistent and vast ideological and narrative structure that studies the universal archetypes and the fundamental human characteristics. We can mention in this regard the work of JRR Tolkien, Isaac Asimov, Gene Roddenberry, George Lucas and other less known authors.

Nonetheless, honest fiction does not claim to have the "final key" for the interpretation of all stories ever known by humans, it does not present one single door as true and authentic as opposed to all others described as false, especially when its direction leads to the erosion of the spiritual and ethical principles of human society. Everything is ok as long as fiction continues to call itself fiction. Problems start when fiction presents itself as a new revealed religion (by name or simply as a matter of fact) of a monolatric type - which means it excludes the validity of other more tolerant religions or tries to absorb them as secondary manifestations of the "true faith" - and sometimes trying to produce "historical/ archeological evidence" to support itself. We have a problem when someone tries to sell us a supreme absolute truth that actually consists of the fantasies of a writer (or a line of writers) presenting stories, scenarios and conclusions constructed specifically to "demonstrate" baseless theories and to stick the label of "false and irrelevant superstitions" on the deepest and most ancient cultural and religious traditions of the planet, yet still giving the impression of quoting them as authoritative references. In short, saying that the ancient Gods were simply tyrannical and war-mongering aliens is a seriously distorted and offensive view, and it must be exposed with a suitable rebuttal: re-establishing the proper knowledge and understanding of the original ancient tradition is the only form of "revolutionary fight" that does not entail any danger of individual or collective damage, but has the power to neutralize any oppression or conspiracy at any level.

There is no doubt that conventional history must be re-written, and we recognize the existence of very interesting data in the stories about extra-terrestrials or aliens. It is even possible that some personalities portrayed as Deities in some religious mythologies have been constructed from the stories of individuals who were not precisely divine, or who might even have been negative entities, as suggested by the theory of the Elohim/Annunaki. But this does not mean that one can take all the forms of religion and spirituality that ever existed on the planet and reduce them to mere alienism, or classify in the same "divine" category all the superhuman or extraordinary entities of all types - divine, demoniac or something else. Each personality, each tradition, each text must be examined accurately and individually to determine whether the conclusions justified in one case should be applicable to other cases as well. Otherwise we would be lumping up all sorts of things in a superficial and ignorant manner.

The same consideration also applies to the personal competence of researchers: for example if someone has invested time and effort to study the Bible in the ancient Hebrew, Coptic or Greek versions cannot automatically present himself as an expert in Sanskrit and in the Indo-Vedic texts such as *Vedas, Puranas, Mahabharata, Ramayana*, and certainly he cannot avoid to honestly and carefully verify his opinions with the direct original sources of Hindu tradition. Similarly, a person who has studied the history of Freemasonry does not automatically become an expert on the history of all past, present and future religions of the planet.

Of course if that researcher has not simply studied Freemasonry (or other occult organizations) but has become one of its members or supporter, we may suspect that his work might be a part of a specific plan of disinformation propaganda aimed at shaping the public opinion: see for example the interesting book *Externalisation of the Hierarchy* (published in 1957) by theosophist Alice A Bailey (1880-1949), where *externalisation* is the gradual preparation of the masses to accept a control system through the propaganda of the Establishment and the gradual presentation of an ideological scenario that had previously been kept secret to avoid alarming the people.

In this regard we can also mention *The hidden life in Freemasonry* (published in 1926), by the other famous theosophist Charles Webster Leadbeater (1854-1934), that speaks of interactions between non-human beings from other planets and freemasons of the 33rd level. Another interesting book is *Messaggi simbolici: introduzione allo studio della scrittura aliena* ("Symbolic messages: introduction to the study of alien writings", by Mario Pazzaglini), in which the analysis of over 150 cases shows that the alphabets presented as "alien" were actually manufactured from hermetic and enochian texts, typically used by the occultist-esoteristic disinformants.

The topic of extraterrestrials and ancient astronauts has become increasingly popular in the last few decades, but in spite of the production of many presentations (including multi-medial ones), very important pieces are still missing in the picture for a vast and complete perspective that can be accepted as realistic. There is a lot of available material in libraries and bookshops and even on internet, but not all information is reliable, and in fact the cumulative effect could cause confusion. Many researchers in the field have openly recognized that some of the circulating information is distorted or unfounded and often mixed with grossly false data, and this could mean that a deliberate disinformation campaign is afoot.

For the most part, the authors interested in the subject are coming from the field of ufology, where we can find over 20,000 events with recorded reports of sightings of unidentified flying objects and more or less humanoid beings supposed to be coming from other planets, often considered as technologically superior to humans but generally not explicitly and directly identified with divine or mythological figures.

On the other hand, some alienist researchers have explored the territory of occultism in various directions, especially on the wave of the colonialist romanticism developed since the 1800s - a current that collects fragments from various ancient religious traditions (Indian, Mesopotamian, Egyptian, hellenistic, mysteric, hermetic, kabalistic, gnostic, mystic, esoteric, alchemic) used and mixed, adapted and interpreted very freely and often superficially, for the purpose of demonstrating new theories that are supposed to be "revolutionary and illuminating" but usually end up creating confusion and fear, because the resulting picture is focused on occult and non-benevolent forces, that are at best indifferent towards the sufferings of the creatures they come in contact with. Such researchers are generally affected more or less consciously by some degree of cultural conditioning, because they tend to see everything through the lenses of abrahamic ideologies, projecting their criteria in an active or reactive manner and thus distorting the picture and the interpretation. This certainly damages or destroys the positive and useful aspects of non-abrahamic cultures, or makes them impossible or very difficult to understand correctly.

An active (or positive) projection presents the abrahamic concepts in a positive sense: it sees other cultures as inferior to abrahamic religions or as their imitations or derivatives, or at best as precursors of the "true faith", because the researcher identifies with the abrahamic ideology or considers it as a valid model. This is the position of the majority of authorities in conventional academia and mass media.

A reactive (or negative) projection is applied by those researchers who oppose the so-called superiority of the abrahamic paradigm or claim to be "neutral as non-believers", but continue to build on the foundations of the abrahamic versions, which they take for granted: thus we have the satanists of various kinds, the atheists who aggressively rant against all forms of spirituality (measured according to the abrahamic concepts and criteria) and those who want to demonstrate the falseness of all religions (Hinduism included) by explaining the Bible from the alienist perspective.

This particular type of synchretism, often perceived as innovative or revelatory, has led some adventurous speculators to create imaginative theories on the "Alien Gods of India", without having any real knowledge of the Hindu scriptures or tradition, and without respecting their correct meaning. Other traditions, too, have been treated with much superficiality and contempt by researchers, but there is no doubt that Hinduism is still the major target of cultural attacks. The defamation campaign against the Indo-Vedic tradition can still be quite successful today because of the lack of genuine information circulating among the public and especially because of the biased presentations created by conventional academics with the purpose of demonizing the "competition" to the abrahamic and post-abrahamic systems, as Hinduism is the last great ancient pre-abrahamic religion survived from the destruction of the past centuries, in a partially damaged but still uninterrupted tradition.

Our publication is meant to help solve this problem, especially by offering genuine information on the Indo-Vedic tradition, information that has been collected with utmost accuracy through almost half a century of personal study on the classical and historical material, and decades of direct research on the field and cross-verification, analysis of the original Sanskrit texts and comparison with a great number of experts especially in India and thousands of activists of the Hindu Renaissance developing in the last decades. In short, it is based on the mission and work of Parama Karuna Devi and our Jagannatha Vallabha Vedic Research Center, established in Jagannatha Puri, Orissa, India (see the Appendix for more details). The result is a logical and consistent synthesis, open to the examination of factors that may be less known by the general public but easily verifiable through the indications about the sources. Specifically for this publication we have invested a further effort to dig even deeper than usual, and in fact we have unearthed some extremely interesting pieces of information.

Another necessary clarification: our Tradition stresses the importance of actual facts and verification of information, but this does not mean that we should give the same value to all ideologies, schools of thought and authors of the various theories - something that would limit our study to the abstract and theoretical level, without any objective benefit or useful conclusion. In this and in all our publications, we observe and present the arguments in full respect for truthfulness, but according to the perspective of original Vedic culture, that usually is not seen in the academic world and even at the level of public opinion and popular media, which is unfortunate because the Indo-Vedic knowledge can be extremely valuable to solve the problems that we are facing today at global level.

This of course does not mean that we want to impose some dogma or beliefs to our readers, but when we speak of God it is absurd to totally rule out all theological interpretations, especially when expressed in authoritative manner, clearly and precisely in the original scriptures and not produced by later speculations of commentators that have introduced non-relevant sources. We invite our readers to continue the verification work directly and to communicate any information or discovery that may improve our presentations: we are determined to follow the genuine principles of scientific research in the best possible way.

The Indo-Vedic tradition radically differs from the Judaic-Christian mythology because the Bible (old and new testaments) does not contain philosophical or theological elaborations or scientific elaboration of advanced technologies that can tell the difference from natural or supernatural phenomena, and therefore it leaves a lot of space for the interpretations of the alienists. On the other hand, the vast original Vedic literature includes theological and philosophical treatises that are extremely deep as well as descriptions and explanations of very advanced technological products (of human/ terrestrial, non-alien origin), so before launching into imaginative elaborations to "explain" Indo-Vedic scriptures as alien-based, a researcher who is intellectually honest should properly engage in the study of the original sources to be able to verify the correctness of the information and beliefs.

We invite all interested readers to explore the subject of Indo-Vedic tradition by consulting our publications, especially the *Introduction to Vedic Knowledge* and the translation and ample commentaries on

Bhagavad gita. Our multi-volume work on *The Awakening of the Mother Goddess* and the Discovery of Natural Religion elaborates on the perspective of historical analysis of various cultures (especially ancient ones) with a comparative study of their different approaches to spirituality and religion and the various aspects of social and personal evolution - issues that we have only partially touched in the present book.

All our publications are available free of cost in electronic format, and at nominal cost in printed format (*printed on demand*, which is more economical than printing out the digital format at home); the solution we have chosen for the distribution of our literature enables us to easily manage new revised editions thus constantly improving the quality of our work, without depending on structures of political power of all types.

Interested readers are invited to correspond through email with the Center and with Parama Karuna Devi to present questions, new information, clarifications, and even proposals for cooperation in various fields.

E-mail: jagannathavallabhavedic@gmail.com

phone: +91 (India) 94373 00906

History or fiction

In the second volume of our work *The Awakening of the Mother Goddess* we elaborated on the problem of the lack of authenticity and credibility of conventional academic historians, an issue that requires a considerable amount of space in itself. But as the concept is extremely important also for the discussion on the true identity of the so-called aliens or extraterrestrials and for the study of ancient religions, we will repeat here some illuminating quotes to this effect.

* "And while telling the fables we have spoken about, because we do not know the truth on the past, but doing our best to approach invention to truth, are we not making it useful?", *The Republic*, Plato (428-347 BCE)

* "On how it can be legitimate and convenient to use falsehood as a medicine and for the benefit of those who want to be lied to", the title of a writing by Eusebius (260-340 CE)

* "History is the planks of a shipwreck; more of the past is lost than has been saved... the most ancient times that are buried in oblivion and silence", from *The wisdom of the ancients*, Sir Francis Bacon (1561-1626)

* "*Mais qu'est alors cette vérité historique, la plupart des temps? Une faible convenue*" ("But what is this historical truth, most of the times? A fable which we have agreed upon"), Napoleon Bonaparte, letter quoted in a biography (1830-1893)

* "Most history is guessing, and the rest is prejudice", from *Story of civilization*, Will Durant (1885-1981)

* "Who controls the past controls the future, who controls the present controls the past", from *1984*, George Orwell (1903-1950)

* "History is written by the victors", Winston Churchill (1874-1965)

Clearly, we cannot put much blind faith in the official version dished out by schools, encyclopedias and media, a version that it recognized as amply fallible and repeatedly questioned at the highest levels of the same official academic authorities. In short, the boundary between history and fiction often becomes blurred and is largely determined by the measure of institutional and political power of those who present a theory. We reject this view as fundamentally anti-scientific.

The genuine scientific approach demands a rigorous reseach and a honest analysis performed in the light of all the available and relevant information: this does not require high academic titles officially recognized by the government, or a detailed knowledge of all the wars, biographies and political events, generally less relevant, on which normally the conventional system insists. More than the lists of names dates and battles, we need a direct perception of the contents of the cultures we study, to clearly separate the objective data from the interpretations and reconstructions of the various commentators, that are only useful if examined as mere theories, and separately from actual facts.

It is therefore necessary for each individual to become responsible for his/ her own beliefs, without feeling compelled to choose a party, a school or a front of opinion to conform to, out of some ill-placed sense of loyalty or consistency. Human evolution must lead to an individual awareness of freedom, on which we can build a responsible and proactive inter-dependence of individuals and groups, as well as of cultures and ideas. Obviously we cannot attain such result simply by "switching party", even in the case the new party offers attractive electoral promises of freedom or liberation, independence, empowerment or a new, miraculous and supreme key to all knowledge. We must stop "following" and start developing our own intelligence and understanding.

To paint a clear and realistic picture of human history we must be very careful and collect information from several sources, giving preference to those that are more direct, verify them as much as possible, compare them and examine them through good sense and intelligence, trying to understand the motivations of the individuals and groups who speak about the issue, and analyzing the objective facts and the situation on the ground without being limited by second-hand rumors.

It is also very important to understand that we should not blindly reject all the information and content offered by conventional academia - in fact a critical approach in individual research cannot be separated from a careful exploration of all sources, especially in the most specialized area, where often illuminating controversies rise among academics of different opinions. Unfortunately such discussions usually remain out of reach for the greater public.

The best method consists in building individually a vision that is truly scientific, as much as possible objective and free from prejudice, learning how to recognize cultural superimpositions and becoming open-minded enough to see things in the perspective of those who have a different vision. It is important to analyze and understand each culture according to the perspective of its own ideological foundations, especially when we want to study non-abrahamic cultures. In fact the most frequent prejudicial bias consists in the abrahamic and post-abrahamic perspective, on which western academia has been built to start with.

In spite of the efforts invested by the Establishment to keep knowledge as a political prisoner, a growing number of people are sincerely trying to penetrate the barrier and cleave out some openings. Their efforts reinforce each other because even temporary or partial failures in this attempt can weaken the monolithic structure of the opposition front, and the work of subsequent waves of honest researchers will find more and more evident gaps on which to hammer forth and break through.

However, it is also true that the besieged guardians of the prison are constantly busy trying to fight back what they consider as illegitimate intrusions, especially by reacting with the time-proven technique of infiltration, hijacking or inculturation (*accomodatio*). So, with the widening of the breach in the academic monopoly controlled by the Establishment, we see that within the masses of people there is a new proliferation of sectarian and exclusive currents of belief (with pseudo-religious characteristics and often disturbing messages) or even openly alienist religions with a general abrahamic or post-abrahamic orientation, usually cloaked in a sort of cheap pseudo-science that is superficial or cleverly ambiguous, but pressing an excessive "cosmic" optimism and a vague and sugary mysticism that have become prominent characteristics of the so-called New Age of the commercial type.

Some alienists have come to the point of presenting extraterrestrials as a sort of wise and knowledgeable elder brothers, descended to Earth to save us from ourselves; psychologist Richard J Boylan (*Extraterrestrial Contact and Human Response*) presents them as a sort of spacemen working as *Medecins sans frontières* ("Doctors Without Borders"), engaged in some charity social work to assist the poor earthlings both materially and spiritually.

At the extreme opposite we find a thriving movement of belief that presents the darkest pessimism of the doomsday type on various levels - environment, society, culture, spirituality - with the result of de-sensitizing (and de-responsibilizing) the public opinion and spreading a sense of passive acceptance of bad things simply out of habit. Within this trend we can also categorize the new myths of the supernatural horror that support a sort of cult for Evil, with satanism and similar currents (vampires, zombies and assorted monsters) and even glorify or idealize psychological suffering, despair or degradation. This trend has been fueled by the spreading of the so-called heavy drugs and psychiatric medication, that are chemical psychotropic substances (artificial or synthetic) designed to confuse and dull the consciousness (rather than making it clearer as usually seen in the natural substances and techniques that work on the subtle level) and that produce dangerous vicious circles of addiction and toxicity. This issue, too, would require a long discussion that we cannot insert here.

We may be excused for wondering whether these two fronts that appear diametrically opposite (excessive optimism, excessive pessimism) could be actually manipulated more or less consciously by the same puppeteers-puppets and with the same motivations, since the focus of their cross-fire leads to the conclusion that the "aliens" (of whatever denomination, ever inter-dimensional) are Gods or Deities that should be worshiped (no matter whether they are "good" or "evil", as long as they are "superhuman") and that the Gods of all religions must be these same aliens, or else they must be considered as an illusory projection of disturbed and desperate minds, as suggested by a certain school of materialistic psychiatry.

According to this perspective, it is easy to reach the conclusion that *Homo sapiens* can only resign himself to the role of "human cattle" for which he was created and cooperate with his owners or creators and their representatives, making himself useful without complaining too much and possibly developing a bit of "healthy" masochism. It is a well-experimented model of business and power that started a few thousands years ago and that, albeit slightly modified at the surface, is still carried on as the very foundation of the concepts of religion, State, government, society and so on. Whether it is presented in the form of history or fiction, by some university professor or by some self-taught author, the result is the same.

Where are they taking us? This is what we should be concerned about.

To unravel the mystery, we need to properly analyze the events of the past. It is said that without really understanding history we are doomed to repeat it. We could add that without really understanding the direction in which we are traveling, we are inevitably destined to be led more or less passively to the destination that others have established for us, like sheep are led by shepherds. And rarely this is to the advantage of the sheep, especially in the long run.

Religion and mythology

In this book we compare the notions of God (Deva, divine personality, semi-divine personality, "God of good" and "God of evil", religion, spirituality and so on) and Aliens (extra-terrestrials, inter-dimensional entities, humanoids, non-humanoids, ancient astronauts, universal community and so on). As a strictly related topic, we will speak about ancient human civilizations and especially the Indo-Vedic knowledge in regard to aliens, spaceships and "forgotten" technologies that represent a true wonder for the greater part of the present population of the world.

To keep the present volume within a reasonable size, we have chosen to limit ourselves to the Gods of the Indo-Vedic tradition, without examining other religions except to sometimes highlight the differences or even incompatibilities on the ideological and cultural levels. It is possible that some characters in the mythologies of various cultures contain qualities that are compatible with alienist interpretations, but it is dangerous to make superficial generalizations, especially when the evidence of those cultures has been tampered and distorted along the centuries, and only a few fragments remain of the original texts. Therefore we are not particularly interested in the rebuttal of such interpretations in fields we are not precisely competent about, especially regarding religions that are relatively less ancient, such as the Greek (hellenic, hellenistic), Roman, Celtic-Norse and even Judeo-Christian, all of which have some cultural value, unlike the recent ideological hodgepodge products such as satanism, freemasonry, theosophy, antroposophy and so on.

Unfortunately many researchers and "experts" tend to manufacture a superficial and simplistic syncretism between various religions, leaning on vague etymological or iconographic similarities to support their pet theories and their cultural prejudice. It is a dangerous game, because artificial cultural superimpositions can produce veritable monsters, as it happens for example when we superimpose slides or transparencies of different images, or even simply images of the same object, photographed from different positions.

The point of this book is that some people claim that the Gods of the various religions are actually deified images of some humanoid extraterrestrials (entirely material and physical, with a precise genetic structure, made of "flesh and blood") who visited Earth in ancient times. A corollary of this hypothesis is the idea that such persons were not divine in the theological sense of immortal, transcendent entities, free from the material limitations of time, space and causality, and especially free from the defects that typical of human beings such as illusion, error, imperfect perception and judgement, defects and so on. This is not an entirely new idea.

The very same current of thought had alrady surfaced in the Hellenistic period in Alexandria, wiith Evemerus (or Euhemerus, Euemeros or Evemeras), born in Messenes (Messina) in Magna Grecia, about 330-250 BCE, who lived at the court of King Cassander of Macedonia, of whom he was a personal friend according to the chronicles of Diodorus Siculus. In his philosophical-utopistic fiction entitled *Hierà anagraphé* ("Sacred History", of which we can find only fragments from quotes, especially from Quintus Ennius) Evemerus claims that the Gods were simply human beings - heroes, kings, queens, warriors and so on - who distinguished themselves for their deeds and later were deified by some political or folkloristic mythological tendency. This extraordinary "discovery" was presented in the journal of an imaginary travel of the author to the (non-existing) island of Iera Pancaia in the Red Sea off the coast of Arabia, that he describes in 3 volumes of imaginative details as populated by a mixture of peoples including "oceanite" natives of 3 races besides Indians, Scythes, Cretans, all ruled by yearly magistrates and by a priestly class. In the history fiction of Evemerus, the "temple of Zeus Triphilius" of the main city of Panara has a pillar of gold with the inscription of all the biodata (birth, deeds and death) of the Gods of Greek Olympus, including Zeus himself. According to this imaginary "reconstruction", Uranus was the first king of the world; his legitimate heir Titan was overthrown by his younger brother Kronos who married his sister Rhea-Opis, with whom he generated Zeus, Hera and Poseidon. After ascending the throne, Zeus freed his emprisoned relatives (his Titan uncles) and had many children from several wives; with his ally the King of Babylon he conquered Syria, Cilicia and Egypt, a country where he received the title of Ammon, and after touring all the lands for 5 times, he finally retired to Pancaia and died of old age.

We do not intend to get deeper into this hypothesis especially here, either to support or to contradict it, although we could say that it is clearly a speculation devoid of any solid basis from the historical point of view and especially it contains serious discrepancies with the "classical" versions of olympic mythology both hellenic (classical Greek period) and hellenistic (synchretic Alexandrine period).

It is not difficult to accept the fact that the "historical" objection is in turn intrinsically weak, because absence of proof is not necessarily proof of absence, and it is not possible to establish that there have never been human beings "of flesh and blood" who had such names and performed similar deeds. We do not even want to deny that in the course of centuries and generations some stories probably based on actual objective facts may have been "embroidered" to become mythology, which consists of largely symbolic representations meant to convey moral, philosophical, spiritual teachings in a literarily attractive form, with a process similar to that of parables or fables, and with the superimposition of images and archetypal values that are universal and eternal.

Our basic objection is rather directed against the exclusively reductive minimalist interpretation of the origins of mythology as a principle, according to which all the Gods of the religions of the planet must be exclusively interpreted as an ignorant exaggeration of the activities of historical persons, individual and mortal, with serious personal limitations and little or no spiritual or wisdom value, whether such persons were human or extraterrestrial, or even malevolent rather than benevolent.

Such dogmatic and absolutist interpretation, grossly materialistic and simplistic, offends the natural feelings of any human being who naturally seeks a deeper and higher meaning in life and perceives a cosmic order, a universal harmony, a transcendental reality beyond superhuman realities, where the earthly or terrestrial level is simply one of the many levels of existence. Some "modernists" believe that a cynical and contemptuous approach is a symptom of intellectual or moral superiority, but it actually is an impoverishment of the human spirit and a basic degradation that can only cause discomfort both at the individual and at the collective levels.

According to the Natural Religion (and to the Vedic tradition, that contains the largest collection of information in this regard that still survives), existence in its entirety is a continuum of awareness that goes beyond space-time dimensions and where a human being can attain different levels of consciousness. This cosmic awareness, that each human being perceives more or less clearly as the omnipresent, omniscient, omnipotent, transcendental and eternal divine existence, is the origin and support or foundation of every thing and every manifestation, including the natural laws. It is not limited by birth, death, mass or position in a physical place, it does not have family or relatives, it does not have a "chosen people" or friends and enemies, it does not give orders or commandments or prohibitions, it does not give rewards or punishments, it is not offended or flattered, it does not make mistakes or repents or changes its mind, it does not engage in covenants or contracts or barters, it does not fight against other Deities, it does not need weapons or vehicles or clothes, it does not need offerings or foods or prayers, it does not need worshipers or followers, it does not care what human beings believe or do not believe, and is not particularly interested in the private lives or personal activities of people.

Nonetheless, the supreme Existence (also called "cosmic" or "universal" but certainly not "extraterrestrial") is conscious and intelligent, and can communicate or relate to the individual beings, who are all parts of its unlimited existence. It can also manifest in specific personalities and appear in various dimensions, but because it does not identify with the typical material limitations of space-time-individuality, its appearance and activities contain a great depth of meanings and purposes, and are always meant to support the universal community of all beings.

To make a crude example, we can compare these divine personal manifestations to a teacher who seems busy learning the multiplication table when he repeats it for the benefit of his pupils, or an actor-director who plays a highly symbolic role in a theater performance written by himself and meant to convey deep moral and philosophical teachings. If the teacher stops his recitation and asks a student to complete it, it is not because he does not know the result of the multiplication and needs suggestions. In the same way, the activities that the actor performs on the scene do not entail permanent consequences or real sufferings, and are not fortuitous or due to chance: each detail is calculated with precision and deliberately applied. And above all, in a cyclical way: in a school curriculum or in a school after another, in a drama performance after another, the script is substantially the same but sometimes with small circumstantial variations that "improve the taste" and make the exercise more interesting and convenient.

This cyclic manifestation that is controlled deliberately to convey messages is not admitted by the reductive perspective supported by Evemerus and his successors, down to Zecharia Sitchin and the other alienists. This reductive perspective may be applied to the figures that in abrahamic mythology are defined as angels or devils ("good" or "evil" individual beings) but certainly not to God (the Godhead) and his/her direct manifestations, that are eternal ontological entities on a transcendental level of consciousness.

Any human being, irrespective of the culture where s/he was born, is naturally able to understand the fundamental ontological principles, the archetypes, that all humans spontaneously carry in their language and intellectual projections. Some fundamental symbols and the vast part of the images are found in all cultures and are interpreted at the subconscious level, a little like deaf and dumb people or persons who do not know a local language are able to communicate instinctively or intuitively by gestures, with a non-verbal language that according to contemporary research often constitutes 80% of the power of communication among all individuals in general. This universal faculty non only covers the primary physical activities (eating, sleeping, sex, defending, heat, cold, joy, surprise, fear, and so on) but also metaphysical concepts such as good and evil, duty, inspiration, veneration, affection, harmony, transcendence, and so on. Besides the expressions of the body, of the hands and the face, and the "subtle vibrations" (feelings, emotions, empathy, pheromones and so on), human communication can be extremely effective through the use of images or symbolic graphic representations, that speak very clearly to the subconscious while bypassing the need for logical and rational faculties that are sometimes absent because of narrow mindedness and prejudice. More recently, psychology has made considerable progress in this field, although the application of results has not always been to the benefit of the public.

The sum total of the universal consciousness is certainly conscious of these archetypes and uses them to communicate and manifest in a localized way as perceivable forms, for the benefit of the limited and conditioned beings. To continue in our example, the teacher writes a mathematical formula on the blackboard to illustrate a law of physics, and the actor-director uses words, music, costumes and gestures to tell a story that carries a message.

This is the true origin of the stories that have been handed down in various forms and mythological embellishments adjusted according to the particular cultures that express them. While it is very much possible that in relatively recent times some limited individuals who were above the human average were cloaked with primary ontological superimpositions (the original manifestations of the universal consciousness), it is foolish and degrading to reduce the result of such elaborations to a mere superstition by people who are ignorant and confused, incapable of understanding technologies, events and objects that were grossly material, since according to the alienist perspective this material level is the only existing and possible reality.

Let us make another easy and practical example: if a person is brave, valorous in battle, powerful and charismatic, one could call him "lion". But it would be foolish or at least ignorant to believe that actual lions cannot exist and the idea of "lion" has always been a superstitious fantasy, or the only possible lions were simply corageous human beings whose figure had been enlarged by popular or political fantasy. We may not have seen a real lion personally, but the shortcomings in our experience are not sufficient to automatically discredit the very idea of the possible factual existence of original lions or their characteristic qualities. Clearly our example has a limited value for the issue we are discussing, because a lion is inferior to a human being under many aspects and does not constitute a wider manifestation of existence and awareness, but we can use it to illustrate the concept of symbolic superimposition as a valid alternative to reductive minimalism.

It is true that the development of patriarchalism and the separation of social classes have removed the interest of the dominant *élite* from the interests of the mass of people to almost complete alienation. In this, the ideologists of Communism see the beginning of "civilization" and "history", while from the perspective of Natural Religion it was the beginning of the degradation of mankind: this is the point of contact between history and religion, or the history of religion, that constitutes one of the pillars of our research.

Along the last 2,000 or 3,000 years, the original religious and spiritual sentiments of human beings have gradually become an instrument of manipulation and control exploited by those who possess the established power based on selfishness. We see for example a rather famous quote attributed to Seneca (4 BCE-65 CE): "Religion is considered true by ordinary people, false by the wise, and useful by the government". From this statement, it seems evident that the cultural fiber of ancient Rome and Greece was alrady damaged and weakened in comparison with the ethical and social parameters of the previous millennia: civilization was not progressing but was rather becoming degraded, as we have analyzed in our work on the history of ancient religions. The present attempt by alienist ufologists to further demolish the natural religious sentiments of people is simply a continuation of this unhappy and cynical tendency, and we could even suspect that it might be motivated more or less directly by political intentions.

The conventional academic elaborations on history, social and political sciences, history of philosophy and anthropology are unfortunately based on this cynical prejudice about the need to subjugate religion to politics, something that is considered the inevitable progress in civilized human society. For example we see *The Origins of Political Science and the Problem of Socrates, Six Public Lectures by Leo Strauss,* edited by David Bolotin, Christopher Bruell and Thomas L Pangle, published by the University of Chicago in 1996, and the seminal work *The City and Man* by the same Leo Strauss, published in Chicago by Rand McNally in 1964. For Strauss the "noble lie" of Plato/ Socrates is justified by the "fact" that the entire structure of the city becomes possible, just and perfect only if the "wise philosophers" (meaning the *enlightened* or *illuminati*) have absolute control over it, and can rule over the multitudes of the "non-wise" by engaging a certain number of "loyal assistants" that are totally faithful and subservient to these "philosopher kings". Strauss clearly states: "even the most rational society, the society according to truth and nature, is not possible without a fundamental untruth", therefore it is necessary to assign "the natural status of the human species to a part of the human species, the citizens of a particular city", who are therefore distinguished from the rest of mankind because of their intrinsic superiority, by which "the fraternity of all human beings is to be replaced by the fraternity of all fellow citizens" where the citizens constitute the superior élitist and privileged category - the *Übermenschen* as opposed to the "human cattle" (*goyim*).

We have mentioned Evemerus' book, but a couple of centuries before him Protagoras had declared: "As far as the Gods are concerned, I have no way to know if they exist or not" - a statement that is not offensive yet, but certainly a symptom of very scarce spiritual or religious understanding or realization. Attempts to rationalize the ancient traditional stories in some "historical" reading had already been made by Xenophanes, Herodotus, Ephorus and Hecataeus of Abdera. Tendencies to mythological fiction had been expressed by several authors of classical Greece, who recognized they had forgotten a large part of the ancient knowledge and thus tried to fill the gaps and make their religious and cultural stories more attractive for the youngsters and the public in general.

Not only they tried to give a "Greek shape" to the names, the characters and the events of the sacred stories of other cultures, but they did not hesitate to invent new mythological characters and events, merrily inserting them in tragedies or "chronicles" that were convenient for their purposes, as well as adapting the still existing popular stories (cutting and pulling just like in the story of Procuste's bed), because a certain dose of fantasy in this regard was not seen as a dangerous aggression to moral values. In fact, Greek intellectuals had a strong taste for parables and flights of fancy (pindaric!), as we see for example in the *Batracomiomachy* ("The war of rats and frogs") usually attributed to Homer and from the very famous fables of Hesop - that however did not dare to use the names of the Gods themselves, but used animal characters or at best some ordinary human beings.

The hellenistic currents of thought in Alexandria, contemporary of Evemerus, had a tendency to elaborate on the Greek mythological tradition with the idea of a golden age of the Hyperboreans - for example by creating the philosopher hero Anacharsis of Scythia or the idealized Merope imagined by Theopompus. However, we know that the Greek contemporaries of Evemerus considered his hypothesis as extreme and outrageous, cynical and de-stabilizing for society in general - or at least they were convinced that his theory should not be made public. Maybe told in private among "enlightened philosophers", but without the general people actually realizing its implications, because religion has always been a fundamental need for the human beings, and without the Gods of

Olympus, people would create new Gods probably more dangerous and destructive, as we can see nowadays.

Even the Romans, who did not had many scruples in writing fictional stories about the deeds of the heroes who founded their city and making them appear to descend from various Gods and demigods, saw Evemerus as a dangerous extremist and feared that the spreading of his theory among the people would be damaging to law and order, and so they put it on the same level of epicureism, a doctrine that could be good for emperors and a few aristocrats in their private lives, but that could not be tolerated among the common people. With the same motivation, the Fathers of the Church took advantage of the fragments of Evemerus' book (especially quoted by Lactantius, Eusebius, Augustine) to denigrate pagan religions and "demonstrate" the superiority of the "historical" Jesus Christ compared to the previous gods (with a small "g"). The idea was also used in the critique to religion expressed by Karl Marx and his successors, so much that still today marxist historians consider it useful for demolishing traditional spiritual beliefs and replace them with the new gods of their socialist or communist (or State) mythology, whose worship will be compulsory for everyone, with the utmost zeal and without objections or "difficult" questions.

The alienist theory simply carries on this current of thought, but with more disquieting colors, because it puts on the same "divine" level all superhuman beings, including the malevolent and dangerous or even the demoniac. Some have observed that the present trend of interest for UFOs and extraterrestrials shows characteristics that are very similar to the obsession for occultism and satanism in the past centuries, that had the effect (apparently deliberate) to distort the perception and the memory of human experiences with the dimensions that we could call "supernatural" but that really are simply "extraordinary". Jacques Vallée, researcher and expert for NASA, has written some books presenting the theory that the alienist movement developed through a deliberate plan of disinformation, created to suffocate the genuine and relevant material under a thick cover of sensationalism that can be easily discredited, on the identical propaganda trend already used by the oppressive governments about satanism and folklore traditions.

Satanism, occultism, esoterism

Alienism as the cult of aliens or extraterrestrials considered as divine entities although they were mortal individual beings with superhuman powers, is distinct from Evemerism, that sees the Gods of Olympus as mere human beings deified by the popular or political tradition. The superhuman powers manifested by the alien-gods can be "explained" with attempts at technological interpretations, but as the fronteer of modern science moves into the territory of quantum physics, the boundary between gross and subtle matter becomes blurred. The mechanistic technology of bolts and screws and carbon or petrol has already been amply outdated even at popular level, although the interests of the market prevent the free distribution of renewable energy and DIY soft "village technology".

To become aware of the true scientific advancements of this last century we must venture into territories that are jealously guarded by the highest academic specialization, covered by deliberately complicated and obscure jargon, and strongly discouraging inter-disciplinary cooperation for communication and knowledge. The most cutting edge researchers are strictly under control and exploitation by the Establishment through a system of arbitrary financements from academic institutions, government, the army and the industry, especially by the multinationals and cartels in various fields.

Somehow something has been leaking through, and from what we can see, the most advanced technology today looks increasingly similar to ancient mythology, and the link is indicated by alienists as the result of "alien technology" recently gifted to earth governments by some powerful "visitors". The idea that mankind received advanced technical knowledge from extraterrestrials should be comforting, but it rather creates fear and uncertainty because its facts remain hidden by State secrecy and especially because the effects of such technology seem to be seriously dangerous for the health of human beings and for the planet as well.

The occultist or esoteric tradition, based on satanism, is built precisely on the same parameters: superhuman beings, possessing dark and terrible powers, make a pact of alliance or covenant with an élitist group of human beings, granting them special material privileges and benefits and demanding in return their obedience, worship and service entailing a certain measure of suffering and oppression for innocent creatures, humans and animals alike. Not even the worshipers remain safe from damages, and in fact the vast majority of the stories ends with the final destruction of the ill-advised and greedy selfish human who has accepted the covenant with Satan.

A great number of movies and entertainment products of the satanist trend contain more or less open references to the primary myth of Doctor Faust, who became famous through the story told by Christopher Marlowe (1564-1693) and later by Johann Wolfgang von Goethe (1749-1832). According to a booklet circulating in 1587 and entitled *Historia and Tale of Doctor Johannes Faustus*, the good doctor of the story actually lived between 1480 and 1540, and the story is almost identical to the one of a certain Teophilus of Adana, who lived around 500 CE and according to the chronicles made a pact with the devil in order to become a bishop.

The concept of satanism is particularly interesting because it is built on the duality between the "God of Good" and the "God of Evil" invented by zoroastrianism and then transmitted through Mani as manicheism and to the gnostic sects, both Jewish and Christian. Zoroaster/ Zarathustra constructed his theology by turning Vedic theology upside down, that is by presenting the Devas as evil beings and Asura Maha ("the great Asura") as the creator and lord of the benevolent spirits. According to the Aryan invasion theory, Vedic ("aryan") civilization was introduced into India by nomadic tribes coming from the Caucasus and still earlier from the region presently known as Iran (a name explained as a derivative of "aryan") and considering the extreme antiquity of the dating of Zoroaster as per his own tradition and by Greek historians, colonial orientalists have concluded that Parsism was the original version of the Vedic tradition proper, that had later come to existence with the rebellion of the followers of the Devas against the "ancient Gods" of Zoroaster. To debunk this absurd myth it is sufficient to carefully

26

read the *Zend Avesta*, as it specifically states that it was the religious revolution of Zoroaster to upturn the cult of the Devas who were previously worshiped.

It is particularly interesting to see that the idea of the Devas as the "younger gods" opposed to the Asuras as the "ancient gods" has been quoted by indologists from a verse in *Rig Veda* (10.124.3), that verification will show as non-existent. True, in *Rig Veda* there is a verse 10.124.3, but it says: "Observing the traveler from another path of life that is not physical, the bird on another branch of the tree, and seeing the original abode of the cosmic *yajna*, I engage in many conscious activities to follow the path of life dedicated to *yajna*. I sing hymns of praise for the omnipotent father who gives life, and I accept my share (of responsibility) in the life of *yajna*, distancing myself from the selfish way of life of the *asuras*". This is a typical example of the lack of honesty and credibility in the academic study of ancient religions and specifically of the Indo-Vedic tradition.

Along history, zoroastrian dualism was taken to a more mystical and philosophical dimension by the hellenistic gnostic movements, Jewish first and then Christian, that added Buddhist concepts (as well as Hindu concepts absorbed through the Buddhist version) borrowed in a rather superficial manner, and remained the foundation of the paranoid and defeatist approach towards the nature of the world and the human beings, of which contemporary culture is still suffering, and that is reflected in the alienist perspective. The existence of a "God of Evil" incarnating evil and being ill-intentioned, who is almost omnipotent or at least immensely more powerful than human beings, produces a desperate and anxious pessimism, by which a human being must surrender to a Savior and blindly obey his orders (as transmitted by the priests) if he wants to have the slightest hope of safety, peace and happiness in a distant future, after his God has triumphed over the Enemy God. In the meantime s/he must patiently endure the restrictions and tribulations that are imposed on him/ her and demonstrate his/ her zeal by fullly engaging in fighting against the followers and worshipers of the Enemy God(s), destroy their temples and "idols", forbid their religious ceremonies, subjugate them politically, convert them or at least enslave them and appropriate their people, their animals, their lands and their wealth.

We know that western demonology, with its various hierarchies of devils and arch-devils down to Satan himself, has been fabricated for doctrinal purposes by Christianity to discredit previous religious traditions and justify its own oppressive political system by projecting some "enemy" to be presented as scapegoat and distract people from the real problems.

Control over the population is based on a sense of fear focused on some mysterious "enemy" who is a constant threat that only the "highest authorities" of the government will be able to tackle and oppose, in a war that requires the complete support of the people. One of the primary concepts of propaganda is the "lurking enemy" and if there is no enemy, it must be invented... the important point is that the government should always point the finger at a suitable "enemy" to keep engaging the attention of the public, so that nobody will start thinking that maybe it is the ruling class that is behaving as an enemy towards its own people. The ideal candidate for the Enemy role is naturally an archetype that represents the things that the government wants to oppose - dissent, diversity, non-conformism, independence, opposition or rivalry: all the varieties of "otherness" as several researchers have remarked, such as Asbjørn Dyrendal, James R Lewis, Jesper A Petersen, Eugene Gallagher.

During the first centuries of the development of the present culture, the Enemy was paganism and in general the Natural Religion that was common to all peoples; as a consequence the fanatic abrahamic mobs rampaged everywhere, destroying or seriously damaging temples, libraries, universities, sacred images and even forests and trees, and slaughtering priests, teachers and devotees. The death penalty was applied even to children who happened to play with some broken old statue or in the ruins of some ancient sacred place. Evidence of such aggression and violence can still be seen clearly in various regions of the world and also in regard to contemporary events, for example in the case of the Buddhas of Bamiyan.

Satanism was a frequent accusation thrown around by various groups of Christians - even against one another, especially towards the more independent sects such as the "Christians of the origins" (such as gnostics, cathars, valdensians, hussites etc) and the Templars, what to speak of the innumerable "witches" victims of the Inquisition, sometimes simply herbalists or midwives, but especially the representatives of the ancient Natural Religions. We can see that the "satanic" devil is depicted with horns - an extremely ancient symbol of power not only during the stone age but also in Sumer, with some traces in Egypt. He often has goat hoofs, like the Faunus Pan and the Satyres of the sacred drama of ancient mysteric religions, and is shown with wings like the planetary Deities in Sumer and Egypt. He carries the trident of Neptune and Inanna, is red like Seth, and is connected with strong sexual aspects that the patriarchal abrahamic ideology equates with obscenity.

He absorbs the characteristics of the "God" of the Abyss, of the Underworld and Death, but also the concept of "rebellion against tyranny and in support of knowledge" expressed in the myth of Prometheus, who had stolen fire from the Olympus to gift it to human beings, and who was severely punished for such action. This perspective (already fully present in Jewish gnosticism) created some positive interest among many "free thinking" intellectuals and even led some people to consider Satan as some kind of patron or deity of scientific research, while popular sentiments have created expressions such as "good devil" or "poor devil", the latter particularly interesting because often used as a synonym for "poor Christ".

It is evident that the name of Astaroth is a distortion of the original Ishtar or Astarte, a name of the Mother Goddess in the semitic cultural region. Lucifer itself is literally "one who carries the light" and represents a distortion of the morning star and the evening star, Inanna/ Ishtar venerated (precisely!) as the planet Venus, that is intimately associated with the all-powerful Sun (as a reflection or companion). Belzebub is a distortion of *Baal zebul*, meaning "the Lord who rules over the Earth" and Belfagor comes from Baal Peor, the title of Baal (literally "Lord") as connected to the city of Peor in Phoenicia. In the Jewish tradition of Zohar, the primary "devil" Azazel (who in the Coptic tradition of the *Book of Enoch* is the leader of the fallen angels or Nefilim, is born from the union of the angels Azael and Aza. We will stop here but the list could continue.

The most important point is that satanism was totally unknown in ancient times before the advent of abrahamic religions, and is very strictly connected especially with Christianity, without which it loses all meaning and reason of being. The first case of satanism registered in history is in 1022, with the trial of two Christian priests accused of worshiping the devil. In 1200 there is the story of one Lucardis, a woman who hoped to see Satan reign in paradise. The collective psychosis spread and in 1486 the two dominican inquisitors named Henry Kramer and Jakob Sprenger produced the notorious *Malleus maleficarum* ("The hammer of the witches") that became the fundamental text on satanism and was reprinted 14 times all over Europe, triggering a further explosion of interest in the subject and not just in a negative sense. In spite of the incredibly cruel and bloody repression, with an estimated 90 million people tortured and killed (abrahamic sources minimize the problem by downsizing the number to a few thousands) in Europe only, from 1200 to the end of the 1700s the power of Satan seemed to become omnipresent, irresistible and obsessive in all social classes - there is even a pope, John XXII (1249-1334), who became famous for his "wizardry" (probably he was a gnostic, but this is a story we may discuss at some other time).

With Renaissance the tendency becomes even stronger, as monarchs, aristocrats and the wealthy merchants that began to rise in society showed great enthusiasm for the thrill of the forbidden knowledge and hoped to obtain special benefits, maybe the secret of the transmutation of base metals into gold, or magic potions for their sexual or political needs. The *gentleman's social clubs* of the 18th century developed an "entertainment" approach that can be described as a transgressive and scandalous pseudo-satanism, as in the Hellfire Clubs, that mushroomed in the 1720s. The most famous was the Order of the Knights of Saint Francis, founded around 1750 by Sir Francis Dashwood the 11th baron of Despencer (1708-1781), that held its meetings first in his villa at West Wycombe and later at Medmenham Abbey, a ruined cistercensian monastery. Its members amused themselves by indulging in all sorts of sensual gratification, toasting to the Devil and mocking Christianity with an attitude that was typical of the aristocrats of the period - strictly in private, to prevent public exposure and scandal.

But it was not a new idea: the model had already been presented by a franciscan (and then benedictine) monk named François Rabelais (1483-1494) in his famous *Gargantua et Pantagruel*, with the impudent and desecrating abbey where the motto was "*fay çe que vouldras*" ("do whatever you wish").

In his *Paradise lost* (1667), the puritan John Milton started (probably involuntarily) the official exaltation of Satan, who is compared in his fall to the destiny of man, condemned for having chosen freedom and personal dignity: "To reign is worth ambition, though in Hell: Better to reign in Hell than serve in Heaven". The book became famous in the subsequent century and was translated in France by Voltaire, inspiring revolutionary and anarchic ideas, so that we find it quoted by William Godwin in his *Enquiry concerning political justice* (1793).

The intellectual and literary interest for the demoniac occultism of "free thinkers" dominated the folk tales of devils, warlocks and hags, but it soon extended to the field to ghosts, vampires, werewolves and various other creatures that are more or less strictly connected to the horror-terror of the "world of darkness" and that in the subsequent centuries became more and more popular and are still a major theme in the present adaptations for cinema and TV. Besides the famous *Frankenstein* (by Mary Wollenstonecraft Shelley, 1818), *The Legend of Sleepy Hollow* (by Washington Irving, 1820), *The Case of Dr Jekyll and Mr Hyde* (by Robert Louis Stevenson, 1886), *The Picture of Dorian Gray* (by Oscar Wilde, 1890), *Dracula* (by Bram Stoker, 1897) and the disturbing tales of Edgar Allan Poe (1809-1849), many other works are produced by a style that became known as "gothic", a definition that refers not only to literature but to all artistic productions such as paintings, music, applied arts such as clothing etc, and that still continues today, sometimes called *goth*.

The most interesting author in this "gothic-romantic" occultist trend is certainly H P Lovecraft (1890-1937), who created a veritable religious mythology around a dark entity named Cthulhu in his story entitled *The Call of Cthulhu* and in other novels about the *Old Ones* or *Elder Things*, with a *pantheon* of ALIEN ENTITIES that are WORSHIPED AS GODS by ignorant people, but in truth are indifferent or actively hostile towards human beings.

In Lovecraft's novels, and especially in *At the Mountains of Madness*, the origin or creation of mankind is attributed to these fundamentally evil aliens as an experiment for the production of slaves (later abandoned), but the main characters (the "heroes") of his stories are academically educated men who bring scientific and rational evidence against the faith and worship for such superhuman beings. Lovecraft admits having found inspiration in the work of German writers Friedrich Nietzsche (1844-1900) the famous author of *Also sprach Zarathustra* ("Thus spake Zarathustra", published in 1891) and Oswald Spengler (1880-1936), author of *Der Untergang des Abendlandes* ("The decline of the West"), a general history of the world published in 1922, that presents world dictatorship ("cesarism" or *kaiserism* in German adaptation) as the only solution for the good of mankind.

Both Lovecraft and his inspirators present ancient civilizations as dark, primitive and barbaric while exalting white racism, but they deeply respect the Jews as a people - Lovecraft even married a Jewish woman. On the other hand, Lovecraft jokingly calls "Yog-Sothothery" the artificial and superstitious mythology he created in his novels. It is not difficult to understand that by "*yog*" he is hinting at *yoga* and the Indo-Vedic tradition, while "*sothothery*" is a neologism crafted from the union of the two words *esotheric* and *sottery*. In this regard we may remember that actor Rollo Ahmed, born as Abdul Said Ahmed in Guyana in 1898 and emigrated to England after WW1, taught Yoga mixed with Voodoo, and there were people (like the famous Dennis Wheatley and wife) who took him very seriously; still today his book *The Black Art* (published in 1936) is considered one of the earliest and most important texts on the history of occultism and in the present revival of *witchcraft* or *wicca*.

The darkly ideas of Lovecraft have been continued after his death by the so-called "Lovecraft Circle" and especially by August Derleth, who is still developing his mythology by inventing stories of wars among aliens, especially between the *Elder Gods* and the *Outer Gods*, the latter defeated and forced to take shelter underground, inside mountains and under oceans. These same themes can be found practically identical in the mythology of alienism and ufology, with the addition of ideas apparently collected from the work of colonial indologists, especially those who admired the *Zend Avesta* and had some notions about the Greek mythology of the Titans and their hostility against the Gods of Olympus, who could in fact be called their "younger relatives". However, it is easy to see that such alienist presentations have been invented deliberately and in some cases even cynically.

We cannot elaborate here on the various esoteric and occultist organizations and on the cultural current of dark "demonology" along the centuries and especially from the 1700s (a time when it started to become a political force) until the present, because a deep analysis would require a thick volume by itself. To conclude our section on satanism proper, we can mention the popular revival of the 1950s, that moved the subject from the intellectual circles of wealthy aristocrats into the masses of consumers, triggering a new wave of collective psychosis until the 2000 - the end of millennium period where we see a corresponding popular interest for the phenomenon of alien abductions and sightings of UFOs (*Unidentified Flying Objects*). Several researchers have connected the two trends, concluding that some or many of the cases of supernatural experiences of a satanic type should actually be explained with a contact with inter-dimensional or ultra-dimensional entities popularly known as "extraterrestrials", as imagined already by Lovecraft and Crowley. This is the origin of the theory of Indian Gods as Aliens.

The perspective on Hinduism

In our study of Hinduism we should be very attentively collecting information from the proper sources and particularly careful not to fall in the traps of colonial indology, that was created with the declared purpose to demolish the credibility of Hinduism, and was represented not only by Britons and Germans, but also by academics of other European nations (especially France and Italy) who followed the ideological current that we can describe as romantic-colonial-fascist mystery. Unfortunately this is still the main source for most people, although the trend is starting to change and a growing number of individuals, both mainstream academics and members of the interested public, are choosing a more authentic and unbiased approach.

The concept that creates most confusion is the definition of "aryan" that became famous particularly with reference to nazi ideology as a special "master race" or "superior race" of tall, blond, muscly men with blue eyes and a specific shape of the head. But the nazis did not invent the idea: they merely simplified it to adapt it to the plan of extermination of the "semitic" Jews by dividing them from the "caucasian" Jews (*askhenazis*) for the famous "holocaust" as we can see from the posters of the government of the period.

In his *Systema Naturae* (1767) the famous physician, botanist and zoologist Linnaeus (Carl von Linné, 1707-1778, the Swedish "father" of the modern system of scientific classification of the species) writes about five human races: the white *Europeanus* of a gentle character and inventive mind, the red *Americanus* obstinate and ill-tempered, the black *Africanus* slow and lazy, the yellow *Asiaticus* greedy and easily distracted, and the wild *Monstrosus* of the native tribes.

Famous philosophers such as Friedrich Hegel, Immanuel Kant and Auguste Comte claimed that the western or European culture was the highest point of the human evolution and approved without reservations the enslavement of the "inferior races". Christian preachers openly supported these views by quoting "the curse of Ham" (by which all the descendents of this son of Noah, of black race, were destined by God to become slaves) and the instructions of ("saint") Paul of Tarsus, who taught that slaves should always be faithful and obedient to their masters and never try to escape their condition because it had been decreed by God. In his *Indigenous races of the Earth* (1857), the American Josiah Clark Nott (1804-1873) put "negroes" on a level of creation between the "Greek" (considered as the beginning of western or european culture) and chimpanzees.

The next step of the classification of the superior race was the transition from "european" to "aryan". The idea of the "aryan race" was invented by the French philosopher Joseph Arthur Comte de Gobineau (1816-1882, *Essai sur l'inegalité des races humaines*, "Treatise on the inequality of human races"), whose book was translated into English by the above mentioned Josiah Clark Nott, with the financial and political support of Henry Hotze (1833-1887), albeit shortened by about one thousand pages - those where Gobineau had described the Americans themselves as a deplorable mixture of races. Unlike the vast majority of the Bible commentators, who classified the various races as descendents of the three sons of Noah (Shem for semites, Ham for africans, Japhet for caucasians), Gobineau believed that only white people could be descendents of Adam and Noah, and therefore semites and hamites were simply variations of the white race, while the other races were not even part of the human species. For Gobineau it was impossible to think that the chosen people of the Bible could be considered an inferior race: "... who were the Jews? I repeat, they were a people skilled in all enterprises, a free people, strong and intelligent, that before losing the name of independent nation in spite of their valiant fighting, had produced almost as many doctors as merchants" ("... *que furent les juifs? Je le répète, un peuple habile en tout ce qu'il entreprit, un peuple libre, un peuple fort, un peuple intelligent, et qui, avant de perdre bravement, les armes à la main, le titre de nation indépendente, avait fourni au monde presque autant de docteurs que des marchands*").

The particular theory of Gobineau identifies the Jews as the "original human race" described as the aryan indo-european stock "coming from Ur, the city of Chaldeans" where the mythical Abraham was born. And who, through the mythology of the Annunaki, provides an important character for biblical alienists such as Sitchin and his followers. Their theory is conveniently propped on the old perspective of the *Zend Avesta* (the religion of Zarathustra), amply leaked into Jewish and Christian gnostic sects. It is precisely from the *Zend Avesta* that Gobineau extracts the definition of "aryan", a term used by Zarathustra to indicate his own followers, worshipers of Ahura Mazda, the "Great Asura" of whom the Devas are enemies; by turning the roles of Devas and Asuras upside down we also upturn the roles of *aryas* and *dasyus*, as we will see later on examining these very important Sanskrit words.

In the *Vedas*, the Devas are the benevolent Deities who manage the universe and the *aryas* are the civilized and peaceful human beings who follow the principles of *dharma* and *vidya* and the social norms of the *varnas* defined as *brahmana*, *kshatriya*, *vaisya* and *sudra*, while the Asuras are demoniac beings and the name of *dasyu* refers to pillaging criminals. In the *Zend Avesta* however the Devas are presented as evil spirits mistakenly worshiped as Gods by the ancient people, the *aryas* are the loyal followers of Zarathustra, the Asuras are benevolent spirits to be worshiped and served, and the *dasyus* are all the unfaithful human beings - that is, those who have no faith in Zarathustra and Ahura Mazda. This is where we find the root of confusion and error, as we will see more specifically in the next chapters.

We apologize for using some Sanskrit technical terms but these are essential to avoid the danger of misunderstanding due to a vague approach. *Dharma* refers to the natural and universal ethical principles, *vidya* is the integrated knowledge of physics and metaphysics, *varna* is the system of social and professional categories that are regulated by precise duties and engagements, and the categories of *varnas* described as *brahmana, kshatriya, vaisya* and *sudra* correspond only superficially with the common contemporary definitions of intellectuals, warriors, entrepreneurs and laborers or servants. Most of the academic and popular confusion on the "Hindu caste system" was originated by distorted presentations of the *varna* system, specifically imposed by the British colonial regime on the basis of racism. We will discuss this issue somewhere else, because it requires a lot of space.

Western academics incorrectly (but more or less deliberately) shaped the idea of "aryan" on the nomadic tribes converted by Zarathustra, that normally lived by raiding, pillaging and enslaving, and practiced a rigid patriarchalism and a sharp social categorization based on birth in a decreasing order of power: aristocratic leaders, priests, vassals and slaves - classes that do not correspond at all to the Vedic *varnas* we mentioned earlier.

The religion of the *Zend Avesta* does not contain philosophy or theology but simply conjurer spells to keep the Devas away, very strict rules for physical purification especially in regard to funeral rites (burial and cremation are strongly prohibited) and fragments of previous planetary mythologies presented in a somewhat confused manner. It seems that such lack of consistency is due to the fact that (according to the traditional stories told by the Parsis) all the Parsi texts were destroyed by Alexander of Macedonia, who also slaughtered almost all the priests; after the dissolution of the Alexander's empire, the Persians started to reconstruct the texts "from memory", inevitably with some irregularities.

Fortunately this has not been the case with the Indo-Vedic tradition, that in spite of repeated aggressions remained sufficiently vital and uninterrupted without the need of being reconstructed from scattered and forgotten fragments. At least until today.

When projected on the "aryan" theory, this primitive vision of Parsism on religion was interpreted as the proof of greater antiquity compared to Indian culture; as a consequence, it was believed that Parsism was the ancestor or origin both of Hinduism and Judaism, considered as contemporary of the Assiro-Babylonian and Egyptian cultures. We shall speak more extensively about the religion of Zarathustra in a later chapter because it constitutes the cultural foundation for the development of the Jewish ideology that created the Bible - the general basis used by almost all alienists in the construction of their mythologies.

The "aryan" theory of Gobineau was very successful among his contemporaries because it reconciled the racial and colonial prejudices of white supremacists with their faith in the Bible. Many subsequent writers, such as French anthropologist George Vacher de Lapouge (1854-1936) in his book *L'Aryen* ("The Aryan", 1899), claimed that classification into this superior and original human race could be determined by using the cephalic index (the measuring of the shape of the head): thus the Europeans with a longer cranium or "dolicocephals" characteristically found in north Europe were natural leaders, specifically created by God to dominate over the "brachiocephalic" (short-skull) peoples considered "sub-humans", an idea already expressed by Nietzsche. Not a new idea: the cruel practices of skull deformation in newborn babies to make them look more similar to the "superior race" go back to the times of the "monotheist" pharaoh Akhenaton (closely connected by CG Jung with the character of Moses in the Bible) and are found in other cultures as well, especially in central and south America, and also among the Huns or Khasa/ Kusha, of whom we shall speak later.

The British colonialists were very eager to pick up this race mystique to justify and promote their conquest of Africa, Australia and north America, but India was immensely more complex and sophisticated compared to the native tribes of those other regions. Many British officers arrived in India and were deeply impressed by the great value of the quantity and quality of knowledge that had already amazed the scholars of classical and hellenistic Greece and even the islamic raiders, who had taken from India the decimal numbers and higher mathematics (algebra, algoritms, etc) and practically the entire science of astronomy known until the beginning of the 1900s. The enormous traditional literature of India included treatises on astronomy, mathematics as well as physics, medicine, surgery, philosophy, theology, architecture, chemistry, metallurgy and so on.

In our work *Introduction to Vedic knowledge* we have explained how Indian culture was perceived by westerners along the centuries, and here we will simply give a few pointers. Among the people who were amazed and awed by Indian culture we can mention for example Louis Jacolliot (1837-1890) a French scholar who was for some time appointed as supreme magistrate in the court of Chandranagar, Lord Warren Hastings (1732-1818) first General Governor of India (from 1773 to 1785), Lord Curzon (1859-1925) marquis of Kedleston and viceroy of India (from 1899 to 1905), Sir John Malcolm (1829-1896) Governor of Bombay, Sir William Wedderburn Bart (1838-1918) magistrate in Pune and General Secretary of the Government in Bombay, Sir Thomas Munro (1761-1827) Governor of Madras (in 1819), Colonel James Todd (1782-1835), Sir Charles Norton Edgcumbe Eliot (1864-1931), Sir William Jones (1746-1794) judge of the supreme court in Calcutta and founder of the Royal Asiatic Society of Bengal, and especially Sir John Woodroffe, also known as Arthur Avalon (1865-1936), general advocate for Bengal during 18 years and then supreme magistrate in 1915, who officially converted to Hinduism and wrote several favorable books on the subject.

Obviously the British colonial government was not very happy to see its officers show such respect and admiration towards a people that was to be conquered, subjugated and exploited, and especially did not have any intention to easily convert to Christianity.

The situation called for the intervention of academic professors to produce translations of the Vedic texts that were adequately distorted and simultaneously beheading the ancient system of educational and cultural formation characteristic of Vedic civilization based on the decentralized system of *gurukulas*. The enforcement of compulsory census on the basis of "birth castes" was an important step because it introduced hereditary social immobility (by preventing individual evolution and any effort to really become qualified as established by the original system) and tried to win the favor of the higher social classes (especially the brahmins descendents of the ancient Vedic *brahmanas*, but also the wealthy merchants and intellectuals) creating a new indigenous dominant class that would be loyal to the British government, formed by "*brown sahibs*" to be trained in the fundamentalist Christian schools and rewarded for their loyalty with important positions in government and academic institutions - "*Indian in blood and color, but English in taste, in opinion, in morals, in intellect*".

In a letter to his father written in 1836, Macaulay declared: "It is my belief that if our plans of education are followed up, there will not be a single idolater among the respectable classes in Bengal thirty years hence. And this will be effected without an effort to proselytize, without the smallest interference with religious liberty, by natural operation of knowledge and reflection. I heartily rejoice in the project... No Hindu who has received an English education ever remains sincerely attached to his religion". In his *Minute* (1835) he wrote tht Hinduism was built on "a literature admitted to be of small intrinsic value... that inculcates the most serious errors on the most important subjects... hardly reconcilable with reason, with morality... fruitful of monstrous superstitions... false history, false astronomy, false medicine... in company of a false religion".

Sir Monier Monier-Williams (1819-1899, author of the English-Sanskrit dictionary still most widely used) wrote: "For what purpose then has this enormous territory been committed to England? Not to be the 'corpus vile' of political, social, or military experiments; not for benefit of our commerce, or the increase of our wealth - but that every man, woman and child, from Cape Comorin to the Himalaya mountains, may be elevated, enlightened Christianized... When the walls of the mighty fortress of Brahmanism are encircled, undermined, and finally stormed by the solders of the cross, the victory of Christianity must be signal and complete."

The German author Friedrich Max Müller (1823-1900) is considered the most important among the founders of western academic indology even in India, where a servile "caste" brahmin (the famous

Tilak) gratified him with the resounding title of *Mula Acharya* of *Go-tirtha*, with a rather questionable literal translation of the name of Müller and the name of Oxford University. In fact in Sanskrit *mula* means "root, primary" while *acharya* refers to an important teacher or master, an attribute that might have been extrapolated from *max* or *maximus*, according to the meaning of "great"; in Sanskrit the English word *ox* is translated as *go* (generically "bovine") and the English word *ford* is translated as *tirtha*, a term that is very rich in symbolic spiritual and religious meaning as the "crossing place" that enables one to go beyond the "river of the phenomenal world" and go from ordinary awareness to the spiritual transcendental awareness.

In their naive perspective, many brahmins honored Müller because according to his theory their "caste" or family ascendence (in Sanskrit, *jati*) was of the "purest blood" and therefore closer genetically to the aryan origins and the British "indo-european brothers" who occupied the highest social position in colonial India. They did not realize that the interest for Sanskrit and Vedic scriptures expressed by those early indologists was candidly destructive. The success of this evil scheme caused the development of strong racist sentiments among Indians, the obsession for skin bleaching in the attempt to look whiter, the irreparable rift between north and south India, and a considerable acceleration in the degradation of Indian culture especially from the perspective of the study and knowledge of Vedic scriptures - all problems that unfortunately are still plaguing India.

Müller was particularly irked by those scholars who, instead of engaging in this evangelical mission, committed the mortal sin of sincerely appreciating Vedic knowledge: "he should know that he can expect no money; nay, he should himself wish for no mercy, but invite the heaviest artillery against the floating battery which he has launched in the troubled waters of Biblical criticism". In another passage of his correspondence, Müller wrote: "the ancient religion of India is doomed ... and if Christianity does not step in, whose fault will it be?". Horace H Wilson, who in 1833 obtained the Boden Chair in Sanskrit at the Oxford University, offered a prize of 200 pound sterlings to the best rebuttal of the Vedic religious system, which he simply considered a collection of primitive witchcraft spells and hoped "to prove that they were fallacies, by means of the sublime spear of the Christian truth". Another early indologist, WW Hunter, expressed the same sentiment: "Scholarship is warmed with the holy flame of Christian zeal".

On the recommendation of Baron von Bunsen, ambassador of Prussia to the United Kingdom, the imperial British government decided to avail of the services of young Müller and offered him a lucrative contract at Oxford to produce the greatest possible number of pages with distorted and biased versions of the Vedic texts and commentaries on eastern religions: this is the famous encyclopedia *The Sacred Books of the East*, in 50 volumes, presenting Vedic scriptures as texts of anthropological and historical interest, putting them on the same level or even below the level of the literatures of Buddhism, Koran and *Zend Avesta*, which were more "monotheistic" and therefore more acceptable for zealous Christians.

Müller wrote in one of his letters: "This edition of mine and the translation of the Veda will hereafter tell to a great extent... the fate of India, and on the growth of millions of souls in that country.... the only way of uprooting all that has sprung from it during the last 3000 years... and that is of a more degraded and savage character than the worship of Jupiter, Apollo or Minerva... It may have but served to prepare the way of Christ... India is much riper for Christianity than Rome or Greece were at the time of Saint Paul."

It was Max Müller who established the foundations of colonial indology, by fabricating the notorious "Aryan Invasion Theory", by which some nomadic tribes of "indo-european" raiders originally from Caucasus or central Asia, endowed with the racial characteristics that are described as "caucasian", had invaded the Indian sub-continent, enslaving and slaughtering the sparse indigenous population - primitive, black, weak dravidians - and bringing the *Vedas*, Sanskrit, slavery and the rigid caste system based on racism, patriarchalism, religious intolerance and so on. The genocide of the natives was survived by a few scattered refugees who fled as far as possible into the south, keeping their original languages (of tamil-dravidian type) and the ancient tribal deities, different from the bloodthirsty gods worshiped by the "pack of blond beasts of prey" (as per Nietzsche's definition) that had settled in the north.

The theory of the aryan invasion from the Caucasus into India has already been completely demolished at a professional level by mainstream academics, because it has no archeological evidence whatsoever. Already in the 1960s the American archeologist GF Dales demonstrated that there had been no clashes or massacres of any kind between dravidian peoples and invaders of a different race, and that Harappa and other cities of the region had been abandoned peacefully and orderly, because of climate changes. Even the "old school" archeologists such as Raymond and Bridget Allchin now admit that the culture and life style of the two populations - the so-called aryans and the so-called dravidians - were practically identical. And certainly anyone who bothers to read Vedic scriptures will be able to easily verify that there is not even one fragment that speaks of nomadism or an original land in the Caucasus or on the Anatolian highlands, but we find plenty of descriptions of the geography of India as it was before 3000 BCE, when the Sarasvati river was a majestic water way, with many advanced and crowded cities along its banks (its valley can still be recognized in satellite photos even if the waters have disappeared) and many other very ancient large cities such as Kasi (Benares), Prayaga (Allahabad), Mathura and Ayodhya were already established on the banks of Ganga, Yamuna and Sarayu (north), Narmada and Sindhu (west) and Godavari and Kaveri (south).

According to Vedic tradition, the most sacred region of the sub-continent was called *brahmavarta* ("the spiritual land") and was between the Sarasvati and the Drisyavati: geological verification has shown that the Sarasvati finally disappeared around 1900 BCE, while the Drisyavati had already disappeared in 2600 BCE. These dates coincide with the Hindu tradition, according to which the Kali yuga, the "black age" in which we presently live, started around 3100 BCE. Indian academics such as B Lal, SR Rao, SP Gupta, Dilip K Chakrabarty, KM Srivastava, MK Dhavalikar, RS Bisht and others have further elaborated on the subject, and we hope that sooner or later also the school texts and the public opinion will be updated. Certainly the faulty presentations with sensationalistic purposes or even politically motivated cannot help, therefore we need to encourage Indian researchers to overcome the cultural inferiority complex accumulated in the past few centuries and to return to the attentive and sincere study of the original texts.

Unfortunately in the meantime the "aryan" mythology has become deeply rooted in the esoteric and occultist field, and consequently also in the fields of ufology and alienism: the authors there speak repeatedly of the alien races called "Nordic" (from the systems of Pleiades, Vega, Ummo, etc), "Blond" (from Telos and many underground settlements and inside mountains on Earth) and even "Aryan" (who are supposed to have established settlements under Antarctica with the help of German nazi scientists). It is particularly interesting to note that such "aryan" aliens are often presented as allies of the sauroid or reptilian race, a kind of aliens that are particularly evil and cruel.

The perspective of Hinduism

According to the Indo-vedic tradition known as Hinduism, and specifically as we can see from the information contained in the texts called *Puranas* and *Itihasa* ("ancient stories"), the etymological, ideological and cultural (maybe even racial, but that is not important) connection that has originated the idea of a "indo-european" people is traced back to migratory waves not towards India but from India and moving outside especially towards the west, in different historical periods and starting from very ancient times, as we can see in the work of many scholars, including Srikant T Talageri (*The Rig Veda and the Avesta: The Final Evidence*, 2008, and previous books in 1993 and 2000). The reason of such migrations is also explained in the tradition of Zarathustra as a "disagreement" about the rules of civil and social life, that caused the departure from the land of origin, later idealized as a veritable "paradise lost".

We have already mentioned the fact that in Hinduism (the present heir of the Indo-Vedic tradition) *aryas* and *dasyus* are two opposite cultures - the first of civilized and peaceful agricultural settlements, and the second engaging in raids and pillaging and generally nomadic. We will now speak about two other very interesting definitions especially for the comparison between *Vedas* and *Zend Avesta*: the concepts of *ari* and *dasa*, respectively "enemy" and "servant". While the word *arya* ("noble") characteristic of the original Vedic culture referred to a human being who knows and follows the principles of natural and fundamental ethics and so he behaves nobly towards all beings, the word *ari* ("enemy") can be applied to those bands of "separatist" renegades who are hostile to the rest of the population and who were exiled, more or less voluntarily and in different waves, from the Vedic social nucleus, and went to settle as *anaryas* ("non-*aryas*") further west, in territories where they could freely choose the life style they preferred. From there, some groups migrated even farther towards the Anatolian highlands, the Caucasus region, and apparently also to the "fertile crescent" of Mesopotamia and other areas. It is natural that such rebellious and hostile communities twisted the original terminology of the *Vedas*, applying the concept of "enemy" (*ari*) to the *aryas*, whom they considered truly "enemies" because they had been chased out by them. From this ambivalent root of *ari-arya* came the modern definition of "aryan/arian" (as in Nazi ideology): it is no wonder that so much confusion and damage were created.

Those who are not familiar with Sanskrit may see little difference between the two words *ari* and *arya*, but here is the key to understand the very serious cultural and ideological upheaval caused by Zarathustra, that seeped more and more dangerously into human society, to finally result in the present disaster at planetary level. Indeed the fundamental problem that caused this global damage is the "separatist" selfish mentality by which a group of persons (nation, tribe, clan etc) becomes ideologically separated from the rest of mankind and from the greater universal community of all beings, pursuing materialistic ends that give advantages only to their group but cause sufferings to other innocent beings. In other words, the mentality of the *ari* ("enemies") is to see themselves as enemies of others and viceversa, on the ideological level, creating artificial and prejudiced differences, as for example those based on ethnicity or race. As we will see later, this mentality was reinforced and legitimized by the contact of *anarya* human beings with non-human races (that we could, albeit imprecisely, call "extraterrestrial") described in the Indo-Vedic tradition, especially with the asuric dynasties of Daityas and Danavas.

It is important here to understand that according to the *Vedas* the definition of *arya* does not entail any racial aspect. In fact the *Rig Veda* (9.63.5) clearly states: *krinvanto visva aryam*, "let everyone become *arya*". It may be useful to clarify that the verbal form of the verse does not express an order to be applied forcibly, but simply an invitation and a wish, therefore we cannot conclude that the Vedic system requires forced conversion as we see with adharmic religions. Many texts describe in detail the ritual procedures (*suddhi, prayascitta, vrata, diksha*) by which a person who was born outside the Vedic system (*antya-ja*) can be integrated into it, becoming *arya* under all aspects. All scriptural and historical evidence clearly shows that in order to become *arya* it is sufficient to embrace the ethical and ideological principles of *arya* civilization, irrespective of the physical racial characteristics or the circumstances of birth, that obviously cannot be changed by a simple decision as expressed in the verse.

We see that in the scriptures of Indo-Vedic tradition, *aryas* can be of many different races: Rama and Krishna have a complexion so dark to seem black or blue, while the complexion of Shiva is compared to the whiteness of camphor and his hair is copper red. Balarama and Arjuna, too, have white skin, while Kunti, Yasoda and Draupadi are so dark that they are compared to "blue lotus flowers". Kapila has blond hair, but this trait is seen as rare enough to be highlighted as wonderful and extraordinary.

The quality of *arya* does not correspond to a social class or caste different from the lower classes, as we see for example in verse 6.22.10 of *Rig Veda*, stating specifically that the *dasas*, the servants or *sudras*, must be considered *aryas* to all effects when they are trained in the ethical and religious principles of *arya* civilization and observe its norms. On the other hand, the persons who were born in families high in *arya* society but degraded themselves by engaging in criminal activities and thus became *dasyu* should be reformed, exiled or killed, as we see for example in *Rig Veda* 10.69.6 and 10.83.1 (and many examples mentioned in *Puranas* and *Itihasa*). We recommend to always verify the references with the original Vedic texts where the Sanskrit text is contained, and not to stop at incomplete quotes or books compiled by authors supporting ideologies that are hostile to the tradition they write about.

Which are the noble behaviors characterizing the *aryas*?

They are the actions in accordance to the fundamental, universal and eternal principles of natural ethics, constituting the basis of the scientific system of social cooperation and personal evolution aimed to the full realization of human potential, up to the attainment of the divine level. In Vedic technical terms, these three dimensions are called respectively *sanatana dharma*, *varna ashrama dharma* and *para dharma*. The *arya* civilization, also called Vedic, includes all three dimensions: undoubtedly it is a daring and ambitious program, difficult to attain, and therefore nobody should be artificially forced to participate if they do not feel up to it. However, it is true that a society composed by persons who are in harmony with *dharma* on all three levels constitutes the ideal example for human beings and guarantees happiness and prosperity both on the material and the spiritual planes.

The concept of *sanatana dharma*, or Natural Religion, is the instinctive tendency of all integral (non-alienated) human beings, in all cultures, in all times and geographical places, and consists in respecting and following the principles of universal ethics (honesty, compassion, cleanliness, self-discipline, and so on) and the voice of conscience. Anyone can do that, even without receiving specific instructions and without belonging to a particular religious faith. One who follows *sanatana dharma* can choose to simply remain on that level, or to make an extra effort to engage in *varna ashrama dharma* and/or *para dharma*.

The concept of *varna ashrama dharma* is more complex and is based on the recognition of four fundamental categories (*varnas*, not to be confused with *jatis*, or birth circumstances) of human beings, characterized by different tendencies and habits (technically called in Sanskrit as *guna* and *karma*) and with specific duties, that we could roughly describe as intellectuals, fighters, entrepreneurs and laborers. All the four *varnas* are expected to observe the fundamental principles of *sanatana dharma* as a preliminary requirement; in regard to *param dharma* (spiritual realization) they can engage in it, but they are not forced to do so. This is the original system, later distorted into the mechanism of the "castes" that we will analyze better in some other publication quoting precise references from Hindu scriptures.

The category of laborers or servants (*sudra, dasa*) includes all those professional occupations based on manual work, more or less specialized: workers in all industries, farm hands engaged in agriculture and animal managing, millers, oil press workers, transporters and couriers, drivers, pilots, messengers, house helpers, janitors, waiters, hospital nurses and physiotherapists, office assistants, warehouse men, accountants, burocrats, cleaners, laundry men, dye workers, cobblers, mechanics, plumbers, electricians, masons, technicians of all sorts including designers, smiths, potters, carpenters, artisans, beauticians, hair dressers, tailors, artists and anyone who earns a living with physical or manual activities. Workers are all those who are engaged in any work by others, meaning they need an employer and a salary, or sell simple objects and even artistic objects that have been fashioned manually as handicrafts, but are not able to become organized commercially because they do not plan, develop or preserve with long term goals: as soon as they have some money in their hands they spend it to enjoy life, and if they receive large sums they tend to squander them uselessly and soon they are broke again or even deep in debts.

It is very important to clarify that *sudras* (*dasas*, or servants) are not "slaves": in the Indo-Vedic system slavery does not exist, because all servants are always free to go away if they want, to choose a different "master" or even to provide for their own maintenance by getting hired temporarily by a variety of customers who pay them each time. The classification is not based on birthright either, because according to the Vedic tradition "everyone is born *sudra*" (*janmana jayate sudra*) and each individual can become qualified for a higher position only through a precise training under the guidance of an expert and responsible *guru*, who will officialize the induction into the most appropriate category according to the results at the end of the studies.

Entrepreneurs (*vaisyas*), who are a step above the *sudras* in terms of professional qualifications, are able to transform resources into wealth especially by cultivating the land (not only by agriculture but also by developing forests, mines, urban settlements etc) and managing, distributing and re-distributing resources and wealth wherever necessary, taking care of the animals and the laborers who depend on them. They can and should contribute gifts and assistance to the well being of deserving and needy people, especially through the performance of adequate rituals precisely prescribed by Vedic tradition, but they are not responsible for the managing of society in general and they cannot occupy government positions or form *lobbies* to influence the government. They are not allowed to accumulate personal or family wealth or "keep court" in imitation of kings; the surplus of valuables or consumers goods must be presented to the kings in the form of taxes or tributes (always voluntary) or donated to intellectuals, to support their work in society, selflessy and without "strings" attached such as demanding or expecting special favors.

Fighters or warriors (*kshatriyas*) work by managing people, taking care of them and protecting them, ensuring the necessary conditions for the well being and the individual evolution of the entire population: this is a full time job, 24 hours a day and 7 days a week, for which they must be ready at all times to sacrifice their own lives and the lives of their families, and everything they possess. This professional category therefore engages in government administration besides internal and external defence, but they never interfere in the personal lives of the subjects (except in case of violent aggression, that must be prevented or stopped immediately) and especially has no right to intervene on religious or spiritual issues, on the transmission of knowledge, on the choices of the subjects in regard to family or residence, and on the normal performance of activities of the various professional categories, except to support the justified mobility from a social or professional category to another for the benefit of the entire society.

Intellectuals (*brahmanas*) must be expert in all the branches of knowledge to be able to teach, advise and guide all the other members of society; they must know not only physical but also metaphysical sciences, and be perfectly competent in their practical application. As a consequence, the training of *brahmanas* requires a much greater number of years and a more rigorous dedication to studying, something that is not feasible for everyone.

Therefore school education was strongly personalized and oriented towards precise categories from the earliest years of instruction: the students went to live in the home of the teacher, who observed them carefully in all circumstances and at all times to establish the real qualities, tendencies and potential of each individual. The purpose of teaching was always to stimulate, facilitate and support the personal evolution of each individual.

In evaluating the students, the teacher can also consider the factor of family and social background, because at the age of 5 (when he is enrolled into school) a child has already absorbed values and models of behaviors, and his family might have expectations in regard to his future engagement, as we see in all cultures. Parents who are university professors, lawyers, medical doctors or politicians, sometimes as heirs of a tradition spanning along several generations, naturally wish that their child will follow their footsteps and the same professional career, and will be disappointed if that does not happen. This tendency is also found in families of craftsmen and farmers who are deeply attached to tradition, although the choice of a more difficult or more responsible profession is generally seen as social progress; the parents may have the impression that their professional heredity is in danger of becoming lost, and be saddened by the idea. However, there is a simple solution consisting in free adoption that is not controlled by the government or non-concerned persons, and therefore it enables all the interested persons to manage their past, present and future relationships in a relaxed and effective manner, and to preserve a supple social mobility, without trauma and anxiety.

In the original Vedic system the choice of professional orientation for each student remains exclusive responsibility of the teacher, who does not have prejudice or attachments or preferences (except the benefit of the student) and is very expert in psychology and behavioral sciences. Obviously the system requires an extremely high level of qualifications for the teacher, something that nowadays has become totally lost. In fact, we need to put special attention not to confuse the original Vedic system with the present Indian society, that is degraded and confused by centuries of decadence and especially by the undue influence of non-compatible cultures imposed by invaders and colonialists. The Vedic system requires complete and independent de-centralization of school education and social management, a pre-requisite destroyed by colonial invasions and by the present tendency to globalization.

The so-called "Hindu Renaissance" already rising in the last few decades wants to revive the still existing embers of this extremely ancient civilization, but to rebuild a stable and functional fire in these conditions is a very difficult work, especially because there are powerful hostile forces that want to prevent this new blossoming of the original knowledge and culture.

Dasyus and Daityas in *Rig Veda*

In order to understand Hinduism we need to go to its sources, constituted by the original scriptures, making an effort to verify the Sanskrit text, which often contains big surprises for those who had only heard speaking of these subjects indirectly, from some academic indologist or mass media opinion maker in documentaries, encyclopedias, school books and so on. However, it is not necessary to become able to make one's own translations: it is sufficient to be able to recognize some key words and properly understand their meaning.

The four collections of hymns (or *suktas*) called *Rig, Sama, Yajur* and *Atharva* are considered by mainstream academics as the most ancient texts of Hinduism, and therefore they are often quoted to illustrate the origins of Vedic culture. Specifically, the *Rig Veda* has been mentioned to support the theory of Aryan invasion, because many important words are found in similar forms both in the *Rig Veda* and in the *Zend Avesta* (the text attributed to Zarathustra/ Zoroaster). According to Vedic tradition, however, these similarities are explained with the separation of the *dasyus* from the *arya* civilization because of their criminal inclinations; the subversion of the values that becomes evident from the comparison between the two cultures constitutes the measure of degradation and not a record of history written by victors on the trivial matter of two rival clans fighting for supremacy or even about a genocide of indigenous populations perpetrated by invaders.

The analysis of the original texts clearly shows how the difference between Devas and Asuras both in *Vedas* and in *Zend Avesta* is always a question of ethical choices: it is easy to establish which ones are more virtuous and evolved if we detach ourselves from the colonial logic that was searching for moral justification in the slavery practiced by the nomadic raiders following Zarathustra. In the Vedic system the word *asura* refers to persons who oppose the Devas (the Devas are also called *sura*, "virtuous"), but includes both human and superhuman beings; while human *asuras* are generically called *dasyus*, superhuman *asuras* are more precisely identified with the clan of the Daityas, that can never be described as Deities or Gods although they sometimes solicit worship from human beings. The fact of being worshiped or venerated by someone is certainly not a proof of divinity, as we can easily see from the example of contemporary celebrities - ball players, actors, singers, and so on. Considering the possibility that the *Zend Avesta* culture is an evidence of *degradation* compared to the original Vedic values as clearly stated by Indo-Vedic scriptures, we will now examine the key concepts of *dasyu* and *daitya*, that explain the difficult and dangerous relationship between those that are sometimes called "alien gods" and their followers-worshipers in the various regions of the planet.

As we have already seen, the word *dasyu* refers to the behavior of raiders and pillagers, who can belong to any ethnic group and any culture, but are opposed to the Vedic *arya* system, that supports the universal community in cooperation with the Devas. The Daityas are specifically a dynasty of *asuras* descending from Diti, therefore the word has a precise ethnic and cultural meaning, although it is extended not only to these "Great Ancients" of pure superhuman race but also to their secondary relatives, as well as to their followers and worshipers and hybrid descendents. In this sense the word *daitya* is strictly connected to the *dasyus*, the human beings who are hostile to the Devas and worship the superhuman *asuras* or follow their principles and behaviors; we also remember that the word *arya* is used as opposed to *dasyu* in Vedic texts and in an upside-down way in the *Zend Avesta*.

Due to limitations of space it is not possible to quote here all the Vedic verses that illustrate these points, but we can bring some examples from *Rig Veda* (1.51.8, 1.117.21, 1.130.8, 4.16.10, 4.26.2) defining *aryas* as opposed to the *dasyus*, highlighting the fact that the *dasyus* are "hostile to Brahman" (*brahmadvishe* 3.30.17, 7.104.2), do not follow the ethical norms of civilized behavior (*avratan, niravratan* 1.33.5, 1.51.8, 1.130.8) and exploit others for their own selfish material advantage (*shushna* 1.51.6, 4.16.11), while *aryas* engage in sacred activities (*yajamana* 1.51.8, 1.130.8 etc). Another interesting detail is that *aryas* give great importance to settlements and agriculture, specifically to the ploughing of fields (1.117.21 and others), something that certainly does not apply to a nomadic life style.

The raiders called *dasyus* ("criminals") are described as "hoarders" in the sense of persons who accumulate wealth without utilizing it properly for the benefit of all beings - a type of behavior that modern culture considers a sign of personal and social success and even a wise previdence to ensure a better future. It is interesting to note that the Sanskrit word *vritra*, that in its form of Vritrasura designates the main enemy of Indra (Indra is the chief of the Devas) precisely means "banker, treasurer, wealth, darkness, mountain, restriction, circle (wheel), noise" and refers to a powerful and evil person (or group) that aggressively "makes noise" disturbing the general peace, and selfishly accumulates and freezes resources and wealth without allowing them to circulate freely in a productive way to improve the life of everyone (see especially in *Rig Veda* 1.33.4, 1.52.4, 1.52.7, 1.54.5, 1.55.1, 1.55.5, 1.61.7, 1.62.4, 1.86.10, 1.101.2, 1.102.7, 1.103.6, 2.14.4, 2.20.7, 3.16.1, 3.30.4, 3.5.14, 4.3.1, 4.26.7, 4.26.10, 4.30.20, 5.77.1, 6.16.27, 6.18.8, 7.99.5, and so on).

Raiders are not interested in producing wealth but pillage it, selfishly accumulating their loot without caring about the needs of their victims or the land they invade, burning and damaging as they like. Verse 1.103.6 even speaks about "dirty money hoarded by speculators", of "dark *asuras* who accumulate wealth despising the poor and robbing the innocent": Indra (or the *kshatriya* who represents Indra) must defeat such criminals by breaking their "armored coffers" and wisely distributing the wealth amassed by those selfish misers (3.30.8, 6.31.4). Other verses offer the metaphor of the clouds that lock in the rain, an image that connects the financial resources of a land to the enlivening water that makes the earth fruitful; this idea has deep roots in the collective unconscious even in the west, as we can see in expressions such as "flow of money", "liquidation" etc.

It is also interesting to note the word *vritratva*, literally "the *status* of *vritra*", referred to a category of people that correspond to such description - something that radically changes the perception of Vritra from the "mythological" point of view. The idea that hoarding and blocking wealth is a criminal behavior also applies to human resources, as we see for example in verses 4.16.7, 4.16.8, 4.16.9, stating that such asuric practice is totally opposite to the "simple and direct administration" of the Vedic *arya* model, where progress as sustainable development is considered important and the government remains localized and de-centralized, easily accessible and responsible, and focuses on protecting the subjects without unnecessarily interfering to obstruct their professional occupations and their private lives. In this regard we cannot avoid noticing the degree of deviousness of the theory by which Hindu orthodoxy (*orthodox* literally means "faithful to the original doctrine") is "conservative" or "opposed to the individual and collective evolution and progress".

An adjective often used in *Rig Veda* to describe the *dasyus* ("criminals") is *ayajva*, literally "those who do not perform *yajna*", where the meaning of *yajna* includes all the actions that are religiously noble and dutiful, aimed at supporting the universe in cooperation between human beings and Devas, based on the performance of human duties within *dharma*. It does not apply specifically to the ritual worship of the Devas, because the various forms of *yajna* include the search for knowledge, the practice of yoga, service to guests, the protection of animals, and the performance of one's professional duties.

A verse from *Rig Veda* (1.33.4) is addressed to Indra (the chief of the Devas) as the ideal *kshatriya* (warrior and ruler in Vedic human society): "O most powerful warrior! You possess many weapons and patrol (the kingdom) alone. Use your power to destroy the wealthy Dasyus who rob the people to selfishly accumulate possessions: may they be killed by you! These criminals do not engage in *yajna*."

The colonial theory of aryan invasion artificially and mistakenly superimposes the two concepts of *dasyu* and *dasa*, that are incompatible because the *dasyus* remain outside the system of *varnas* and *dharma*, while the *dasas* (meaning the *sudras*) are very much a part of it, as we have already mentioned. Under no circumstance the servants or *sudras* commit or have committed criminal (adharmic) activities such as robbery or pillage, which are clearly specified as the characteristic life style of *dasyus*; in case a member of any *varna* (not only *sudra* but also *vaisya, kshatriya* and even *brahmana*) committed some criminal action in violation of ethics he must immediately be expelled from the *arya* system and becomes a *dasyu*, irrespective of his birth, social position, genetic or racial origin. In this regard it is interesting to know that the literal meaning of the word *varna* is "worthy of being accepted" and refers to the ethical and professional qualifications required to become a member of one of the four social categories of the Vedic system. The word "caste" and the concept of seminal descendence or birthright that comes with it, do not have anything to do with the Vedic system of *varnas* (social occupational categories) and if the *dasyus* do not engage in *yajna* it is certainly not because someone is preventing them on the basis of some birth prejudice.

Therefore the *dasyus* are identified with the categories outside Vedic society, the *anarya* ("non-*arya*") tribes called *bahlika* ("external") that include *mlecchas, yavanas, khasas* and so on. The *Mahabharata* is particularly rich in this type of information, but we cannot quote all the passages as they are too numerous and large; those who are interested can consult the following: Adi parva chapter 223, Sabha parva chapters 2, 43, 50, 52 and 57, Drona parva chapters 4, 23, 34, 90, 100, 118, 177 and 190, Bhishma parva chapters 9, 75, 82, 103 and 118, Santi parva chapter 328, Udyoga parva chapters 39 and 86, Karna parva chapter 20, 44, 56 and 74, and Anusasana parva chapter 103.

To summarize these passages very briefly, we can say that according the *Mahabharata* both the rulers and the subject of such "external" kingdoms are considered less civilized in comparison to the *arya* kingdoms because they do not observe the hygienic norms of cleanliness and purity, normally drink alcoholic beverages (have cellars to keep liquors) and eat meat including beef (there is mention of a recipe of garlic beef and another of meat and flour, but without details on the procedure). They have excellent horses, perfectly trained, that they sell at a very high price, and also nimble and swift donkeys that can endure long journeys; they trade in wool and hides (especially sheep and deer), carry long swords and scimitars and especially battle axes.

Along history, some groups of these *dasyus* and *anaryas* have chosen to associate with the ethnic and cultural communities of superhuman beings known as Daityas and Danavas, and it is quite possible that from their settlements in the external territories they may have migrated for various reasons especially towards the west, both in the north and in the south, creating "arian" but non *arya* nations. Such nations could be called "tribes" or "kingdoms" by their *arya* contemporaries, because the number of inhabitants or the amount of wealth were not important factors in evaluating the degree of civilization.

Many of these "tribes" in fact were neither technologically backwards or financially poor, rather the opposite (see the verse above mentioned calling them *dhaninah*, "wealthy"); in the Vedic system the degree of civilization is not measured according to the amount of sense gratification or accumulated money, the possession of particularly sophisticated devices or the size of the buildings. In general, elegant simplicity was considered a quality rather than a defect, and wealth was considered useful only when used for the benefit and progress of the individual and society: there was no hoarding of unused goods, something that until recently was commonly condemned as "miserliness" even in western societies.

Nonetheless ancient Indian civilizations, including the external ones in the valleys of Indus and Sarasvati, enjoyed considerable prosperity and abundance, not only for the quantity and quality of food but also for the appreciation of beauty and well-being, with a high level of health and longevity. They were thriving in trade, transportations (especially on water ways), traveling and cultural exchanges; there is evidence of exporting goods towards Mesopotamia and Egypt, such as gold, lapislazuli, sesame and sesame oil, spices, medicines, extracts, cosmetics, pigments, the famous indigo (a name apparently connected to the name "India"), fabrics, precision instruments and even decorative animals such as peacocks. It seems that the name *meluha* originally came from sesame, called *ellu* both in the Sumerian language and in the languages of south India, and amply exported towards Mesopotamia by sea routes.

The Mlecchas frequently mentioned in Vedic scriptures (especially in *Puranas* and *Itihasa*) have been identified by many researchers with the inhabitants of the legendary Meluha, a very prosperous kingdom that had strong commercial ties with Sumer, and that was probably located in the region presently known as Punjab (from the Sanskrit *pancha apa*, "five rivers"), that some identify with the mythical land of Punt mentioned in Egyptian texts. In this perspective it becomes apparent that possibly some of the advanced cities of the Indus and Sarasvati valleys discovered by archeologists starting from 1920 were actually the settlements called Mleccha as non-*arya* (meaning, not subject to the demanding ethical and religious rules of the *arya* kingdoms) and therefore allowed non-vegetarianism and the use of animals for food.

In fact in several ancient cities in the Indus valley archeologists have discovered non-vegetarian food remnants, something that triggered hot controversies among contemporary Hindus to establish whether their Vedic ancestors were vegetarian or not, and what they were eating precisely. Evidently this problem does not have much to do with a sincere desire of imitating the original Vedic civilization, because from the scriptures and from the archeological finds we know very well that the staple foods in ancient times were sesame and barley, today very difficult to find in India but essential for religious ceremonies according to the original texts, while millet (that almost nobody uses any more) constituted the basis of the diet especially for those who were engaged in intense physical work. On the other hand, contemporary Indian markets are flooded with potatoes, chilli peppers, tomatoes, pumpkins and even maize (all originating from the Americas and therefore introduced to India not before the 1700s), not to speak of the typically British tea with biscuits.

The percentage of vegetarians in India has dropped drastically during the last century, without counting the "local traditions" that are typically based on meats (Kashmir, Punjab, etc) or fish (Bengal, Orissa etc). In Vedic scriptures, non-vegetarian people are called *chandalas* or *mlecchas* or non-*aryas*, and although they were tolerated on the territory they could not be part of the *varna* social system; the degraded system of the castes and the myth of meat consumption as the source of the physical strength and power of the British have confused the picture, and unfortunately today we have some caste brahmins and even "*dharma* activists" who insist in trying to demonstrate the irrelevance of vegetarianism in Vedic religious practice.

Conventional archeologists typically present the settlements in the Indus (and Sarasvati) valley as the origin of a "dravidian" Indian civilization, destroyed by the invasions of the "aryan nomads" according to the theory of the colonial indologists. As we have already mentioned, many Indian researchers and even some westerners who appreciate Hindu culture have presented the OIT (*Out Of India theory*) to replace the classic AIT (*Aryan Invasion Theory*), but still some pieces are missing from the puzzle, and we could certainly contribute to the overall picture with the knowledge of these non-*arya* kingdoms clearly and profusely mentioned in Indo-Vedic scriptures. The necessary information can be found in Vedic texts: we just need to look for them. And especially, we should not be contented with the old and obviously biased translations, that were made deliberately confused and denigratory by colonial indologists and still remain the main or sole source usually available. We should rather put sufficient effort to produce translations and commentaries that are easily understood by the modern public, but they are able to convey the original message in all its relevance and power.

Harappa and Mohenjo Daro are likely to be two classical examples of *mleccha* (*meluha*) settlements at the margins (both ideologically and geographically) of Vedic civilization, that still shared many cultural and knowledge aspects, but chose to abandon their cities after damaging climate changes, to search for new territories. However, it is not unlikely that the rulers of these *mleccha* communities had at their disposal a wide range of vehicles, including flying *vimanas* (spaceships or airplanes) mentioned in many Vedic texts as we will see in a next chapter, because such technological knowledge is not intrinsically based on ethical or religious considerations, and in fact it is widely known that the use of *vimanas* was common to Devas and Asuras and even to human beings.

The mass of the population (*mleccha* or *arya*) may have used similar vehicles or more ordinary transportation according to their means and abilities, because the *vimanas*, in those times just like today, were expensive crafts and thus relatively rare, which needed special fuel, servicing by specialized technicians and expert pilots to drive them. The biggest aircrafts, that could transport a larger group of people, also needed adequate spaces for landing and parking and therefore must have been less numerous.

Vimanas of all sizes could be built and driven also by people from the "external kingdoms" who did not follow the ethical and spiritual values and teachings of the Vedic system but used its material technological aspects, including many rituals that one could call "magical" because they interacted with the subtle dimensions to modify the structure of matter. Actually *asuras* and *dasyus* too perform religious ceremonies including fire rituals, but although they are rather proud of such practices, their actions cannot be called sacred (*yajna* or "sacrifice") because they are not directed to the service of God intended as the totality of all beings in the universe. The rituals performed by the *dasyus* always have some selfish purpose and even if sometimes they are called *yajnas*, they are such in name only, as very clearly statement in *Bhagavad gita* (16.7-18).

It is very important to understand the connection between the *dasyus/ayajvas* described in Vedic texts and the *anarya* tribes that emigrated to the west, mixing with other asuric cultures and building the foundations for the development of the doctrine of Zarathustra, that we will analyze more deeply in a next chapter.

God in Hinduism

As we have already mentioned, Vedic tradition connects the *aryas* with the Devas and the *aris* with the Asuras. In fact this concept is also found in Zoroastrism, but turned completely upside down, supporting the separatist perspective of the *aris*, who are the followers and worshipers of the Asuras, who consider the Devas as their "enemies" to the point of presenting them as evil and diabolical beings. This confusion appears evident from the common etymological origins of the two opposite words "divine" and "devil", and several other connected words.

In other less complex cultures the polarization between "good spirits" and "evil spirits" is less prominent and diversities have subtler differences that are more compatible with each other. Unfortunately it is not easy to get fully immersed in the mentality of ancient cultures that have already disappeared, wiped out by the iconoclastic fury of abrahamics and post-abrahamics, but there are traces that can be found and integrated properly to make the picture clearer. By examining the versions presented by ancient cultures in relationship to the idea of divinity, we notice that the concept of God as supreme and total existence, ontologically transcendent and eternal, is distinctly different from the limited and temporary existence of individual persons who possess more or less considerable superhuman powers, and who are described by local mythologies as gods (with a small "g").

The original Indo-Vedic tradition, still alive at present in a certain measure thanks to the huge expanse of its literary evidence and disciplic transmission, offers a valuable perspective to access a genuine level of perception of ancient civilizations, and to establish the correct relationship between the two concepts of Good and Evil and the understanding of a transcendent reality that is beyond both of them. In the previous section about religion and mythology we have already mentioned this concept of God as transcendent Existence, that can be naturally and instinctively perceived by any human being without consideration of specific cultural, religious or ethnic affiliations. In this regard we have mentioned the concept of Archetypes, examined more elaborately in our work on *The awakening of the Mother Goddess*, and specifically in the first volume dealing with the Natural Religion, while the second volume discusses the development of these concepts along the course of known human history.

The exploration of the concept of God is essential to properly understand the concept of Deva. We are aware that it is impossible to insert a long theological elaboration here, and so we will simply touch the main points that are directly connected withe the subject of this book. Furthermore, because the required explanation is based on very precise technical concepts, we are compelled to use a bit of Sanskrit in our elaboration, hoping it will not become too difficult to grasp. We will try to be as clear as possible.

The supreme God (technically defined as *brahman*) is pure existence and awareness (*purusha*), that potentially contains all manifestations (*prakriti*) both spiritual and material, past, present and future, in all dimensions. The fundamental unity of the supreme Divinity (God) is never diminished because to its complete nature, that includes both the male principle (*purusha*) and the feminine principle (*prakriti*); as these two aspects are apparently distinct from the original One, the ontological principles manifesting as male and female are constantly engaged in what we could compare to a dance of union, or according to some symbolic imagery, the Sacred Marriage.

This is the origin of the concept of trinity, represented by Vishnu as the non-manifested One, the primary and complete Brahman (not to be confused with Brahma the creator of this particular universe), from whom Shiva and Shakti manifest as the Father and the Mother of the cosmos and of all beings. Later, with the patriarchal and especially colonial influence this original Triad was covered by the concept of Trimurti replacing Shakti with Brahma, who technically could be considered a form representing the Mother of the universe, because he gives shape to all material existences, generating them from his own body. However, the body of Brahma is substantially different from the human body because it is immensely "subtler" and therefore generally defined as "mind" (see the characteristic term *manasa putra*, "son of the mind").

We will now discuss the concept of *avatara*.

The ontological principle (also called *tattva* or "existence") of the supreme God can express itself in various measures (*svamsa, vibhinnamsa, atman*) and descend (*avatara*) on a level that can be perceived by the senses, to perform specific pre-organized activities (*lila*) meant for the evolution and sustenance of the universe (*rita, dharma*).

We have already presented the concept of the supreme ontological principle in the previous chapter on religion and mythology, explaining that the *avataras* (visible manifestations) of the supreme

God can be compared to a school teacher or an actor-director who utilize expressions, words, gestures and scenography that have been designed specifically to convey a message required for the evolution of individual beings. Because their awareness is always transcendental to the activities they perform, they are not limited by circumstances, and the nature of their birth and death (generally defined as "appearance" and "disappearance" to highlight their extraordinary character) is not subject to the laws that govern the more ordinary levels of material existence.

The specific form of the divine manifestation is determined from time to time by the space-time *continuum* where the principle of transcendent existence chooses to appear and act.

According to the degree of consciousness of each manifestation, these *personalities of Godhead* express a different degree of power and qualities, forms, names, activities, and so on. The immediate expansions *svamsa* at the origin of the existence of the universe are called Vishnu, Shiva and Shakti, who constitute a level of awareness unlimited and inconceivable for a materially limited mentality, because they are not limited by duality, time and space. Here we are still on the level of the trascendental Unity, even if temporarily manifested at a level that can be perceived by material senses. The apparent individuality of such manifestations is determined by the specific mission of the *avatara* and can be translated into form that, albeit always divine, have the appearance of human or superhuman beings, or even of animals that are however quite extraordinary such as Varaha, Kurma and Matsya (respectively boar, tortoise and fish).

Let's see for the example the *avatara* Rama (or Ramachandra), who is the main character of the epic poem *Ramayana*, mentioned by alienists to try to support their theories. Actually Rama is a direct manifestation of the Supreme God (*svamsa*) but he is not a Deva or administrator of the universe: he is a human being, born on Earth in the human *kshatriya* dynasty known as Surya vamsa, as the son of king Dasaratha and his queen Kausalya - both totally human under all aspects. So although he is an *avatara* of Vishnu, Rama plays the role of a human being and ideal prince (*maryada purushottama*); in this capacity he offers ritual worship to the Devas and especially to Shiva and Shakti.

Another special character in the *Ramayana* is Hanuman, often superficially and simplistically considered a "monkey" because of his physical description, that includes a tail and rather monkey-like facial features. Obviously the "animal" interpretation does not explain how Hanuman and all the Vanaras (literally "residents of the forest") are very much capable of speaking, wear clothes and ornaments, use weapons of which some quite sophisticated, live in palaces and have a professionally organized society with architects, army generals and kings. The conundrum is not solved by saying that they were monkeys to which popular fantasy has conferred special powers, because then *all* the information on the Varanas should be considered *equally* "mythological" and one could just as well theorize that they were actual human beings who used to wear masks and animal disguises, as we see in shamanic cultures. In fact many researchers have started to consider the hypothesis that the "monkey" character of the Vanaras could be a totemic symbol rather than a genetic feature. We could even suggest the existence of some humanoids (who may have had some kind of tail) who in that distant historical period enjoyed a rather high level of life although they lived in the forest. In any case, this Hanuman described in the *Ramayana* is certainly not presented as one of the Devas who manage the universe, but he is recognized as a *svamsa avatara* of Shiva, and is therefore transcendental to temporary and limited individuality.

On the other hand the enemy of Rama, called Ravana, foolishly presented by some alienists as a "Deva" or "god" is actually a Rakshasa (Asura and Daitya) endowed with superhuman powers but having a demoniac orientation, and much more limited in level of awareness and therefore in ontological existence compared to Rama and Hanuman. Thus, claiming that the *Ramayana* describes "a war among gods" is preposterous, because among the characters of the entire story *there is not even one single* Deva.

Regarding the use of *vimanas* or spaceships during the events described in the *Ramayana*, even a small amount of investigation will reveal that such airplanes or space ships were not used by any Deva but rather by the Rakshasas (Asuras). The most famous is the airplane called *pushpa* or *pushpaka vimana*, originally belonging to Kuvera, the chief of the Yakshas and lord of hidden wealth, who was related with Ravana as son of the same father, Visrava Pulastya Rishi but from a different wife, exactly like the Adityas and the Daityas are all sons of Kasyapa Rishi. Kuvera occupies the position of Deva as one of the universe administrators (*vibhinnamsa*) thanks to his elevated level of awareness, that is not connected to his racial origin. However, Kuvera has no part in the story of the *Ramayana*, because although he had originally been the king of Lanka, he had been ousted by Ravana, who had appropriated his palace and his *vimana* too. This airship, the *pushpaka vimana*, was in possession of Ravana, and when Ravana was defeated and killed in the Lanka battle, Rama received it as a gift from Vibhishana ("the nice brother" of Ravana); at that time Rama takes that particular *pushpaka vimana* and uses it to return to his capital Ayodhya. We need to remember that Rama had reached the island of Sri Lanka not by flying in his *vimana*, but by walking on a bridge of stones that is still partially existing today, and is called Rama Setu (literally "the bridge of Rama") or also *Adam's bridge*, a name given by British colonialist because of its obvious extreme antiquity.

Similarly in the story of Krishna, narrated in the *Mahabharata* and especially in *Bhagavata Purana* but also in other less known texts, we see that Krishna was not an administrative Deva but an *avatara* (*svamsa*) of the transcendent Godhead, born on Earth (precisely in Mathura, a few kilometers from present day Delhi) in the Yadu branch of the other great Vedic human dynasty, the Soma vamsa or Chandra vamsa, as son of two totally human beings - prince Vasudeva and his wife Devaki. The idea of the "virgin birth" cannot be applied to the advent of Krishna because Devaki had already had 6 sons (in the "normal" way) and a miscarriage before the birth of Krishna, and Vasudeva is under all aspects the husband of Devaki; besides, the *Bhagavata Purana* clearly states that Krishna "passed from Vasudeva to Devaki". Princess Devaki is a noble but normal human being, while *parthenogenesis* refers to the independent generation of a divine offspring, that is possible through an absolute power of the Genitrix Goddess (or, with patriarchalism, of a male God) where only one parent exists.

In the abrahamic distortion the "virgin birth" of Jesus does not confer any divine power to Mary, but simply refers to a miraculous human pregnancy because it leaves an intact hymen even after child birth (as per gynecological exam specified in the Gospels) demonstrating the "purity" of the particular woman and therefore her "market value" as superior to that of "dishonored" women who have been deflowered. In no ancient culture we find any positive value in the concept of virginity in the abrahamic gynecological sense; until a few centuries ago in non-abrahamic cultures/ religions the idea of "virgin" simply referred to a young woman who had no marriage relationship or family duties based on matrernity. The fact that a woman had had sexual intercourse (or not) was totally irrelevant, because the concept of sex was not considered a disqualification or sinful association.

Let us go back to Krishna. In spite of the fantasies of alienists, Krishna did not have a *vimana*, but used land vehicles, or sometimes war chariots that remained on the ground. The particular case of Garuda does not indicate a machine but a sentient being, devotee or servant, described as eating and performing other physical activities, and having adventures of his own.

The so-called "sky battle" against Salva's aircraft was actually a defense fight *from the ground* against the air attack brought by an ordinary human being, named Salva, who was determined to avenge the death of his friend Sisupala, cousin of Krishna, killed by Krishna himself. This Salva is a normal human being, certainly not a Deva or a god or even a divine *avatara*: also in this case the idea of the "war among gods" is totally unfounded.

After obtaining an aircraft of the *saubha* type, that the text clearly described as built by the Asura Maya Danava (who was also not a Deva), the above mentioned Salva drives it over the city of Krishna, called Dvaraka, and starts to drop projectiles of various types, while Krishna was away participating to the Rajasuya ceremonies of another cousin, Yudhisthira.

The sons of Krishna and the other warriors of the dynasty, who had remained at home, organize an anti-aircraft defense from the ground, also countering the simultaneous attack on land by the army of Salva, that had laid siege to the city. We see that the eldest son of Krishna, Pradyumna, leader of the defense forces, rides on a normal war chariot described specifically in the episode where he is wounded and loses consciousness, and his chariot driver Daruka takes him back into the city to revive him. In this case as well, the defenders of the city and the relatives of Krishna are described not as Devas but as human beings of a human dynasty, born on the Earth from ancestors who were also originally from Earth.

Krishna arrives while the battle is still going on, but he is not flying on a *vimana*: it is from the ground that Krishna shoots down Salva's aircraft, so Salva is forced to abandon ship and to continue fighting on foot, until he is killed by Krishna on the battlefield. We leave it to the readers to figure out how it is possible to conclude, from these events so clearly described in details by the original texts, that the fight between Krishna and Salva was "a war among gods who were flying on spaceships".

In the same way, in the Kurukshetra battle described in the *Mahabharata* we do not see even one single Deva taking part to the fighting, although the text repeatedly mentions "divine" weapons: according to the secondary Vedic scriptures called *Vedangas* and specifically the *Dhanur Veda* (the *Veda* of military science), any human being who was sufficiently qualified could learn to use divine weapons, but certainly this did not raise him to the position of Deva or divine *avatara*.

It is true that the *Mahabharata* does not speak only of the battle of Kurukshetra but also narrates of other wars in different times and places, as told by the characters of the central story during their conversations where we see *vimanas* (airships or spaceships) but these are often used by Devas and Asuras and sometimes by human beings. The *Mahabharata* is an immense text, that in various editions comes up to 200,000 verses, and the battle of Kurukshetra is only one of many events and subjects, albeit the most important one. For those who are interested in the subject, we have prepared a summary of the *Mahabharata* for the first Appendix to our work on *Bhagavad gita* (which is a part of the *Mahabharata*) and also in the third volume of our *Introduction to Vedic knowledge*.

Another point in the story of Krishna that has been muddied more or less explicitly by alienists refers to marriage, conjugal relationships and offspring. The alienist theory claims (more than "suggesting") that Krishna, as an extraterrestrial being descended to Earth out of greed and lust, was sexually attracted by earthly women and united with them, generating a descendence of "demigods" to perpetuate his genetic heritage, maybe with artificial insemination (but then we cannot see why aliens should be described as lusty). Generally the presentations of alienists and their debunkers insert in their videos some images of Radha and Krishna to illustrate such theories, and someone maybe slightly more informed also utilized the BBT painting (property of the Bhaktivedanta Book Trust) showing young Kunti who meets Surya, from whom she will have a son, Karna, who is one of the heroes of the *Mahabharata*. Of course, we have also seen the picture of Surya meeting Kunti presented as an image of "Krishna the Sun God", but that is another demonstration of ignorance by "debunkers" who evidently are not much better than the alienists they are trying to expose.

Speaking about Karna, his extraordinary birth from the Sun God Surya (not Krishna) does not make him a Deva by any description; in the story we see that everyone (including himself) considers him as an ordinary human being and a rather unlucky one for that. The secret of his birth will be revealed only after his death, when Kunti asks her other sons (the five Pandavas) to perform the funeral rites for Karna, who had been their secret eldest brother.

And speaking about the Pandavas, who technically are the only persons in Hindu "mythology" to qualify for the definition of *demigods*, their birth from Kunti and Madri as sons of the main Devas - Indra (Arjuna), Vayu (Bhima), Yama (Yudhisthira) and the twins Asvini kumara (Nakula and Sahadeva) - is certainly not presented as a special divine right to the succession on the throne, of which they are legitimate heirs only because they are the legal sons of Pandu, the human husband of Kunti and Madri. And in fact they are called *pandava*, "sons of Pandu". In the entire *Mahabharata* they are described as simply human beings, although favoured by the Devas and blessed with special gifts.

The divine origin of the Pandava brothers is also irrelevant for their offspring, of which the only survivor to the Kurukshetra war is Arjuna's grandson, named Parikshit, who will continue the dynasty as a normal human being, without claiming any divine genetic superiority. The same situation is described with reference to the descendents of Krishna, the Yadu dynasty, that were annihilated in a fratricidal fight even before the disappearance of Krishna himself; the only survivor was Krishna's grandson Vajra, who went to live with Arjuna in Hastinapura as an exiled prince because Krishna's capital city Dvaraka had been submerged by the ocean. Nothing more is said about the descendents of Vajra, and the descendents of Parikshit are described as ordinary kings of a totally earthly character.

One last important observation is the fact that the Devas who generated the Pandavas (including the "secret 6th" Karna) had not descended spontaneously because they were atracted to earth women on whom they imposed their lusty attentions, but they had been deliberately called with a specific *mantra* by the family of Pandu, because Pandu was unable to generate an offspring directly and wanted to have heirs indirectly as per the Vedic system. In case a king - for any reason - was unable to beget a son, the queens had the option of uniting with some special person to conceive a very qualified heir. Kunti had already experimented with the *mantra* when she was a very young girl, secretly giving birth to Karna but abandoning the child because she was confused and did not know how to take care of him. With Pandu's permission, Kunti called the three primary Devas, then she gave the *mantra* to Madri, the other wife of Pandu, who used it once to call the two Asvini kumaras, getting two sons at one time.

From the description of the *Mahabharata* it appears clearly that the called Devas consented to impregnate the two queens only as a favor and not because they wanted to, and certainly they were not motivated by sexual desire. There is no other passage, in the *Mahabharata* or in any other text, where we see a Deva descending, with or without a spaceship, because he was attracted by earthly women, to generate a semi-divine descendence; those who have this tendency are always below the Deva level, usually Asuras or at best Gandharvas. There is only one particular exception regarding Indra, but his escapades are not with ordinary women, and are certainly not meant to procreate a semi-divine offspring; since Indra's court is famous for its Apsaras - the incredibly beautiful dancers expert in sexual seduction - it is difficult to imagine why king Indra or any of his associates would want to have encounters with ordinary terrestrial women.

The other famous example, also narrated in the *Mahabharata*, speaks about the descent of the Goddess Ganga, the personification of the Ganges river, for whom king Santanu had fallen desperately in love. After much hesitation and after establishing very precise conditions, Ganga consented to marry Santanu and gave birth to the famous Bhishmadeva, but the union of Ganga with Santanu was very short, because the king was unable to understand and respect the mysterious activities of Ganga and so, according to the agreement, the Goddess left him. In this case, too, Bhishmadeva remained a *non sequitur* from the genetic point of view, because he never married and did not beget even one single child, to keep the promise made to the father of Santanu's second wife, Satyavati, who did not want his descendents to have potential competition in the succession to the throne. The narrow-minded scheme failed causing disastrous consequences for the kingdom, because Satyavati's sons were unable to beget even one single heir, and Satyavati had to call for help from Vyasa, an extraordinary son she had had from Rishi Parasara before her marriage with Santanu. But Bhishma had no descendents.

We have already seen that Krishna did not land in India from a spaceship, but he was born in Mathura in the palace of king Kamsa, from two perfectly human parents named Vasudeva and Devaki. The idea that he "descended from Vaikuntha" refers to his ontological nature of *avatara* of the transcendent divine, rather like ordinary human beings "descend" from the subtle to the gross dimension when they are conceived and take birth in totally normal circumstances. The only difference is the level of awareness, that in the case of the genuine *avataras* of the transcendent God is complete and perfectly controls the material elements and the development of events, while conditioned souls are dragged here and there by "destiny".

Krishna is not a Deva but he never falls under the control of sexual lust, and his conjugal relationships are always described in all texts (especially in *Bhagavata Purana*) as expressions of blessing explicitly requested by the interested women. The *Bhagavata* informs us that Krishna married more than 16,000 women, but we should not imagine a situation similar to the *harems* where in fact the islamic invaders locked up thousands of girls purchased as slaves on the market or forcibly removed from their families. To each of his wives,

Krishna gave a luxurious personal residence that she was free to leave at all times.

Krishna was never the king of Dvaraka, because he preferred to leave the throne to his grandfather Ugrasena. Ugrasena had been imprisoned before Krishna's birth and during the 16 years of reign of the usurper Kamsa, and was freed and reinstalled to kingship by Krishna himself who killed the evil tyrant. The main wives of Krishna were Rukmini, Satyabhama and Jambavati; Rukmini had personally written a letter to Krishna, begging him to save her from a marriage arranged by her family, while Satyabhama and Jambavati had been happy to marry him to cement State alliances. Kalindi boldly asked Krishna to marry her when she met him on the bank of the river Yamuna, while Lakshmana, Mitravinda and Bhadra chose Krishna during their *svayamvara*, a ceremony in which the *kshatriya* princesses of the royal order could watch and evaluate the qualities of the participants to the games. The others are the 16,000 girls, whose names are not mentioned in the *Bhagavata* or other texts, who had been rescued by Krishna after his battle against the Asura Bhauma, who had kidnapped them and kept them captive; all of them asked their rescuer to remain under his protection, and Krishna officially married them.

All the children of Krishna were considered human beings and not demigods or carriers of some special divine "genetic heritage", and their dynasty ended during the lifetime of Krishna, as we have already mentioned. It is true that *Puranas* and *Itihasas* speak of "test tube babies" but these are children of human beings, conceived in the traditional way and then cloned, or children generated by Apsaras (heavenly nymphs, not Goddessess) by collecting the sperm of human males, especially Rishis who had become particularly powerful by their realizations in Vedic science. And in any case, the result of such conceptions is always considered as a normal human being, and not the special descendent of a semi-divine race, destined by genetic right to dominate on the masses of the population.

Regarding the relationship of Krishna and Radha, whose images are often pasted inside the videos produced by alienists, the theory of the extraterrestrial who descends because he is sexually attracted to some earthly woman is even more preposterous. Apart from the fact of

Krishna's birth on Earth as we have already mentioned, his relationship with Radha and the other *gopis* of the cowherd village named Gokula Vrindavana started in their early childhood, because Krishna had been smuggled to Gokula by his father Vasudeva, who wanted to save him from Kamsa's violence, and was secretly exchanged in the middle of the night with the baby girl who had been born from Yasoda, the wife of the village chief Nanda. On the other hand, Radha was the daughter of Vrishabhanu, the chief of a nearby village named Varshana, and often the children of the area used to meet in the pastures or on the bank of the river Yamuna, from which the girls regularly fetched water. The *Bhagavata Purana* specifically explains that Radha had fallen in love with Krishna and she was not the only one, because many other girls were fascinated by that most handsome boy, whose complexion was so black as to seem blue, and who played the flute in such an amazing way.

It is necessary to remember here that all Vedic scriptures and especially the stories of the persons recognized as divine *avataras* contain many levels of meanings, as we have already explained with the example of the school teacher and the actor-director who plays a role in a script. The great *acharyas* who are universally recognized have explained the deep symbolic implications of the love affair between Krishna and Radha and the other *gopis*, from the archetypal depiction of the soul aspiring to the union with the transcendental God, to the movements of planets and constellations, and the text of the *Bhagavata Purana* is full of explicit references to the transcendental nature of Krishna as the supreme Soul of all beings and the foundation of the entire universe.

Radha and the *gopis* take the unilateral decision to ask the Devas (and specifically Goddes Kali, also called Katyayani) the blessing of being able to marry Krishna, and from this point onwards there is the development of love games, because Krishna consents to reciprocate the love of the *gopis*, and even so, only after much hesitation. However, neither Radha or any other *gopi* ever had a child from Krishna, and certainly the idea of a semi-divine descendence of an alien with the terrestrial victims of his libido ends *not with a bang but a whimper*, to quote a famous expression TS Eliot (*The hollow men*, 1925).

Obviously, all this information and its conclusions refer to the *avataras* of the transcendent God and the individual Devas, and not to the Asuras of various races, who are famous all over the Vedic texts for their material lust and for a strong tendency to sexually attack women of all races and backgrounds, and sometimes even men.

Once again, our message is confirmed: the superhuman characters that alienists want to present as Devas are actually mere Asuras, not necessarily extraterrestrials, but nonetheless extremely dangerous.

The individual Devas

To better understand the difference between the *avataras* of God (such as Rama and Krishna) and individual Devas (as persons in administrative posts in the universe) we need to compare the nature of the emanations *svamsa* and *vibhinnamsa* (who are *avataras*, meaning they are on a transcendent ontological level manifested in various degrees on the tangible level) with the individualized manifestations (*jiva atman*) who can temporarily occupy dynamic positions and roles connected to the elemental *vibhinnamsas* in relations of dependency or derivation.

Here we find specifically the personalities of the Devas, who work as administrators of the universe, as subordinate and secondary assistants in the functions of creation, maintenance and destruction of the cosmos. Some confusion may rise from the fact that such "jobs" can be taken up temporarily by some *svamsa* or *vibhinnamsa avatara*, but we hope that this brief note will be sufficient to give a glimpse of a possible ramification towards a further field of elaboration, without losing sight of the logical thread that we are following now.

The Devas are secondary expansions (*vibhinnamsa*) categorized according to functional hyerarchic principles, each with their different roles in the immense cosmic drama, in administrative positions. All the Devas, by definition, use their powers only for the universal good; some very evolved human beings are therefore somehow assimilated to the category, as we see for example in the expressions *nara-deva* ("human *deva*"), *bhu-deva* ("*deva* of Earth") or in the suffix *deva* sometimes used as a title of respect accompanying the name of a person, albeit rarely and especially for kings. In this regard it is also useful to clarify that the title of *deva* indicating a human king does not mean that the king reigns because of a divine right of investiture through the endorsement of priests or because of genetic heritage as a descendent of hybrid aliens as suggested by alienists: it rather means that the *position* of King is to the administration of the kingdom just like the position of Deva is to the administration of the universe - that the King has the duty to feed and protect all subjects and make sure that resources are properly distributed.

Corresponding, but much more frequent, is the suffix *devi* (feminine of *deva*), that is used as a respectful title to address any woman, as the feminine form itself is considered a direct manifestation of the Mother Goddess as ontological principle, while the masculine form in itself is considered a secondary manifestation of the Mother Goddess and not of the "Father God".

We can thus understand that the Devas are relatively limited persons, whose powers and individuality are determined by their particular level of consciousness, although that is much higher than the normal human level. If we want to try a rough comparison, we could say that the secondary Devas are to the primary Devas like the Adriatic sea is to the Atlantic ocean, while the human being is merely a puddle: that is water in all cases, but in a totally different category. If someone has only seen puddles, even large puddles, he does not have the intellectual instruments to understand the vastity of the Atlantic ocean, and if he tries to measure it by multiplying the area of the biggest puddle he has ever seen, he will easily become confused. If we tell him that in the Atlantic there are (or were) thousands of whales, he will only think we are crazy or superstitious ignorant "dogmatists".

The Devas exist. The Gods exist. And certainly they will not stop existing if a contemporary human being becomes convinced they are merely aliens or their existence is a superstitious projection. A human being can alienate himself from the harmony of the universe, but his existence in those conditions is certainly not the highest point of evolution, but rather a sad condition of disease and suffering that damages everyone - the individual, society in general and even the planet itself, as we can easily see by having a look around in the world we presently live in. With their insistence on Aliens as a supreme reality, alienists have alienated themselves and created more and more alienation among the people. To stop this disaster, it is urgent to help the greater possible number of persons to understand the deep reality of existence, and to rediscover the proper harmony with the natural order of the universe.

At the highest levels the Devas are archetypes, meaning they are fundamental components of cosmic existence, naturally recognizable by any human being in any culture. As such, they are eternal and immortal, but they also can manifest as *avataras* by consciously descending into our material universe, appearing and disappearing according to the necessity of their specific mission.

In their administrative functions, even the relatively less high Devas participate to a certain degree in the divine ontological qualities, meaning they are considered immortal or almost immortal (in the sense that they continue to exist for the entire duration of the universe), omnipresent or almost omnipresent (in the sense that they can manifest in all places and even in multiple forms) and omnipotent or almost omnipotent (in the sense that they have the ability to manipulate subtle and gross matter). In the Vedic perspective, however, such characteristics are potentially present also in the human beings of this planet (earthlings/ terrestrials) who can develop them through the techniques of yoga, although the process requires a lot of effort. Of course, it is not easy to understand the subtle point about the Godhead, so we should not be simplistic about our analysis: the fundamental concept in Vedic knowledge is that God (transcendent supreme Existence) is existence and awareness that transcends individuality, so trying to understand the Devas as "not God" by applying the individuality concept is not going to work very well.

Specifically, the Vedic tradition highlights the importance of connections and correspondences between the levels called *adhidaivika*, represented by the personalities of God or Devas, *adhibhautika*, represented by the material elements including all the various factors of existence and not just the gross elements, and *adhyatmika*, represented by the individual awareness of the human being who has the duty to actively cooperate with the entire universal community, tuning in with the highest possible level of consciousness.

It is very evident that such a network of correspondences and connections cannot simply apply to a race of "flesh and blood" extraterrestrials, no matter how greatly endowed with superhuman powers, that remain subject to strong limitations of space, time and individuality.

Let us try to explain this concept better, because it will make it easier to understand the idea of divinity in the ancient world as it was applied at various levels. All the Devas basically engage in the study and managing of the fundamental principles of existence at cosmic level; this gives them a deep knowledge of the laws of the universe and an almost complete control over matter, including the matter that constitutes their bodies, and of the practice of spiritual science that leads to liberation through the evolution of awareness or consciousness.

They recognize and worship the supreme Existence, that corresponds to the concept of God - absolute, omnipresent, omniscient, omnipotent, present in the hearts of all beings, and foundation of the existence of all beings. They do not identify directly and individually with this universal Existence, but they intimately participate to it through awareness. Some of these beings are so advanced in the knowledge of the various dimensions that their awareness transcends the individual level and direcly taps into what we could call "collective super-conscious" or "God's mind". This possibility also exists at human level, as we have already said. From here we get the concept of superimposition of the ontological characters of the Deity to individual personification of deities who represent it in archetypal way - but in the case of the Devas, who constitute the original model of the idea that later seeped into other cultures, such personifications possess by definition not only the mythological attribution but the specific functions as well.

In other words, the Devas are "transcendent" to the degree in which they have already realized (not "seeking") Transcendence (that *is* God as ontological Existence) and therefore they are directly part of it: this ability is determined by their identity position. It is an eternal ontological position for the *svamsas* such as Vishnu and Shiva and their *avataras* and direct emanations and for the main forms of Adi Shakti, but it is an acquired position for the administration Devas, the lesser Devas and even for all human and humanoid beings. It is not easy to understand this, because on the level of Existence (Brahman) all realities are actually One, so differences or distinctions are simply determined by the degree of awareness: *svamsas* are ontologically and eternally complete awareness, that by definition is non-dualistic.

The level immediately after the *svamsa* (Vishnu, Shiva, Shakti) is the elemental *vibhinnamsa* (the primary Devas) such as the personifications of Sky (that is, space) and Earth, Sun and Moon, Fire, Air, Water, Rain, Rivers and Ocean, Mountains, Stars and constellations (including the planets), Dawn, Night, Numbers and geometrical Shapes, verbal Expression, the human sub-personalities (Mother, Father, Warrior, etc) and even physiological functions (nourishment, healing, death etc). As we can see, the concept of "elements" is not limited here to the usual 4 or 5 described as earth, water, fire, air, ether, but they include all the various factors and components of Existence.

These "elemental" or "archetypal" Devas cannot be killed because they are not limited by a separate individual body, but they directly manifest in all the forms connected to their respective functions, and they disappear temporarily with the end of the cycle of universal manifestation to reappear at the beginning of the next cycle. They are therefore eternal, although in a sense individual and distinct, that is, not on a completely transcendental position.

The personifications of these ontological principles contain a power that is greater than the individual being's; in fact it is possible for the individual being to tune into their level of consciousness and acquire qualities and powers to be used in one's own personal life. This scientific process is called "worship" but it is substantially different from the abrahamic concept, as the human being that is engaged in it must identify with the worshiped Deity, installing it within himself as "soul of his soul" (*param atman*). The tantric tradition, so often ill presented and not only in the west, details its specific method and its requirements; unfortunately many original texts have been lost and presently they are available to the public in rather recent copies and are in many cases incomplete or distorted. Incompleteness is somehow deliberate, because the original tradition is fundamentally mysteric or initiatic, meaning it must be transmitted by the qualified *guru* to the qualified disciple on the exclusive responsibility of the *guru*, otherwise it must remain "secret", or veiled by ambiguities or gaps.

It is important to understand that such secrecy has nothing to do with the esoteric-occultist perspective developed in relatively recent times, that explains élitarism with political or racial motivations. We should rather compare it to the strict discipline of a school specialized in professional training in highly technical fields that could be very dangerous, such as the categories of airplane pilot, designer of high voltage electrical systems, neurologist surgeon, and so on. It is foolish to expect to be able to enter lightly into such professional activities simply after reading a generic book or listening to a public lecture on the subject, even inventing extemporaneous solutions that appear to be easier compared to the descriptions in texts that seem to be too technical for an independent beginner. Of course nothing is completely impossible, but we should not underestimate the danger of damages, which become immediately evident when we look at the western esoteric-occultist scenario that claims to be based on "*tantra*" (for example with the notorious Crowley and theosophists).

Less "intense" than the elemental Devas but more numerous (about 33 million) are the administrative Devas, secondary manifestations or "assistants" of the elemental Devas: they live on planetary systems we could call "heavenly" (Svarga) and easily travel from one planet to another in wonderfully decorated spaceships. In general they are described as "angel-like" but they have extremely powerful weapons. They never wage war against each other (as some alienists claim) but they rally together against the forces of chaos and oppression, to protect the universe and its good functioning. They are substantially different from the concept of "angel" (from the Greek *angelos*, "messenger") because they are not messengers of God, they do not have wings and do not sing in choirs; if we want to find similarities with the angels of abrahamic mythology, we need to look for the Gandharvas, a race of Upadevas or "sub-*deva*", a category that is lower than administrative Devas.

It is easy to try to make a comparison between the Devas and the Annunaki of Sitchin, because both groups are called "divine" as superior to human beings for physical constitution as well as for technological knowledge. But it is a wrong comparison, because even if we accept the idea that the interpretation of the Annunaki is correct (and could very well not be), while Sitchin's Annunaki are a more or less homogeneous category of aliens who fight among themselves, Vedic tradition clearly explains that besides the Devas there are Asuras, who are always the enemies and opponents of the Devas. It is also important to note that in Vedic tradition the Devas (even those less important) never try to impose themselves (or their offspring) as kings or leaders of human society, while the Asuras have often violated this universal rule of non-interference, also mating with humans and having offspring; therefore it is more likely that superhuman beings similar to Sitchin's Annunaki should be categorized as Asuras and not as Devas.

All Devas are strictly vegetarian and are horrified by the idea of blood sacrifices or holocausts (human or animal) but they are willing to befriend those who show good qualities and offer medicinal aromatic herbs, clarified butter or pure milk products, grains, fruits and leaves, flowers and clean water possibly taken from a sacred place. The Devas accept but never demand offerings from human beings and even more so they never demand their loyalty and exclusive obedience, and they never directly intervene in human history.

The examples of personal interaction between Devas and human beings are extremely rare, because normally they are limited to apparitions or astral projections (a bit like holograms) to give blessings; it is even less frequent to have cases of mixed procreation (as in the famous case of the Pandavas) but these are never due to a lusty desire of the Devas, but are always a special blessing particularly, spontaneously, and explicitly requested by the concerned human (female or male). Unlike the Asuras, Devas do not find human beings as sexually attractive because in regard to evolution they are as different from human beings as human are different from animals such as cats and dogs - considering that the Devas respect and love human beings that are evolved enough, but a little like evolved human beings respect and love their affectionate hairy four-legged friends.

On the other hand, Asuras can also have beautiful females that are better than humans, but they are not so interested in beauty, and they rather prefer dirtier sex and especially rape.

The main individual Devas mentioned by the hymns of *Rig Veda*:

* Surya, the male aspect of the Sun, who has 12 emanations called Adityas, one for each zodiac sector and precisely:

* Indra, the warrior aspect, the kingly power, that carries rain and lightning,

* Parjanya, a manifestation of the Sun in rain, not to be confused with Indra,

* Dhata, the creator or "destiny", of whom Brahma Prajapati is a secondary manifestation,

* Bhaga Vivasvan, a manifestation of the Sun in fire, not to be confused with Agni,

* Amshumana, a manifestation of the Sun in wind, not to be confused with Vayu,

* Vishnu, the manifestation of the Sun's omnipresence, not to be confused with Narayana,

* Varuna, the manifestation of the power of Sun in water,

* Mitra, the manifestation of the Sun in moon and ocean,

* Pusha Aryama, the manifestation of Sun in grains,

* Tvasta, the manifestation of the Sun in trees and herbs.

The ontological trinity of Brahman (Vishnu, Shiva, Shakti) only appears as a reflection, for example in the qualities associated with Indra as representative of the supreme Reality in the material world, or in the Rudras who are manifestations of Shiva as Kala Bhairava, or in the figure of the original Goddess, Aditi the mother of all Devas, who manifests in many forms, such as:

* Sarasvati is the flowing word (Vak, literally, "word") exactly like the majestic river that takes her name; it also includes the concepts of knowledge, sound, music,

* Lakshmi is the principle of beauty, fortune, auspiciousness, wealth, prosperity,

* Savitri is the feminine aspect of the Sun (not the wife of Surya, because the wives of Surya are Samjna and Chaya), personifying the power of feminine energy and creation; another name of Savitri is Gayatri, the Mother of Vedic knowledge and of all the sounds from which syllables derive (meaning the letters of devanagari alphabet) and thus *mantras,*

* Bhumi or Prithivi (literally "the vast") is Mother Earth, who is invoked together with Dyaus or Space, who is also in female form, and not male as many have claimed for the purpose of aligning the Vedic system with the other ancient cultures studied by colonial academia (especially to connect the name of Zeus or Deus pater).

Other feminine aspects of Devas mentioned in the hymns of *Rig Veda* are: Usha (dawn, the moment of illumination), Ratri (night, the moment of silence), Rati (attraction) and Kamadhenu (the cow, the image of plenty).

Other primary Devas mentioned in the hymns (*suktas*) of Vedic *samhitas* and sacrificial oblations during the *yajna* rituals are:

* Agni, fire, who by consuming the ritual offerings distributes them to the Devas; among the various forms of Agni there is also the "belly fire" (*jatharagni*) that is the digestion power that consumes the food we eat and circulates energy all over the body,

* Vayu, wind, present within the body as *prana,*

* Asvini kumaras, the power of healing, manifested in the form of two twins sons of Surya,

* Yama, death and justice, also called Dharma; he presides over the subtle dimensions between life, death and rebirth, and controls Pitriloka and the "planetary systems" called Narakaloka, consisting in the dimensions called Atighora, Raudra, Ghoratama, Dukhajanani, Ghorarupa, Tarantara, Bhayanaka, Kalaratri, Ghatotkata, Chanda, Mahachanda, Chandakolahala, Prachanda, Varagnika, Jaghanya, Avaraloma, Bhishni, Nayika, Karala, Vikarala, Vajravinshti, Asta, Panchakona, Sudirgha, Parivartula, Saptabhauma, Ashtabhauma and Dirghamaya. Narakaloka is only vaguely comparable with the abrahamic concept of "hell" and is more similar to the Tibetan concept of Bardo, but has nothing to do with the lower planetary systems such as Atala, Vitala, Sutala, Talatala, Rasatala, Mahatala, Patala.

Less known in popular tradition are the other archetypal personalities to whom various hymns of the *Rig Veda* are dedicated: Soma (the moon), Ritu (the cycle of seasons, the laws of nature), Rudra (destruction and pain) who in turn manifests in 11 sub-forms, Brihaspati (the priest), Visvakarma (technological ability), Kshetrapati (the principle of protection of Earth). Other hymns are dedicated to forms that we could call "composite": Indra-Varuna (the water that falls as rain), Mitra-Varuna (light reflected in water), Indra-Vayu (the storm), Indra-Vishnu (royal majesty), Indra-Agni (the power of the warrior), Indra-Soma (the power of health), Agni-Soma (the offering of the medicinal tonic into fire).

Some hymns of *Rig Veda* also address groups such as the Adityas (the manifestations of Surya mentioned above), the Marutas (manifestations of Vayu), the Visvedevas (the assembly of the Devas) and the Ribhus (the collective technical knowledge of the universe), as well as several components of daily life: food (as grains, *anna*), water (*apas*), the trinity water-grass-sun, the hawk (as a metaphor of the individual soul), the mountains, the clarified butter for the offerings, ritual oblation, the word, the mind, the rivers, the forests, faith, creation, the religious connection between husband and wife, the duality produced by illusion, he who performs the ritual, weapons, and the horse.

In other Vedic texts, especially in the *Puranas*, there is mention of Brahma, the architect of this particular universe ("son" of Vishnu that means his secondary manifestation) and the various manifestations, forms and *avataras* of the original trinity of Vishnu-Shiva-Shakti.

Among the most prominent forms of Vishnu Narayana we find Rama, Krishna, Narasimha, Varaha, Vamana, Kurma, Matsya, but there are also partial forms such as Parasurama, Kalki, Mohini (who has a feminine form but is not a manifestation of the Mother Goddess), Narada, the Kumaras, Garuda, and so on: none of these innumerable forms can be described as "Deva" except for the general nature of his mission in the world. Among the main forms of Shiva we find Isvara, the several Bhairavas, Sarabha, and the secondary forms of Skanda or Kartikeya (the principle of war) and Ganesha (the principle of intelligence and determination), who are symbolically presented as his "sons". A very famous *avatara* of Shiva is Hanuman, closely connected to the *avatara* of Vishnu named Rama.

Among the primary forms of the Mother Goddess (Aditi) we find Durga (the material world), Kali (eternal Time) and the other forms we have already mentioned (Lakshmi, Sarasvati, Bhumi). The secondary forms of Durga, who interact with the secondary forms of Shiva and Vishnu, are Parvati, Gauri, Uma, Sati, Bhuvanesvari. The secondary forms of Kali are manifested to neutralize particularly powerful Asuras and to protect the universe: Chandi, Chamunda, Mangala, and so on. The secondary forms of Lakshmi are listed as the various aspects of prosperity such as victory, royalty, maternity, agriculture and so on. A "composite" form of Lakshmi and Bhumi is identified with spring and fertility. These forms and manifestations cannot be precisely defined as administrative Devas because they belong to the superior ontological category of *tattva* (Brahman).

A complete discussion about these aspects of the Personalities of God would require a rather large volume in itself, so we now return to the quick excursus on the various levels of beings that reside in our universe according to the Vedic scriptures.

At a level below the administration Devas we find the Upadevas ("sub-*devas*"), listed as Gandharvas, Apsaras, Siddhas, Charanas,

Sadhyas, Vidyadharas, Kinnaras (centaurs), Kimpurushas (sphinxes), Valakhilyas, Kalakeyas, Suparnas and others, down to the 400,000 human or humanoid species mentioned by the Vedic tradition. The Upadeva category includes the individual beings who have been elevated to the higher planetary systems (Svargaloka) and who are the "subjects" of Indra.

In the cosmological descriptions offered by the *Puranas* there are various planetary systems, both above and below Earth, with their different populations; there is information also about inter-dimensional portals that can be accessed especially from dusk to dawn and during certain astronomical moments, and about parallel realities where time flows at a different speed. There is a special position for the Pitris, the ancient ancestors of human (terrestrial) *aryas* who, thanks to their own virtuous merits and those of their descendents are enjoying the opportunity to live at the court of Yamaraja as advisors and members of his assembly; in their honor every year Hindus perform a series of ceremonies called *pitru paksha* and offer ritual oblations for the deceased.

Among the 400,000 human species (differences are calculated on the basis of the level of consciousness) we can also count the Vanaras, the "monkey men" already mentioned with reference to Hanuman, and who according to the Vedic tradition lived in the forests beyond the Vindhya mountains, and also the two tribes of the "bears" and "wolves" respectively, that are mentioned in the *Puranas* especially with reference to the migrations of the rebellious *kshatriyas* defeated for 21 times by Parasurama, and who went to seek shelter in the territories inhabited by these tribes and mixed with them. The "bear" tribe of the Vindhya mountains appears both in the story of Rama and in the story of Krishna; its chief or king is called Jambavan, and princess Jambavati became one of the 8 main wives of Krishna (according to the *Bhagavata Purana* she gave him 10 children).

Non-divine superhuman beings

At the extreme opposite of the Devas we find the general category of the Asuras, that is traditionally opposed to the Devas because Asuras are motivated by separate selfish interests; they do not give any importance to the benefit of the universal community and in fact they try to exploit it in every way for their own immediate and materialistic advantage. The category of Asuras, like the category of Devas, has different levels of personal power, by birth or by acquisition. Although generally the Asuras are heavily identified at material level (and therefore strongly identified with racial considerations), the definition of *asura* is not exactly genetic, but refers to a mentality that in some species is considered as cultural tradition (especially among Daityas and Danavas) and therefore it can be confused with a racial category.

Thus some human beings, too, can be defined as asuric, or as it is often said a little imprecisely, "demoniac". The asuric mentality or nature is described in details in *Bhagavad gita* (chapter 16) as opposed to the divine mentality or nature; the fundamental difference consists in the fact that the *asura* has a selfish approach, based on dualism, that pits a personal selfish interest (individual or collective) against the total universal benefit, while a divine mentality supports harmony, cooperation, well-being and progress for all beings. In fact the divine mentality is by definition aware(ness) of the intimate unity of all beings, who are parts of the One (Brahman). The clashes between Devas and Asuras, described especially in the *Puranas*, are reflected by the clashes in human society between the opposing fronts of *arya*

and *ari*, who follow the same values and behaviors of the two superhuman factions to which they offer worship respectively.

Contrarily to what abrahamics believe, Devas and Asuras are not "angels and demons" and do not fight "for the power over the human soul" (either individual or collective), but for the control of material resources. The Devas engage in the protection of the universe for the benefit of everyone (not only for the benefit of their own followers or the followers of the "Supreme God") while the Asuras make all efforts to become the masters of the universe for the advantage of "their party". Under no circumstances the Devas act as "avenging angels" or hurt any human being or animal, and they never wage war against human beings or destroy their cities - not even as a mistake while they are fighting against the Asuras. So to claim that Mohenjo Daro or Harappa (or other human cities) have been destroyed "by fire showered by the Devas" is a totally baseless interpretation, completely unacceptable for those who know Indian scriptures well.

In the case of the Asuras, the power of control over material resources includes human beings, who are treated as slaves and cattle to be exploited materially. The Asuras do not have any use for the so-called "human soul", especially because the living being does not "have" a soul but "is" a soul, and therefore the soul cannot be separated from the living being any more than heat can be separated from fire. Furthermore, because it is purely spiritual, the soul cannot be touched by corruption in any way, any more than our hand can touch the sky.

For the purpose of our elaboration, we are particularly interested in the superhuman Asuras of the dynasties known as Daityas and Danavas, but especially in the clans of Rakshasas, Yakshas and Nagas, who interact more frequently with human beings and therefore they are more known in various cultures at global level also under different names, as we will see later on. From the racial ("genetic") perspective, the administrative Devas and the superhuman Asuras are very similar because they are related, divided only by different choices about ethical values. On the ontological-macrocosmic level, this relation indicates the need of a polarization of values that triggers action, because it is only through action (which is the exercise of free will and choice) that individual beings can evolve. Positive and negative tendencies exist in each embodied being and the cosmic adventure, the eternal "struggle between good and evil", goes on daily for everyone at the individual level - but it is not controlled by Devas and Asuras.

Rather, at a deeper level, transcending the phenomenal, the *roles* of the Devas and Asuras (not the Devas and Asuras individually) personify or exemplify positive tendencies to be cultivated and negative tendencies to be overcome: they act like characters in a gigantic theatrical play enacted on the scene of the entire universe, with the purpose of engaging and instructing all the "pupils of life" who participate or watch. Not all the actors and spectators are aware of the nature and the purpose of the play, but the roles are assigned according to free individual choices, and the director always tries to insert messages that can be clearly read. While the Devas consciously play their role in the universal play, the Asuras are conditioned by ignorance and so they passively live their roles, although superficially they seem more active and independent.

The fundamental difference between the Vedic vision and the so-called monotheistic vision is in the fact that the Asuras are not "Gods of Evil" who control the material world, but still immature or unevolved individuals who are conditioned by ignorance and are making a seriously wrong evaluation of Reality, and whose destructive choices must be counteracted by the positive activities of wise and evolved persons. To summarize the general message of the play in a simple aforism, we could say, "evil is nothing but a lack of understanding of good". Several corollaries ensue (for example, "each problem is an opportunity") but we will have to elaborate about this somewhere else, because we should not stray too far from the purpose of this present book.

According to Vedic hagiography, Aditi is the mother of the 12 Devas collectively known as Adityas ("sons of Aditi"), of whom the most important is Indra, the king of the higher planets.

Diti, sister of Aditi, is the mother of the Daityas ("sons of Diti"), who consider themselves as rivals of the Devas and therefore their enemies; they live in the lower planets under the Earth (Rasatala, Talatala and so on) together with the Danavas. Indeed, the Danavas ("sons of Danu", another sister of Diti) are another important lineage in the scene of the Asuras and traditional allies of the Daityas; particularly famous is Maya Danava (Ravana's father in law), an extraordinary architect and designer, specialized in large spaceships such as the Tripura ("three cities") destroyed by Shiva and the Saubha of Salva brought down by Krishna. The son of Maya Danava, Bala, is famous for having created 96 "mystic powers", or wonders of subtle technology to manipulate matter in extraordinary ways.

Like other members of his clan, Maya Danava is not totally malevolent towards all human beings, and sometimes he reciprocates their acts of kindness with gifts (even wonderful gifts) as we see in *Mahabharata* (Sabha parva, chapter 3), in the episode where he builds a palace for the Pandavas and presents them with objects of huge value that had belonged to king Vrishaparva and had ended in the treasure of the Yakshas. Equally famous is the king of the Daityas named Bali Maharaja, who in spite of his birth and his position is a great devotee of Vishnu and in his palace on Sutala has a temple dedicted to the *avatara* of Vishnu named Vamana. On the other hand we have for example the Kalakeyas and the Paulomis, two lineages in the Danava descendence, respectively sons of Kalaka and Puloma, both daughters of Vaisvanara son of Danu; these two sisters also married Kasyapa Rishi and generated a great number of descendents, who resided in a space city orbiting around the Earth.

Here it is important to understand that "marriages" and "reproduction" on a superhuman level have modalities that are quite different from the human level; they are not based on "artificial insemination and genetic manipulation" but on materialization, that we can describe only approximatively as based on the control of bio-magnetic frequencies. Explaining the "reference technology" is like trying to explain the functioning of telephone to someone who does not have the least idea of what electricity or radio waves are: if an ignorant person does not accept metaphors and symbolic language, we risk being labeled as crazy or superstitious.

Under the Earth there are other planets, known as Atala (we are not going to embark in elaborations on unlikely linguistic connections with Atlantis), Vitala, Sutala, Talatala, Mahatala, Rasatala and Patala, which have the same size of the Earth and are called *bila svarga* or "subterranean paradises", because the Daityas, Danavas and Nagas who reside there enjoy a very high level of quality of life, possess great wealth and know many pleasures, also because they are very expert in medical science and keep their bodies in full health and potency, especially at the sexual level. The houses, gardens, lakes and pleasure places are even more wonderful than those of the heavenly beings, but they never see the Sun because they are subterranean, so time is not divided into days and nights, and the light is provided by the jewels decorating the heads of the great serpents who live there.

These artificial cities have been constructed by Maya Danava, the amazing architect who besides spaceships can make excellent houses, fortified walls and gates, assembly halls, temples and even hotels for tourists. On the last planet at the bottom of the "bubble" of the universe, in the region of Patala, live the Nagas. This valuable information can also cast more light on the esoteric-occultist legend of Agartha or "hollow Earth", for which inside our planet there is a mysterious and extremely ancient city of beings that are very advanced technologically; Agartha could then be simply a sort of "hallway" or corridor between Earth and the lower planets.

Another interesting subject is about the inter-dimensional portals connecting the so-called subterranean planets down to Patala, the region of the universe inhabited by the Asuras and especially by the Nagas, that we could call "reptilians". Tradition has localized several of these portals or "wells", one of which is at Sheshanaga (Benares, Varanasi), another at Patala Bhubanesvara (Uttarakhanda, Himalaya), another at Patalkot (Madhya Pradesh), another at Patala lingam Arunachalesvara (Tiruvanamalai, Tamil Nadu), and another at Belesvara (Puri, Orissa). These are only the most famous, but it seems that all the localities traditionally associated with the Naga cult were built in the vicinity of one of such portals, more or less hidden, generally in caves or under water.

These inter-dimensional passages (a sort of *wormholes*) connect the seven lower planets with Earth: with the appropriate knowledge human beings too can use these portals and even settle in the lower planets, provided they have permission from their residents - somehow like the present system of visas obtained from Consulates under the recommendation of local sponsors. We should not make the mistake of confusing the higher planets with the "paradise" of abrahamics and the lower planets with their "hell"; probably the majority of the people who dream about going to paradise, to the heavenly planets or even to the Vaikuntha planets expecting them to be places of sense pleasures actually end up in the lower planets.

Rakshasas, Yakshas, Pisachas and other similar beings live on planets situated within dimensions that are parallel to the Earth and can be accessed through the space called *antariksha*, extending for about 1,300 km above the Earth surface. These are the beings (that cannot certainly be called Devas) who most frequently use *vimanas* (spaceships) to visit Earth because they find it rich in "game" not only animal but human as well. Their colonies on Earth are always hidden a little out of the way - in forests, inaccessible valleys, or even in tunnels and caves within the mountains or underground. Because of the human demographic explosion on planet Earth with the industrial revolution and especially after WW2, these small colonies were probably forced to abandon several localities that used to be isolated and quiet; we could imagine that such developments must have irritated them a lot, pushing them to search for new power and residential solutions that may be an even bigger danger for humans.

We shall now connect with the subject of occultist satanism to comment on the term "demon" that is often utilized to refer to superhuman Asuras and especially Rakshasas. It is important to understand that the word "demon" does not constitute a precise translation, as in the course of the centuries it has been modified with a semantic luggage that was alien to its original meaning. In Greek culture, both classical and hellenistic, the *agathos daimon* was a friendly and protective spirit, just like the Roman *genius*. *Agathos* actually means "good" and refers to a sort of benign protector similar to the ghost of a great ancestor. Other cultures too speak about friendly or at least potentially benevolent spirits, but these are not divine or transcendental, and rather remain strictly localized.

Things took a turn for the worse because of the radical dualism introduced by Zoroaster and later by abrahamic religions, that have gradually transformed the concept of "demon" in an extremely negative sense, as secondary manifestation of an "Evil principle" that has been called "Satan". If we remove this superimposition, the *daimon* appears again as an ambiguous entity, powerful and not always benevolent, that must be propitiated with offerings and prayers, and that can grant huge benefits and gifts when pleased, and inflict terrible punishment if offended or enraged. Worshiping such beings, however, does not make them "divine", not even in the eyes of their worshipers.

In the Indo-Vedic system of knowledge, this category includes several species that we could call superhuman. Some superhuman races have a more strongly negative in respect to the others: besides the Yakshas, of whom we will speak more in the next chapter, we can briefly mention the Rakshasas are typically asuric by cultural tradition, the Nagas are slightly less, the Yakshas even less, but they are still very dangerous. Potentially dangerous, but more often benevolent are the Gandharvas, Charanas, Vidyadharas and Apsaras. They sometimes unite in alliances among themselves and sometimes with some human groups, more or less degraded.

The Rakshasas correspond largely to the descriptions of orcs, trolls and evil man-eating giants, but unlike the trolls of some fiction they are very intelligent, endowed with great powers and expert in black magic and especially in *shape shifting*; they are sexually and genetically compatible with the human species but have a strong tendency to sexual violence and they often hurt their victims with humiliating sexual actions and slavery. Some special genetic traits are transmitted to their hybrid descendence, that they consider a "superior race" to humans; "ordinary" humans are considered and treated like cattle, also for food. Rakshasas sometimes consume animal blood and flesh, but they prefer human blood because their subtle perception savors the "vibrations" of suffering, fear and despair of their victims, and human beings are more sensitive and active than animals in this sense. Like the Yakshas and even more than them, Rakshasas are interested in gold, so much that Hiranyaksha ("eyes for gold") the brother of the more famous Hiranyakasipu ("comfortable gold bed") caused a very serious geophysical imbalance by overmining Earth; to remedy the situation Vishnu manifested as the *avatara* Varaha, the primeval "boar" (we elaborate on the theme of the sacred boar in the second volume of our work *The Awakening of the Mother Goddess*) who killed Hiranyaksha and restored our planet to its proper position.

The Nagas (also called Uragas) are described as serpents or dragons, with or without wings, and could be defined as "reptilians" but they are perfectly compatible with the human species on the genetic level, so much that Rishi Astika was the child of the Nagini Manasa and Rishi Jarutkaru, and Iravan was the son of the Nagini Ulupi and Arjuna the Pandava. The Nagas are very dangerous because they possess great powers and a strong dominating tendency; they enjoy sacrifices of human blood but they are also very expert in the art of medicine and elixirs (not just poisons). The Yakshas, that are particularly interesting for us, could be compared to elves, fairies, gnomes, dwarves, leprechauns, nymphs and so on, and they are less powerful than the Rakshasas.

The Gandharvas are particularly expert in singing and dancing, but they also have very powerful weapons, as well as spaceships and a very advanced technology. The Apsaras are heavenly dancers or courtisanes, something between nymphs and angels, but under no circumstance they can be called "the wives of the Devas"; they like to seduce important men such as Rishis and powerful *kshatriya* kings, but they show very little interest in their offspring and generally abandon it at birth - as for example Drona (from Gritachi), Kripa and Kripi (from Janapadi), Shakuntala (from Menaka). The Kinkaras are low-rank servants, generally employed by the Yakshas as security guards and janitors. Even lower in the scale of importance we find a great variety of sprites, ghosts, vampires of a more or less disturbing nature, described in Vedic tradition as Vinayakas, Dakhinis, Pretas, Vetalas, Kusmandas, Bhutas, Pisachas, Kapalikas, and so on.

We will now speak about the connection with occultism.

We see that generally the *asuras*, the category of beings that we could call "demoniac", are known as expert "magicians" capable of manipulating matter at the subtler levels, and who show considerable powers including control over other beings, and in fact they often sadistically enjoy watching the sufferings they inflict on other beings, oppressing and exploiting them for their selfish and opportunistic purposes. But these activities are based on illusion. Verse 9.12 of *Bhagavad gita* states: "(Those who) cultivate delusional desires, engage in delusional activities and delude themselves about possessing knowledge, but are confused by a mistaken consciousness, certainly take shelter in the illusory nature of *rakshasas* and *asuras*" (*moghasa mogha karmano mogha jnana vicetasah rakshasim asurim caiva prakritim mohinim asritah*).

The illusion mentioned in this verse is also called *maya* ("that which is not"), because the individual being can never really control Nature, because Nature is immensely more powerful than him. The perspective of "magic" by which the adept tries to acquire a "supernatural" power is actually a delusion, and by creating negative karmic reactions it imprisons the "wizard" to great future sufferings, as we have already seen while discussing the concept of satanism.

The motivation of this type of "wizardry" is illusory as well: it is based on deceit (*na satyam tesu vidyate*, 16.7), atheism (*jagad ahur anisvaram*, 16.8), sense gratification as the supreme purpose of life (*kim anyat kamahaitukam*, 16.8) and performance of horrible and cruel actions that cause damages to the universal community (*ugra karmanah kshayaya jagato ahitah*, 16.9). The *asuras* aim at accumulating more and more material power and wealth and do not hesitate to eliminate through violence anyone who may stand on their path and is therefore seen as "enemy" (16.12-14). The primary criteria to recognize *asuras* are based on the fact that they do not hesitate to cause sufferings to others (*karsayantah sarira stham... tan viddhy asura niscayan*, *Bhagavad gita* 17.6).

The character of the aliens described by Sitchin and others in the same line is therefore much more similar to the Daityas or Danavas, Rakshasas, Yakshas or Nagas, that are categories very different from the Devas, but they could ignorantly be mistaken for "gods" in the sense of entities showing extraordinary and superhuman power. Daityas, Danavas, Yakshas and Nagas are dangerous but not necessarily evil, and they reward with material benefits the human beings who serve and worship them, but they oppose the concept of an absolute and omnipresent God because they want to take the supreme position for themselves.

Their typically materialist mentality is well described in *Bhagavad gita*, with chapter 16 totally dedicated to the differences between the qualities of the Devas and the qualities of the Asuras. Another verse of *Bhagavad gita* (17.4) reveals that the human beings influenced by ignorance and greed are naturally attracted to worship and serve the Asuras: *yajante sattvika devan yaksa raksamsi rajasah, pretan bhuta ganams canye yajante tamasa janah*, "Good people worship the Personalities of God (the Devas), those who are influenced by greed and lust worship Rakshasas and Yakshas, and those who are in the darkness of ignorance offer sacrifices to ghosts and other types of lower beings."

This helps us to better understand the fascination that some archetypal or superhuman figures (fairies, vampires, goblins, orcs) have on human beings and the considerable investments engaged in the attempts to exorcize them or repaint them in nice colors as we have recently seen in popular entertainment culture.

Daityas, Danavas, Yakshas

We have mentioned the Asuras descendents of Diti and Danu, two of the wives of Kasyapa Rishi, whose sons are traditionally enemies of the sons of Aditi, the first wife of the same Kasyapa.

In turn, Daityas and Danavas have produced descendents, some of "pure" race and others of mixed race through unions with human beings; to those, we need to add the people who have chosen to enter their clan for one reason or another. Genetic and racial considerations are a factor limited to the internal relationships of the clan, while rivality towards different "nations" (as those of the Adityas or Devas) constitutes a more important factor. This dynamic can still be observed in the abrahamic-based ideologies, that are keen on the internal distinctions or divisions on the basis of descendence (racial or institutional) but in a lesser degree compared to their constant war against non-abrahamics, non-believers or pagans of all denominations.

It is also interesting to note the social structure in Zoroaster's tradition, where the *nmano* (family) consisted non only in the father-mother couple (*nmanapatis* and *nmanapathni*) and sons, but included also all the *aryaman*, that are adopted sons, servant/ vassals as a group of "loyal followers" exactly similar to the *clientes* of the Roman *pater familiae* and the Greek *metoikoi*, as well as to the *kin* of *frith* in Celtic and Germanic tribes. Because the *nmano* was strictly patriarchal, women were excluded from the lineage of power, with the strange exception of the daughter of the daughter of the brother of the father of the family - a rule that was apparently introduced at some special historical time, probably to solve a succession problem, and then survived out of tradition. In turn, families (*nmano*) were united in the *vis*, a sort of *clan* that we could describe as the equivalent of village if it did not refer to peoples that were largely nomadic; while the tribe (*zantus*, under the *zantupatis*) had an ethnic and cultural meaning (its members are called *dahyu*, originally "*dasyu*"), and the *clan* (*vis*, under the authority of the *vispati*) represented the judicial and social authority ruling over *faide* or blood vengeances, arranged marriages, heredities, alliances and military and political ventures. All the tribes together formed a "nation" under the ceremonial authority of a king called *dahyupati kshayathiya* (it is not difficult to make the connection with the Sanskrit *kshatriya*).

All the "others" were called *anya* - in Sanskrit literally "others" or "foreigners/strangers". The slaves, both the acquired ones and the ones "born in the house" had no relevance in the power structure and were compared to cattle, especially because they came from "foreign" populations.

The "nation" of the Daityas has this name because its dominant family descends from the two sons of Diti (Hiranyaksha and Hiranyakasipu), cousins and half-brothers of the Adityas sons of Aditi. The stories of this very high "black aristocracy" and its genealogical ramifications are described in Vedic scriptures and especially in the *Puranas*; among the most famous historical descendents of Diti we may mention Prahlada and his grandson Bali (very important cultural exceptions because they are virtuous devotees of Vishnu), Virochana, Bana, Kumbha and Nikumbha. The descendents of Diti have developed a vast clan of allies of similarly aristocratic and powerful lineage, such as the Rakshasas and Yakshas descending from the sons of Pulastya Rishi and Surasa (another wife of Kasyapa) and especially the Danavas, who are the innumerable descendents of the 40 sons of Danu, another sister of Aditi and wife of Kasyapa. As we have already mentioned, besides the direct descendents of these superhuman lineages, the extended nation of Daityas and Danavas, Rakshasas and Yakshas also includes all the hybrid and even ordinary human beings that are the equivalent of the *clientes/metoikoi/kin* for the asuric aristocracy, especially around the Danava clan, that was the most numerous.

We will now speak of the human Danava "nation", consisting of the followers and associates of the superhuman Danavas and especially of their descendents, whose presence is shown in the human history of the last millennia. It is important to note that the human Danavas (called *dasyus* in Vedic texts) have cultural and often even racial traits that are almost identical to those of another group of hybrid humans descending from the Yakshas, the Khasa, of whom we shall speak in the next chapter because they are particularly important in the history of occultism of the last centuries.

Already in ancient times, the human Danavas moved to the north-european region, although the veneration for their Great Mother Danu is found also in the names of many rivers in central Europe (Danube, Don, Dniepr, Dniestr and the river Danu in Nepal); we may remember that in the *Zend Avesta* the word *danu* literally means "river". We also remember the tribe of the Danes, giving its name to Denmark, the Danai ancestors of Mycenean Greeks (sons of Perseus son of Danae) that are a blond people as described by Homer, the Denyen (one of the famous Sea Peoples who invaded the Mediterr-anean around 1500 BCE) and the Dinars in the Balkans (Dinaric Alps). Some have connected the Danavas with the mysterious "tribe of Dan" mentioned in the Bible: the most famous of these Danites was Samson (the long-haired strong man); an unusal characteristic of the tribe of Dan was that its economy was based on sea travels unlike all the other tribes of Israel, that lived on sheep and cattle.

Even more interesting is another more recent "danite", the famous Simon Magus mentioned in the *Acts of the Apostles* 8.9-24 and in the *Acts of Peter*, where the apostle personally clashes with this Simon, who was originally from the village of Getta in Samaria, where the tribe of Dan had settled. According to Josephus and Justin (the martyr, also native of Samaria), almost all Samaritans in those times were followers of this Simon, considered "the origin of all heresies, including gnosticism" by Justin, Ireneus, Hyppolite and Ephiphanius. This Simon preached that the First Thought of God (equivalent to the Logos in the Apocalypse of John), called Ennoia (feminine), had descendend into the lower worlds to create the angels; this entity was the Christ, and those who follow him will be saved not because of their actions but by divine grace - a concept that is still very important for many protestant Christian sects. Very similar gnostic doctrines were taught by Valentinus (and his followers known as valentinians), Basilides (basilideans), Sethians (who venerated Seth as the revealer of knowledge, Sophia or Barbelos, of whom Christ is the manifestation) and the ophites (who worshiped the Serpent as symbol of Christ).

Charles Upton has stated that the God-serpent Dan-bhala, worshiped in the synchretic religion known as Voodoo, partially derives from an heterodox form of Etyopian Judaism. To better understand that statement: Charles Upton, born in 1948, calls himself "sufi and metaphysician" and has written various books published by Sophia Perennis (a typically gnostic name), such as *Cracks in the Great Wall: UFOs and Traditional Metaphysics, The System of Antichrist: Truth and falsehood in Post-modernism and the New Age, Legends of the End: Prophesies of the End Times, Antichrist, Apocalypse and Messiah from eight religious traditions, Shadow of the Rose: The Esoterism of the Romantic tradition, Vectors of the Counter-Initiation: The course and destiny of inverted spirituality.*

In Irish mythology, Danu or Dana is the Mother of the Tuatha Dé Danann (literally "the people of Goddess Danu", where *tuatha* means "nation" or "kingdom") and corresponds to "mother" Dôn in the Welsh *Mabinogion*. According to Cormac Mac Cuilennáin (Irish bishop and king of Munster from 902 to his death in battle in 908), another name of Danu is Anu (should we totally revolutionize the concept of Anunnaki here?), whose genitive form Anann corresponds to the more frequent Danann. It is important to understand that she is not a "Goddess" from the ontological perspective or with regard to the administration of the universe; compared to the male Personalities of God, the feminine Personalities are more difficult to categorize because the primeval Goddess directly manifests in all the spiritual and material forms in the universe. We remember that in Vedic tradition all women are called "*devi*", or "goddess" as natural representatives of the Mother Goddess, Nature herself. Also the Irish meaning of the word *dia* (nominative of *dé*, that is the genitive form) does not refer to "God" from the ontological point of view but includes the superhuman beings and in general all beings who are worthy of veneration. In the case of the Danu mentioned in Vedic tradition, the divine quality can also be connected to the fact that she is one of the sisters (a younger sister) of Aditi, the mother of 12 important Devas, besides the fact that she is the venerated mother of the superhuman beings who are ancestors of the Danava clan.

According to the *Lebor Gabála Érenn*, the Tuatha Dé Danann, descendents of Nemed, founded four cities in northern Ireland (Falias, Gorias, Murias and Finias), from where they carried the Cauldron of Dagda, the Spear of Lugh, the Stone of Fal and the Sword of Nuada, then they moved to the south of Ireland riding on dark clouds and landing on Conmaicne Rein in Connachta; subsequent versions of Christian copists speak of ships that landed on the coast of Conmaicne Mara and burned soon afterwards, something that was probably mentioned to downsize the story of the "dark clouds". Researchers calculate that the first kingdom, under Nuada ("of the Silver Hand"), ended in 1897 BCE with the battle of Magh Tuireadh in which the native population was defeated. The second battle, named Magh Tuireadh, was against the Fomorian, while in the third battle the Danann had to accept the arrival of a wave of newcomers who had similar powers and who allotted them "the underground".

Unfortunately the traditional Irish and British stories in general have been heavily polluted by the manipulation by the Christian monks who have compiled them ("downsizing" the protagonists as Evemerus had done) and thus reshaping the general mentality of people according to the same perspective, so that the ancient religion has only left collections of more or less disturbing fairy tales and folkloristic beliefs that do not contain any ethical value or wisdom any more.

Reductionist interpretations have led in the 1800s to the theory on the "Dinaric race", proposed by Joseph Deniker, Carleton S Coon, Hans FK Günther Jan Czekanowski. Their genetic traits would be white complexion (but without the rosy cheeks of the nordics), hair from black to dark brown to dark blond, eyes of various colors, long face, tall and thin body build, long and thin nose and very large feet. The German anthropologist Victor Lebzelter also postulated the existence of an intermediate race, called Noric (something between Nordic and Dinaric), a word derived from a province of the Roman empire corresponding to present south Austria; the physical traits include white complexion, blond hair and light eyes.

The category of Yakshas is famous not only in Hinduism but also in Jainism and Buddhism, and in Indonesian cultures as in Thailand, Bali and so on. In south India (Karnataka, Kerala), initially organized at Udupi by Narahari Tirtha disciple of Madhvacharya, an artistic genre developed under the name of Yakshagana ("the Yaksha people") with figurative-oracular aspects, similar to the forms of dance-theater of the Bon tradition of Tibet and apparently also of the Iranian Daivagana - where the *daivas* are defined according to the categories described by Zarathustra. This Yakshagana art form combines dance, music, dialogues, elaborate and symbolic costumes, a strong make up and scenographic techniques to present stories from *Ramayana, Mahabharata, Puranas* and so on; sometimes the actors go into a trance and people ask them questions as it is done with an oracle or spiritist medium.

We could say that the Yakshas have superhuman powers, in the sense that their technology enables them to manipulate matter and move through dimensions; they have a long history of residence on our planet and specifically in the Himalayan region, but their presence seems to have been recorded also in other regions, such as north Europe, where they have probably been the origin of stories on elves, fairies, goblins and so on. As a people, the Yakshas are often mentioned in Vedic stories, with a complete genealogy of their origin in the *Mahabharata*, Adi parva, chapters 65 and 66, and other passages in Valmiki's *Ramayana* and in the *Rig Veda* where we find the war of the ten kings and specifically mentioning Suda, the king of Panchala, who had fought against the Yakshas on the bank of the Yamuna river.

One of the most famous episodes of the *Mahabharata* is the close encounter of the five Pandava brothers with a Yaksha who lived in a sacred lake (Vana parva, chapter 310) and had taken the form of a heron. Considering them as intruders, the Yaksha killed one after another four of the Pandavas who had ventured there to fetch water, and finally engaged the eldest, Yudhisthira, in a philosophical conversation to test him. Pleased, the Yaksha brought his brothers back to life and blessed them. On another occasion (Vana parva, chapter 139) the Pandavas visit the main kingdom of the Yakshas in the company of Lomasa Rishi; that passage in the *Mahabharata* contains a description of the journey and geographical references that identify the place as the area of Gangadvara around Kailasa and Manasa sarovara in Tibet. Specifically it mentions the mountain Mandara or Gandhamadana as made of white rock, the residence of Kuvera with 80,000 Gandharvas, 360,000 Kimpurushas and innumerable Yakshas of various forms.

In the Sabha parva of *Mahabharata* (chapter 10) we find a description of various assembly halls, including the fabulous palace of Kuvera, considered one of the best places in the universe for social entertainment, attended by Shiva himself, Lakshmi and Yama and other Devas, and by the most famous among the Yakshas, Guhyakas, Rakshasas (including Vibhisana), Pisachas, Gandharvas and Apsaras, and by the great Rishis as well. This palace is in the middle of the lush forests and waterfalls of mount Mandara, on the banks of the river Alaka Ganga or Mandakini and its affluents Bahuda, Brahmavadhya and Brihadvati, and contains the parks known as Citraratha and Nandana kanana (one of the favorite places of Shiva) especially rich in jasmine and lotus flowers; a force of thousands of ferocious Rakshasas named Krodhavasa (literally meaning "always angry") stand guard in adequate uniforms. Kuvera had another palace in Lanka, but his half brother Ravana took it by force, also appropriating the *pushpaka vimana* that was kept there. The Himalayan region is not the only settlement of the Yakshas, who are also described in the Khandava forest and on the Mahendra mountains (Bhishma parva, chapter 9) and on the north bank of the Sarasvati river (Shalya parva, chapter 37). The home of Visravasa Rishi, the father of Kuvera, was on the bank of the Narmada river (Vana parva, chapter 89).

On another occasion we see that Bhima, the second of the Pandavas, engaged in battle with some Yakshas (Vana parva, chapter 160) headed by Maniman (also known as Manibhadra), a personal friend of Kuvera; after the battle Kuvera himself arrived on the spot, wishing to meet the valiant Bhima. We also find another battle engaging Arjuna and Krishna against the inhabitants of the Khandava forest - an assortment of Yakshas, Rakshasas, Nagas and other races (Adi parva, chapter 229). Another important episode of *Mahabharata* is the story of Sikhandini (previously known as Amba), who became a friend of the Yaksha Sthunakama in the forest where he lived in a cave, and he transformed her into a male under her request (Udyoga parva, chapter 194). The chief or leader of the Yakshas is named Kuvera, but he is also called Vaisravana ("son of Visrava") or Ailavila; in the region of Tibet he is known as Bishamon-ten, while Jains call him Saravanabhuti. Some call him Kamesvara because he fulfills desires and Dikapala ("guardian of the directions") because his kingdom extends northwards and thus is a border region for Vedic civilization.

In the *Bhagavata Purana* we find 3 chapters in the 4th canto dedicated to a war campaign against the Yakshas. King Dhruva's brother, Uttama, had been killed by a Yaksha in a forest on the Himalayas; Dhruva goes alone to the capital of the Yakshas, Alakapuri, and challenges them to battle. Kuvera's army, consisting in 130,000 warriors of various races, armed with conventional weapons and "special effects" of magic illusions, is defeated by Dhruva, and the slaughter stops only when Svayambhuva Manu, grandfather of Dhruva, intervenes to pacify his grandson; at that point Kuvera himself arrives, acknowledging Dhruva's valor and thanking him for his restraint.

In Shanti parva (chapter 289) it is said that Kuvera is Indra's banker; also the local tradition at Tirupati temple (Tirumala) dedicated to Vishnu Venkatesvara ("Lord of Lakshmi") says that Vishnu got a large loan from Kuvera to organize his own marriage with Lakshmi: still today the donations left by devotees and pilgrims in the *hundis* to "help Vishnu to repay the debt" have made this temple the wealthiest religious institution of India, although its resources are presently appropriated by the local government, that uses them for other non-religious purposes or even for anti-Hindu activities.

The iconographic images of Kuvera, particularly numerous in the area of Mathura (where we still find also many images of the Nagas) generally show him sitting comfortably, playing the harp, with a drinking cup and a mongoose pet, or with a royal battle club. The Yakshas in general are often depicted with a rather visible paunch, sometimes holding a cup in their hand and a bag of gold, or holding a cauldron with both arms. In various other images they hold a bottle with a long neck, or a basket with a garland, a vase, a club, a trident or other objects that are not easy to identify. In many images they sport a beard, in some they are quite short in stature but with a large head (looking dwarfish) or pulling grimaces or showing prominent teeth. Yaksha women are normally depicted as very beautiful, with a round smiling face and voluptuous bodies, often near a tree with which they seem to merge.

The name *yaksha* has been variously interpreted by linguists; many believe it is connected to the root *yaj* and therefore can be translated as "one who is offered worship". Some have "explained" the Yakshas as "nature spirits" because they usually reside in forests, caves, lakes, trees and so on, but many Yakshas live in palaces or at the gates of cities or temples and palaces as guardians and protectors (*sasana devata*), as stated in *Harivamsa* and in Buddhist and Jain traditions. A Jain legend told in a text in *prakrita* language entitled *Antagadadasao* speaks of the Yaksha Moggarapani, worshiped by a gardener of Rajagriha named Ajjunaka; when the gardener and his wife were attacked by robbers, Moggarapani came to their help giving the gardener superhuman force by which he killed the entire gang. Again in *Mahabharata* (Vana parva, chapter 65) it is said that people who travel through solitary regions usually offer worship to Kuvera and his army general Manibhadra (depicted with 6 arms and riding an elephant, and also mentioned in Valmiki's *Ramayana* together with Maniman and Manistragvi) for protection from dangers. The Yaksha named Sarvanubhuti and a number of Yakshinis (Chakreshvari, Ambika, Padmavati and Jvalamalini) were very popular especially in north India, so that several temples have been dedicated to them still between the 10th and 13th centuries of the current era.

The Devas themselves sometimes ask Kuvera's help at difficult times: in the Vana parva (chapter 160) Kuvera participates to the great assembly of Kusasthali, accompanied by a guard of 300 Yaksha soldiers. Yaksha warriors led by Amogha and Jambhaka fought in the army of Kartikeya and against the Asura Mahisha (Vana parva, chapter 230). On another occasion (Shanti parva, chapter 342) the Yakshas helped to recover some sacred texts that had disappeared.

The Khasas

In our elaboration we are especially interested in examining the possibility that the occultism of the esoteric type, connected to Zorastrism and gnosticism (and ideologies of the same family, such as theosophy and ariosophy), originally derived from the contact of some human cultural groups (especially *dasyus* or ex-*arya* renegades) with the Yaksha civilization, creating a cultural-linguistic-ethnic movement that could actually be described as "indo-european" although not "aryan" but rather "arian". The definition could also be applied, with some variations, to many peoples of antiquity, from the Celts to the Hyksos, from the Dores to the Pelasgians and for good measure even to Elamites and Assyro-Babylonians, postulating that such civilizations, quite different from each other, had been originated by distinct and subsequent movements of migration by people who dropped out from *arya* civilizations and mixed with other populations.

The most relevant group in this analysis is the Khasa tribe or culture (in the two forms Khasa and Saka), that seems to be the connection, more or less uninterrupted, between Asura (Ahura), Zoroaster, manicheism and the Judeo-Christian gnostic currents with Yaweh/Yaldabaoth, the Khazars, the Cathars, the Templars, esoteric occultism from the 1600s to date, Satanism in various versions, and the mythologies of alienists and ufologists. On the same line, or in recognizable ramifications, we could also make further connections that someone could label as "conspiracy theories" but this is not the purpose of our book.

As we have already mentioned, in Vedic times there were several "fronteer" populations in the Bahlika or "external territories". The kingdoms of Sindhu, Gandhara, Malla and Kekaya, although considered "on the border" respectively on west and east, followed the *arya* model because their inhabitants had joined the Vedic community by accepting to become reformed as *vratyas* ("persons who take vows"). Other kingdoms or tribes, not in the *arya* category, kept regular contacts with *arya* peoples in the more central region of Bharata varsha and often shared or preserved some cultural characteristics.

Among these, the lists (especially in *Mahabharata* but also in the *Aitareya Brahmana* and other texts) mention the tribal kingdoms of Khasa and Saka (the ancestors of Parthians, Scythes and Turks), Mleccha (from Meluha, in the Sindhu/Indus region), Yavana (or Yona, ancestors of Ionics), Pulinda (mountain people who lived on the Vindhyas, Madhya pradesh, but are still present in Assam and north Bengal), Pulkasa (a community of descendents of former *kshatriyas* who had been ostracized because of their lack of qualifications), Kalinga (present day Orissa), Anga (present Bengal, whose kingship was given to Karna by Duryodhana), Madra (the native place of princess Madri, second wife of king Pandu), Kirata (the ancestors of the Mongols in the eastern region), Huna (the ancestors of Huns), Andhra (still today there is a State of Andhra pradesh in India), Abhira (nomadic shepherd tribes from present day Rajasthan), Kuninda (mountain people from the Shivalik range), Sumbha (probably the ancestors of the present day Gonda or Gunda, a word that in Indian languages has taken the popular meaning of "brigand" or gangster), Tangana (ancestors of Telanganas in the present day region next to Andhra), Kambhoja (the native region of Duryodhana's wife), Sabara (still present as different tribes in various regions of India, and from whose tradition we have received the image of Jagannatha), Nishada (a tribe of very dark complexion, probably the ethnic type still present in the Andaman islands), as well as Trigarta, Barbara, Parada, Sauvira, Darada, Malava and Salva, on which we do not have detailed information.

In the war of *Mahabharata* there were also some Rakshasas (the most prominent was named Ghatotkacha and was son of Bhima and the Rakshasi Hidimbi) and prince Iravan (son of Arjuna and the Naga princess named Ulupi): these persons are described as endowed with superhuman powers and skills, but still mortal and certainly not Devas.

We will now examine the connection between Khasas and Yakshas. Still today, in the local languages of the Himalayan region there is an equivalence between the word *yaksha* and the word *khasa*, mentioned in *Bhagavata Purana* (2.4.18) in the list of the most famous non-aryan peoples and in the *Mahabharata* among the groups that participated in the Kurukshetra war, as we have already seen. The Khasas are also mentioned in *Brahmanda Purana, Matsya Purana, Vayu Purana, Vishnu Purana, Markandeya Purana, Kalika Purana, Brihat Samhita, Sanat kumara Samhita* and in the Tibetan chronicles entitled *Dpag-bsam-ljon-bzah* ("The wonderful Wish-fulfilling Tree"). The *Manu Samhita* explicitly says that they were degraded *kshatriyas* who had abandoned the Vedic system; all over central Asia the word Kazakh is still used to refer to persons who have chosen not to accept any authority or rule and are therefore totally independent.

As a cultural-ethnic group, the Khasas still live in Kashmir, Himachal pradesh, Garhwal, Kumaon, Nepal, Sikkim, Bhutan and on the hills of Bengal/ Bangladesh and Rajasthan, and we know that at least 2,000 years ago a group of Khasas emigrated to Afghanistan and to the Zagros mountains in the present Irak-Iran region. Descriptions of Khasas say that they were/ are tall and of robust body build, with long and straight nose and white complexion; they have always been excellent hunters and shepherds but also farmers. They offered the first agricultural products to God, oblations to ancestors and animal sacrifices to the Yakshas. Their traditional Deities (that we could call "State Deities") were the Sun in the form of horse (under the name Kas-shu), and the Mother Goddess under the name of Himadevi or Umadevi (where *hima* means "icy mountains"). Their religious practices included a form of shamanism called Jhakri, still today widespread in the region of Darjeeling and similar to the Tibetan tradition of Bon.

Among the descendents of the Khasas still living around the Himalayas we should mention the Gurkhas, a cultural-ethnic group connected to the *guru* Gorakhnath (11th century) and his geographical center Gorakhpur; the name is explained as a derivative of *goraksha*, "protection of the cows", and refers to a nomadic tradition of cowherds that were well prepared to fighting - if we want to compare them to a classical western example, we could call them "cow boys". If we choose the form Gurkha instead of Gorkha we could also make an etymological connection with the word Guhyaka, commonly used as a name for the Yaksha warriors in Vedic literature, and that refers to their skill in ambushes (*guhya* means "hidden").

103

The original Khasa tribes and their reformed leaders the Kshetris, together with the Gurung (maybe from *gaura-anga*, "golden white"), the Thakurs (literally "lords") and the Magar joined together to form a principate and then the kingdom of Gorkha; later they were joined by the tribes named Tamang, Kirant Rai, Limbu, Sunuwar and Tharus. Under the Maharajadhiraj Prithivi Narayan Shah the kingdom of Gurkha became the kingdom of Nepal; because in the course of time the kingdom had also absorbed other communities such as the Newars, in 1865 a new legal code promulgated by then prime minister Jung Bahadur Rana (also of Khasa origin) downsized the definition of Gurkha as one of the many ethnic groups of the kingdom. The kings who wanted to appear "less barbaric" started to circulate the rumor that their lineage came from the Rajasthan hills and took the title of Pahari or Prabattia ("people of the hills"); for the same reason the Gurkhas or Gorkhalis eventually dissociated themselves from the name Khasa, although this was still retained by the peoples who emigrated towards north-west in previous centuries, as we will see later.

Until 1800 Nepal was known under the name of Khas-des ("the country of Khas") and still today the national language of Nepal is the Khas-kura. Furthermore, the words Khasa and Prabattia (or Pahari) continued to be used as synonyms, and the social status of the *chettris*, the Khasa *kshatriyas*, continued to be lower than the famous Rajputana. The history of the region also includes various attempts at *arya* reformation performed by *brahmanas* who came from the plains to instruct the *chettris* in a life style that was more compatible with the Vedic system; some of these families however decided to take the title of "reformed" without changing their habits, but they became famous as Matwali Chettri, "drunken *kshatriyas*".

The other branch of Khasas, the Sakas (Sakai, Sacae, Skythai, Scyth), is even more famous because Greek and Roman historians used this denomination to indicate all the peoples of the euro-asiatic region that followed a generally nomadic life style. It is true that some ancient authors (Herodotus, Strabo, Plinius etc) mention many names of peoples in this region, but as Plinius commented, the issue is extremely controversial because many sources give contrasting information. Ancient historians also make connections between Scythians and Arames (Arameians, Amorreans) whom Herodotus calls Amyrgi, as well as with the Mardis or Amardis (who lived around the Caspian sea and were already harrassing the people of Sumer), the Massagetians, the Turanians, the Magis (ancestors of the Medians) and the Kassites. Instead of paying tributes to the kings of the various nations, these raiders demanded a sort of "mafia payment" without which they directly came down to take whatever they wanted especially from the caravans that traveled along the famous Silk Road, between Mesopotamia and Europe on one side, and China on the opposite side, passing through Persia, Caucasus and the region north of the Himalayas.

Zoroastrian sources recognize that the Sakas were "arian raiders among civilized arians" and were the origin of the Turanian people, later defined as Turkish and Iranian; similarly Herodotus (485-420 BCE) and Strabo (63 BCE-24 CE) describe them as nomadic barbarians constantly engaged in battles and raids. Actually they were a mixture of several ethnic groups, clans and tribes, of which some (if few) were settlers engaged in farming, united by alliances and common interests, as already observed by Plinius (*Historia naturalis*, 6.19) noting the differences in the descriptions offered by various authors, who evidently had come in contact with different tribes. Among the other tribes, the Parthavas (Parthians, from which Farsis and Persians), the Dahis (Dahae - Danavas?) and the Sistans (or Sisthans, from Sakastan), the kingdom of Rustam (the ancestors of Rus from which the Russians), the Tashkurgan (Kurgan) and the Khotan of Kashgar, as well as the peoples of western Tibet and Himalayan hills.

An interesting characteristic described by ancient historians is the Sakas "used to drink juices"; the Parsi historians see this tradition of "drinking the *haoma*" (*soma*) as the demonstration that such peoples had already embraced the doctrine and culture of Zoroaster, because the consumption of the *haoma* is an integral part of the rituals of that religion. The *soma* is the juice squeezed from the stalks of *ephedra*, a plant rich in medicinal qualities, sometimes mixed with the juice of the stalks of wild willow or other plants such as the pomegranate, but in no instance it is described as a fermented drink as imagined by colonial indologists who wanted to justify their own booze culture. In ancient Vedic culture the juice of the *soma* is an important ingredient in the rituals called *soma yajna*, where the worshipers presented offerings to the Devas and then consumed the remaining juice. The two great Persian emperors Cyrus (555-529 BCE) and Darius (521-485 BCE) imposed the religion of Zoroaster to the entire region under their control, so that there are still many *dakhmas* ("towers of silence"), ruins and artifacts from the Zoroastrian culture, at Khwarizem (on the bank of river Oxus, in the region between Kazakhstan, Uzbekistan and Turkmenistan), Tashkurgan and Kashgar (at the center of the mountain ranges of Kunlun, Kara Kunlun, Hindu Kush and Tian Shan).

Again, Zoroastrian sources state that in the ancient Iranian language, Khor is the name of the Sun and develops into the names Khorasan, Khvarizem, Khorasmia, Chorasmia and Chorsares (a nome attributed by Plinius to the Persians). We could also notice the similarity with "corsars", suggesting an ancient equivalence with the Sea Peoples, also described by their contemporaries as blond nomadic raiders; the connection between the words *corsar* and *courier* and *to course* could be easily explained with an original root as *kar* (Sanskrit *carati* "it moves", Greek *karpalimos* "rapid"), also connected to the terms "cart" and "carry".

The Saka tribes were hit heavily by the conquests of Alexander of Macedonia (356-323 BCE), who found Zarathustra's religion offensive and had all the copies of its scriptures burned and its priests dispersed. With the fall of Alexander's empire the Persian region was fragmented into 240 principalities as stated in the *Karnamak kar* ("The Book of Deeds"); the Parthian princes engaged themselvs in reconstructing the religious tradition by gathering the priests again and compiling the texts still remembered orally. Thus their leaders were called *pahlavan*, "champions" (of Zoroaster's religion), from which the term "paladin". The name became the title of an important royal dynasty that survived to our times with the Shah Reza Pahlavi, the last Iranian emperor deposed by the islamic revolution of 1979, and who was still bearing the title of Aryamehr ("Light of the Aryas", obviously in the Zoroastrian sense).

As we have seen, the earliest Khasas had white complexion and blond or red hair, apparently inherited from their Yaksha ancestors, and carried these bodily traits into the first migrations to the west. Their pride for their racial descendence and the sense of clan did not prevent them from genetic mixing with other tribes, especially when they found women who were particularly attractive; this is why for example the present population of Nepal has a considerable amount of Mongolian blood, as we can see from the light brown complexion and the almond-shaped eyes. Such characteristics are less evident in the Khasas who live in Kazakistan, Tajikistan and Afghanistan, or in descendents who took up different denominations, such as Kazakh, Cossack of the Don region, Krymchak, Kumyk, Csángó of Moldavia, slavic Subbotnik and still others in Turkmenistan, Uzbekistan, Kyrgyzstan, Azerbaijan, Romania, Transylvania, Bulgaria, Hungary, Moldovia, Crimea, Russia, Georgia, Armenia, and so on.

In this regard we can mention the idea of the so-called Turanid race, presently considered as an "obsolete theory" and certainly targeted by disinformation propaganda, but associated with the Turanian languages of which nobody denies the existence and are a combination of uralic and altaic components. According to *L'Histoire Générale des Huns, des Turcs, des Mongoles, et autres Tartares Occidenteaux* ("General history of Huns, Turks, Mongols and other western Tartars", by Joseph de Guignes, 1721-1800), *Sketches of Central Asia* (by Ármin Vámbéry, 1832-1913), *L'histoire de l'Asie* ("History of Asia", by Leon Cahun, 1841-1900) and various other books especially by Hungarian researchers, the Turkish peoples were originated from Turanic stock, a Caucasian race with a certain percentage of Mongolian blood.

This identification blurs from racial to ethnic to ideological, as shown by the example of the Finns and Magiars who historically considered themselves "European whites" simply because they were Christians by religion; the confusion between race and culture could come from the asuric prejudice by which the human followers of the superhuman Daityas and Danavas and their hybrid descendents had a tendency to imitate them in a servile way and honor their intrinsic superiority, as we also see even in other ancient cultures less obsessed with racism. However, it is a fact that the Kyrgyzi of Yenisey have blue eyes and the ancient funerary masks of their tradition, found in the Minusinsk valley, show them with long noses and red cheeks. Even more interesting, the *Zend Avesta* mentions the Turans as an important ethnic Iranian/ Persian/ Anatolian group - in other words, the inhabitants of the very region where Parsism was born.

Another very interesting people, rather less known, is the Gutes or Gutians, originally from the Gutium region of the Caucasus, not mentioned by the Greek historians but appearing in the Assyro-Babylonian documents and even in the Sumerian texts, and that Julius Oppert (1825-1905) connected with the Goths (Gutones, the people from east Germany that had a primary role in the fall of the Roman empire) already identified by Ptolemy in 150 CE as the Gutes of Scandia, who lived in the region of the Zagros mountains, just this side of the Caucasus.

First of all, a few words about our good Julius Oppert, who is certainly not incompetent on the subject we are examining: born in 1825 in Germany from Jewish parents, he obtained French citizenship because of services rendered to culture, in 1857 he was appointed professor of Sanskrit and comparative philology at the Bibliotèque nationale de France - founded in 1368 and that in 1896 was the largest library in the world and in 1920 had 4,050,000 volumes and 11,000 manuscripts. In 1869 he was appointed as professor of philology and Assyrian archeology at the Collège de France and in 1890 he became president of the prestigious Académie des Inscriptions et Belles-Lettres (55 French members, 40 foreign associates, 50 French correspondents, 50 foreign correspondents). Among his works, *Historie des empires de Chaldée et l'Assyrie* ("History of the empires of Chaldea and Assyria", 1865) and especially *Ecriture anarienne* ("The writing of the Anarians", 1855) in which he speaks about the Turanian language, related to Turkish and Mongolian, that he considers the earliest language of the Chaldeans and the origin of the cuneiform alphabet. We cannot but notice here that the name of the people mentioned by Oppert, "anarians", sounds even too explicitly similar to the Sanskrit *anarya*, a word on which we have already elaborated.

The career of Walter Bruno Henning (1908-1967), historian, linguists and scholar of religions, started with a doctorate thesis entitled *The Middle Persian verb of the Turfan texts* (1933), still regarded as a fundamental text for the study of Iranian philology. In 1937 Henning married the famous egyptologist-semitist of German Jewish origin, Maria Polotsky, and moved to England where he was university professor for many years and engaged in a long academic controversy, specifically on the datation, the origin and the importance of Zarathustra. Henning wrote *The Khwarezmian language* (1956) and *Zoroaster: Politician or Witch doctor* (1951), mainly as a response to the elaborations of Henrik Samuel Nyberg (*Irans forntida religioner*, "The ancient religion of Iran, 1937) and Ernst Herzfeld (*Zoroaster and his world*, 1947). The non-controversial part of his research is focused on the Tokharian language found in texts from the region of Tarim (north-west China) in the 8th century CE; Henning believed that the Parsis had originally come from the Caucasus region known in the Hellenistic period as Bactria and that presently corresponds to Pakistan and Afghanistan, and that they had moved eastwards only later.

That ancient population (connected to the present Kurds) was identified as the Turians who in 2000 BCE were descendent of the Gutes and the Tukris, two peoples that had reached Mesopotamia and established the foundations of the Assyro-Babylonian civilization around 3000 BCE. The Gutes are even mentioned in Sumerian documents because between 2147 and 2050 BCE they had developed a royal dynasty that lasted several generations; in Sumerian they were called Gu-tu-umki or Gu-ti-umki. Elam, too, was conquered by the Gutians about 2100 BCE. The Babylonian texts (*Chronicle of Weidner*, about 500 BCE) describe the Gutians as "unhappy" mountain people, nomadic, rapacious barbarians, who did not know how to honor the Gods, and whose kings ruled for a maximum of 5 years. The Assyrian chronicles seem to use the word Gutes to refer also to the peoples known as Medes or Mannaes; at the times of emperor Cyrus of Persia, the famous general Gobryas was described as "the governor of Gutium". Henry Hoyle Howorth (historian, 1901), Theophilus Pinches (assiryologist, 1908), Sidney Smith (historian, 1928), Leonard Woolley (archeologist, 1929) and Ignace Gelb (assyriologist, 1944) state that the Gutes were blond-haired and white in complexion, on the basis of the observations by Julius Oppert, who in 1877 published some tablets describing the Gutes and Subaris as *namrum* or *namrûtum*, "of fair color". Similar statements had already been made by Georges Vacher de Lapouge in 1899.

Gamkrelidze and Ivanov used the research made by Henning to build a theory on the middle-eastern origin (from the German *urheimat*, from *ur*, "original", and *heimat*, "fatherland") for the indo-european peoples; obviously dating can cause quite a bit of confusion if we postulate that the indo-european peoples only appeared in 1500 BCE while the Assyrians were already well established several centuries earlier in Mesopotamia, which is still considered by most academics as the "cradle of human civilization". Speaking of Assyria and Zoroaster, we cannot but notice the connection with Ur of Chaldea and between the name Ahura Mazda and the name of Ashur, the Assyrian Deity of the Sun (in Egypt called Aton and worshiped by the "monotheistic" pharaoh Akhenaton) who gave his name to the Assyrian empire and then to modern Syria, where the first "gnostic" Christian congregations developed (see Damascus). In the end, we can clearly see that these subjects are all strongly tied together.

Khazaria

Enter the Khazari, a people whose name really looks like the name of the Khasas of *Mahabharata* - and in fact they seem to be their descendents, albeit mixed with several. other tribes. The ancient Khazar Khanate or kingdom of Khazaria was formed by nomadic clans of Khasa raiders that, as we have already seen, had already been operating at least since 800 BCE in the steppes of the euro-asiatic region along the western side of the Silk Road, traveled by caravans connecting north Europe (especially Russia) with the middle east and China.

At this point we could wonder what is the connection between the Khazars and the issue of aliens and Indian Gods, since the subject seemed to have been exhausted with the description of the hybrid Yaksha descendence called Khasa - a discussion necessary to demolish the myth of the "arian" race of blond and blue-eyed aliens that are supposed to have come down from the Pleiades or from Nibiru to give us civilization and save us from ourselves and who are supposed to be the Gods of all religions. Well, an adequate understanding of the Khazars is required to clearly understand the cultural terrain from which the myths of esoterist occultism developed in the colonial period, when "satanism" became acceptable culturally as long as it donned new clothes, preferably oriental and mystic or even the prestigious mantle of erudition in philosophical-speculative or classical studies. So we continue to collect the pieces of the puzzle and the general picture will become increasingly clear.

The Khazars were a basin of confluence for a variety of cultural currents:

1. the nomadic raiding tribes of hybrid human descendence (*dasyus* who rebelled against the Vedic values) mixed with the superhuman Yaksha race of the Daitya clan,

2. tengri-siberian shamanism of the Mongolian tribes of Turkish language, with the worship of the sun, the sky, the fire, the ancestors, and the awareness of the existence of a number of superhuman beings, generally malevolent or dangerous, such as orcs, giants and goblins,

3. the Parsism of Zarathustra, imposing the concept of a monotheistic State religion, presenting the Devas as devils and the Asura Mazda as the supreme God; on the background of the first local "conversion" in the Caucasus there was a superimposition of refugees from Iran and surrounding areas when Parsis became persecuted by other powers (especially Islam and orthodox Christianity),

4. talmudic and rabbinic Judaism fleeing from the destruction of Israel by the Roman empire,

5. the various Jewish gnostic, hermetic and kabalistic currents fleeing from the destruction of Alexandria in Egypt and from the middle east in general because of the persecution by fundamentalist politicized Christians that controlled the Roman empire,

6. Jewish merchants and bankers, not only those who normally lived or traveled along the Silk Road but also those fleeing from the persecutions in Arabia and middle east in general since the beginning of Islam,

7. various groups of "Christians of the origins" more or less aligned among themselves, apochriphal, gnostic, hessenes, therapeutics, hermetics and so on, who were not satisfied with the politicization

imposed by Constantine and with the conclusions of the first Councils, and were generally considered "Jews" (as Jesus was anyway),

8. a non-specified variety of people who came in different waves or sparsely from different regions - individuals and groups who shared a same desire for personal independence and rejected both Christianity and Islam, such as pagans, atheists, agnostics, or simply free thinkers or adventurers.

We want to clarify that the perspective of our analysis has nothing to do with racism or similar prejudices; according to our opinion (that incidentally is the same position of the original Vedic culture) any individual or ethnic/ cultural group should be free to live according to their own values, beliefs and traditions, naturally as long as these do not become a "justification" for criminal aggressions against innocent people. Furthermore, according to the same principles we firmly believe that any individual or ethnic/cultural group should be free to change their own values and beliefs ("to convert") and embrace a tradition that is different from the one they were born in or in which they had temporarily entered, as well as to remain in the tradition that gives them satisfaction, and that any individual or ethnic/cultural group should be free to choose the geographical region where they want to live, especially if it is a place they consider sacred as per their faith.

In the case of places considered sacred by different religious traditions - such as Hinduism, Buddhism and Shamanism in the Himalayan region - pilgrims and residents should be able to live peacefully in an atmosphere of sacred meditation and perform simultaneously or sequentially the rituals they want to observe, always avoiding offensive or aggressive behaviors that are not suitable to the idea of religion as a value for elevation, peace, morality and so on, generally presented as the public image by religious propaganda.

We shall now briefly examine the history of the Khazar Khanate from the ethnic perspective. The Sakas and Khasas from the Caucasus, already suffering from an increasing aridity and desertification of the land in the region, were joined by waves of other groups, remembered as the Uli Juz ("ancient or great horde"),

Orta Juz ("central horde") and Kisi Juz ("young or lesser horde"); with the centuries the word Juz became Zhuz (*juz* originally meant "hundred", a rather effective concept to refer to the ideal number of members of a single clan). From about 650 to 965 CE the various tribes became organized in a veritable empire that dominated the entire region of Caucasus, the Black sea and the Caspian sea, down to the Urals and the river Dnieper, including the steppes of Volga and Don and east Crimea. Besides directly controlling these territories, Khazaria had a powerful cultural and political influence of the entire region down to Irak and Syria, Anatolia, the Balkans, Bactria, north-western India and central Asia to the border with China.

It was a "cushion" betweeen the Bizantine empire, the Ummayad-Abbasid Islamic empire and the Chinese empire, also geographically and politically absorbing the impact of the independent nomadic hordes that were culturally compatible with the Khaganate structure. In the north they had the Rus tribes while in the south the Sassanid empire was the least dangerous: the greatest pressure came from the two politically organized emerging religious powers - Byzantine Christianity and expanding Islam. Both fronts were anxious to increase the numbers of their converts, and the leaders of the Khazars were still officially "pagan". After analyzing the situation, the Khazar king concluded that it was more convenient to choose a third option, Judaism, that left a greater autonomy to the government and had less rules on the ideological level. In fact Judaism merely forbids what is considered idolatry, blasphemy or sexual immorality, but it does not force its members to convert pagans or give special demonstrations of religious zeal, and gives no restrictions in the fields of trade and finance or professional occupation, except for the observance of one day of complete rest every week (on Saturdays).

Between 965 and 969 the Rus king Sviatoslav I of Kiev waged war against the Khazar capital Atil and finally conquered it, probably finding relatively little resistance from the residents that might have been tired of the difficulties created by the fact of being nailed in that particular geographical position and besieged from all sides. At that point the various groups (that had remained distinct and with nomadic tendencies) finally separated, each on their own way and especially westward, crossing the Balkans and north Italy, dispersing mostly in Germany but also in France and even farther north into

Russian territory; many researchers see this as the origin of the Cossack, Askhenazi, Rom gypsies and even Cathars. The groups that went eastward adopted Islam more or less superficially, turning into the populations of the countries with names still ending with "*stan*" (in Sanskrit *sthana*, "place, residence"): Afghanistan, Pakistan, Kazakhistan, Uzbekistan, Tajikistan, Kyrgyzistan, Turkmenistan. They also created ethnic and cultural enclaves in Mongolia and China, where they were called Hasàkè Zú ("Kazakh tribes") and where still 56 tribes are recognized by the government.

In Russia the famous Cossack are called *kazaki* (in Ukraine *kozaky*, in Poland *kozacy*, in Hungary *kozakok*, from the Cuman word *cosac*, "free man"); settlements became evident since the 1300s especially in less populated areas in the valleys of Dniepr, Don, Terek and Ural, later joined by merchants, farmers and refugees from other areas. In 1552 Dmytro Vyshnevetsky, cousin of Ivan the Terrible, formed the first military corps of Cossacks, the Zaporizhian Horde, as a garrison to a fortress on the island of Khortytsia on Dnieper; the rules of the corps combined the ancient Khazar traditions with those of the teutonic knights Hospitaller, under the authority of an elderly patriarch who carried the title of Ataman. While men were away in military campaigns, the women of the clan got organized to raid and pillage the surrounding villages, as told by Leo Tolstoy in his novel *The Cossacks* (1863).

Kazakhistan, with capital Astana (that replaced old Almaty), is presently the largest continental nation of the world, with vast uranium and petrol reserves, as well as chrome and zinc. In ancient times there was a lot of gold as well, but it seems to have been exhausted, except for a few mines still remaining in the north-east. Some sources have noticed a surrealistic and strongly masonic-illuminati symbolism in the architecture of Astana, but those could simply be coincidences produced while trying to create a very modernist image, probably to counteract the environmental disaster of the region, aggravated by the toxic waste dumped here in the Soviet period and the pollution of the nuclerar experiments especially in the north-east.

In Turkish language, the Khazars are called Tatars; it is interesting to note that the Turkish words *kez* and *qaz* refer to nomadic habits and raiding, while *qas* literally means "terrorizing". The ancient Turkish word *khasaq* precisely indicates the type of cart used by the Kazakh to carry various belongings and especially the *yurt*, the typical round tents with support poles and felter coverings, also used by Mongols and Huns.

According to the linguists Vasily Radlov and Veniamin Yudin, the name *qazgaq* comes from the same root of the verb *qazgan* ("to acquire", "to gain") and thus it would apply to a type of greedy person who is seeking profits and acquisitions. During all the middle ages the word *kazakh* has been used to indicate any individual or group that had acquired independence from rules, and was used by Timur (Tamerlan) to describe his own rebellious youth (as *qazaqliq* or "qazaq-icity"). In the 1600s the Qazaks of the steppes were differentiated from the Cossacks of the imperial army simply by replacing the letter "q" or "k" instead of "kh" at the end of the name; in the Kypchak language the word means "nomad, vagabond, brigand, corsair, independent raider". In medieval Chinese texts the name Khazar is always accompanied by the word *tujué*, that means "Turkish".

In Hebrew, the Khazars are called Kuzarim. There references in Hebrew language about Khazars are particularly relevant because between 740 and 920 CE the Khazars officially converted to Judaism and the Hebrew language (with some important modification) even became the State language, as we can see from the list of the monarchs, that changes names from Tong Yabghu to Bulan, and then to typically biblical names such as Obadiah, Zachariah, Manasseh, Benjamin, Aaron, Joseph and David. In the *Expositio in Matthaeum Evangelistam* ("Explanation on Matthew the Evangelist", by Christian of Stavelot, about 860-870 CE) the Khazars are described as the descendents of war-mongering peoples (Gog and Magog) originally from the Caucasus, converted to Judaism and duly circumcised. It is interesting to note that according to the Bible, Magog was an important descendent of Japhet (the first ancestor of the white race, different from the descendents of Shem or semites and Ham/ Cam or Africans); the *Book of Ezekiel* contains a prophecy by which Gog, hailing from the region of Magog, will pillage the various nations a short time before the advent of the Messiah, who will establish the eternal kingdom of Israel according to the promise of Yahweh, while the *Apocalypse of John* depicts Gog and Magog as allies of Satan in the final clash between angels and devils before the Last Judgement.

The famous Jewish-Roman historian Josephus explains that the Khazars are the Scyths, "that means the descendents of the Biblical Magog" and the Fathers of the Church identify them from time to time as Huns, Khazars, Mongols or other nomadic tribes, or even with the "10 lost tribes of Israel". In the *Romance of Alexander*, a cycle or collection of legends about Alexander the Macedonian compiled between 300 and 1700 CE, in medieval Greek, Latin, Arab, Armenian, Syriac, Hebrew and various other vernacular European languages (and imitated in France by the famous *Roman* or *Chanson de Roland*), Gog and Magog are described as kings of impure nations, chased by Alexander into exile beyond a mountain pass (echoing the Roncisvaux of Orlando the Paladin) and imprisoned by a wall built by Alexander himself. In many versions they are described as cannibals (eaters of human beings) and Islamic geographers positively identify them with the Turkish tribes of central Asia, with Mongolian components.

A letter by king Joseph states that after the conversion, "Israel had returned (*yashuvu yisra'el*) with the people of Qazaria through complete repentance (*bi-teshuvah shelemah*)". The geographer Ibn al-Faqîh (al Hamadani, about 900 CE) wrote in his *Mukhtasar kitab al-buldan* ("Brief treatise on lands"): "all the Khazars are Jews, but this is a recent development". Ahmad Ibn Fadlân, who went on a mission along the Volga (921-922) to study the Rus or Varangian (Vikings, tall blond people, described as abundantly tattooed and fond of combing their hair every day) and serve as an advisor to the Bulgar Khan (the Muslim ruler of Bulgaria) in his war against the Khazars, confirmed that the Khazars were Jews. It even seems that the Khazar king considered himself as the defender of all Jews including those outside his own boundaries, so much that he organized retaliatory expeditions when Byzantine Christians or Islamists attacked some Jews; for example he ordered the destrujction of the minaret of a mosque in Atil to avenge the destruction of a synagogue in Dâr al-Bâbûnaj.

Askhenazi

Since the elaborations of the majority of alienists are based on the Bible, and the elaborations of the majority of esoterists are based on the Jewish-Christian gnostic movements or on Kabalistic esoterism, it is reasonable to dedicate a small chapter to the story of the Khazars after the end of their empire.

The conversion of the Khazars is directly confirmed by Jewish authorities such as Judah Halevi (1075-1141, Jerusalem) and Abraham ibn Daud (1110-1180, Toledo, Spain), and by many other researchers and historians belonging to the Jewish religion, who connected it to the origin of the Askhenazi Jews, of typically Caucasian ("arian") race, an idea that strangely some people accuse of "antisemitism" or "racism", probably because it complicates the picture of the relationship between nazism and sionism, a subject on which we cannot elaborate in this book as we do not want to stray too far from our original topic. However, as we will now see, the subject has been proposed and supported very openly precisely by the highest Jewish authorities, therefore we do not find anything controversial in the reported facts.

It seems that the first to suggest the connection between Khazars and Askhenazi (the European Jews of white or caucasian race) was Abraham Eliyahu Harkavi (in 1869), followed by Abraham Firkovich (in 1872) elaborating on the origins of the Karaites of Crimea, a Jewish sect of Turkish language to which he belonged personally. But people especially noticed Ernest Renan (1823-1892), who clearly spoke in a public lecture at the Cercle de Saint-Simon, in Paris on 27th January 1883, about the conversion of the Khazars as the crucial factor in the origin of the large population of Jews in the region along the Danube and southern Russia. Maybe his declarations made more noise because as an expert on semitic languages and author of the *Histoire du peuple d'Israel* ("History of the People of Israel", in 5 volumes), he did not belong to the Jewish community and presented the subject to the general public instead of keeping it within the internal debates of the rabbis that had never agitated anyone. In his studies on the history of Christianity, Renan had been particularly traumatized by the persecution against the Cathars and the Huguenots, movements of Christian gnostics originally from the Balkans. It could also be interesting to note that Renan was the first scholar to point out inconsistencies in style, time frame and logic in the biblical texts, and that he wrote no less than 50 books including *Histoire générale des systèmes comparés des langues semitiques* ("General history of compared systems in Semitic languages"), 8 volumes of *Histoire des origines du christianisme* ("History of the origins of Christianity") and some other intriguing ones, such as *Mission de Phénicie* ("The mission of Phoenicia"), *La réforme intellectualle et morale de la France* ("Intellectual and moral reform of France"), *Qu'est-ce qu'une Nation?* ("What is a Nation?"), as well as a famous lecture to the Sorbonne on *Islam et Science* ("Islam and science", 1883).

His studies, however, led him to the conclusion that different races have different inclinations and abilities and therefore should be engaged (that is, *forcibly engaged by the government*) in different capacities. Here it could be interesting to note that among Khazars there was a very strict social order, with ak-Khazar ("white Khazars") and qara-Khazar ("black Khazars"); the white ones were described mostly with white complexion, red hair and blue eyes, while the black ones were dark complexioned. The discrimination continued during their expansion in Hungary, where the Khazars called themselves "white Oghurs" and the Magiars were called "black Oghurs".

The idea of a connection between Khazars and Askhenazi was proposed again by Joseph Jacobs (1854-1916), Anatole Leroy-Beaulieu (1842-1912), Maksymilian Ernest Gumplowicz (1864-1897, related to the famous Abraham) and by anthropologist Samuel Weissenberg (1867-1928, from Ukraine, mentioned by the *Jewish Encyclopedia*). In 1909 Hugo von Kutschera (Austrian, Catholic but recognized as expert in the field) wrote a monography entitled *Die Chasaren, Historische Studie* ("History study on the Chasars"), followed in 1911 by Maurice Fishberg (1872-1934, also a Jew emigrated to USA) with *The Jews: A Study of Race and Environment*. Other historians quoted on the issue are Tadeusz Czacki and Isaac Levinsohn - who have extremely interesting family names.

The idea was proposed also by Yitzhak Schipper (Polish Jew, historian, economist and passionate Zionist) in 1918, by HG Wells

(1921) and by the anthropologist Roland B Dixon (1923), as well as by Sigmund Freud (1931), Samuel Krauss (1932) and by Abraham N Poliak, professor of medieval history at the Tel Aviv University, in a monography in Hebrew language (1942) where he concluded that the Jews of east Europe had certainly come from Khazaria. In 1955 Léon Poliakov stated that "it is common knowledge that the Jews of east Europe descend from a mixture of German Jews and Khazars"; the same declaration was also endorsed by Ben-Zion Dinur and Salo Wittmayer Baron.

This Salo Wittmayer Baron (1895-1989), born in the high Jewish aristocracy of Galicia (Poland, formerly Austro-Hungaric empire), son of the president of the Jewish community (an important banker) and ordained rabbi at the theological seminary of Wien in 1920, was convinced by Rabbi Stephen S Wise to move to New York to teach at the Jewish Institute of Religion; later he became president of the Association called Jewish Cultural Reconstruction (founded in 1947). Clearly, hardly a person who can be accused of antisemitism or lack of knowledge on the subject, having been tenured professor in the faculty of Jewish history, literature and institutions, and director of the Center of Israel and Jewish Studies at Columbia University (from 1929), as well as having been awarded a dozen of *honoris causa* doctorates by various universities in USA, Europe and Israel, and praised by Yosef Hayim Yerushalmi as "undoubtedly the greatest Jewish historian of the 20th century" and by his own official biographer as "the architect of Jewish history".

Baron dedicates almost one entire chapter of his *Social and Religious History of the Jews* (published in 1957) to the Jewish kingdom of Khazaria and its impact on the formation of the Jewish communities in east Europe. He describes the conversion of the Khazars as the last mass religious phenomenon, started by a considerable group of Jews fleeing from the continuous wars between Byzantium, the Persia of Sassanids and the Abbasid and Ummayad Khalifates. According to his evaluation, after the fall of the kingdom of Khazaria there was another diaspora to north towards Russia, Ukraine and Poland, and west towards Pannonia and the Balkans, and then gradually towards Germany and France, where between 1000 and 1100 there was a flourishing of Jewish literature. He does not seem to make a connection with the Cathars but the etymological similarity is irresistible, also considering that in the Balkans the slavic populations converted to a type of Christianity with strong gnostic influences - a common trait of Christianity and Judaism. However, Baron observes that Maimonides and the other commentators of that time, disappointed and worried for the lack of interest towards study in the young Jewish communities of the medieval eastern Europe, would be surprised to see how the Jews from eastern Europe had become the spear-head top leaders of the entire Jewish people.

Another very interesting person who has written on the subject is Arthur Koestler (1905-1983), with his famous *The Thirteenth Tribe* (published in 1976). Son of Adele Jeiteles, heiress of an important Jewish family from Prague that had moved to Wien, Koestler went to live in a *kibbutz* in Palestine, then he obtained a job as foreign correspondent for the prestigious publishing group Ullstein Verlag based in Berlin, and in 1931 he became a member of the German communist party. After several adventures, in March 1942 he was appointed at the Ministry of Information of the United Kingdom, where he produced propaganda material for films and newscasts, including the essay *On disbelieving atrocities* (on the nazi extermination of the Jews), published on the *New York Times*. He became an intimate friend and house neighbor of George Orwell and Bertrand Russell, and was granted permanent residence in USA with a special decree of the Government, Private Law 221 Chapter 343 dated 23rd August 1951, specifically named "For the relief of Arthur Koestler". In 1968 Koestler was awarded the Sonning Prize "for his extraordinary contribution to European culture" and in 1972 he was honored as Commander of the Order of the British Empire. Besides novels and essays on politics and history, he also wrote about "oriental mysticism", neurology, psychology, evolution, genetics and "paranormal"; he also financed the KIB Society (named from the initials of the names of the founders, Koestler, Inglis and Bloomfield) which after his death was renamed The Koestler Foundation, as well a chair in parapsychology with a fund of about 1 million sterling pounds at the Edinburgh University.

The issue of the ethnical and geographical origins of the Askhenazi had already turned into politics (presumably "antisemitic") at the conference of Versailles (1919), with a public bickering between a Zionist Jew (unidentified) and Joseph Reinach, a Jewish member of the parliament of France, who declared that the creation of a State of Israel in Palestine was not justified because the vast majority of the European Jews "descend from the Khazars, a Tartar people from southern Russia that converted en masse to Judaism at the time of Charlemagne".

We take the opportunity here to clarify again, and in a most explicit way, that we do not agree with this Joseph Reinach. If the Jews, to whatever race they belong according to their genetic heritage (Askhenazim, Sephardim, Mizrahim or anything else), want to live in an "Israeli nation" centered on Jerusalem and build a new great temple, we have no objections whatsoever. We are not racist at all, which means we do not believe that belonging to a particular race constitutes an intrinsic right to occupy a particular territory; the issue of the cultural identity of a land is a different problem, because places preserve or should preserve the history of the events and civilizations that lived and worked to build them, and this heritage should be respected and appreciated by newcomers - whether they are coming by birth or by immigration.

However, it is difficult to understand how one can give a label of "antisemitic racism" to the objective observation that Askhenazi Jews are not genetically of semitic race. Maybe we should change the definition in "anti-judaism" and eliminate the racial factor? But even reading the "anti-semitism" concept as "anti-judaism", we cannot understand how all these very respected Jewish historians who recognize the ethnic origin of the Askhenazi could be accused of anti-semitism, or how red hair, blue or green eyes and a white complexion (sometimes with freckles) of a very high percentage of Jews also in Israel (98%) could be ascribed to some "palestianian conspiracy".

Maybe the most resounding argument about the ethnic origins of the Askhenazi is supplied by an article (signed Andrew Tobin) in the *Times of Israel* on a study published by Shai Carmi, professor of informatics at the Columbia University, USA, in cooperation with over 20 medical researchers at the Universities of Yale and Columbia, Albert Einstein College of Medicine at Yeshiva University, Memorial Sloan-Kettering Cancer Center and Jewish University in Jerusalem. According to the documented analysis of the genetic factors, the ethnic line of the Askhenazi descends directly from a group of only 350 people; their physical traits are illustrated in an internet article with a photo from the exhibition named *Redheads* organized at the Dizengoff Center by Nurit Ben Sheetri.

To complete the picture we can quote the analysis of the two Jewish scholars Max Weinrech (*History of the Yiddish language*, 1894-1969) and Solomon Birnbaum (*Grammatik der jiddischen Sprache*, "Grammar of the Jiddish language", 1891-1989), mentioning French and Italian influences - and this again reminds us of the Cathars. The *yiddish*, abbreviation of *yidish taitsh* ("German Hebrew"), was born from a mixture of ancient German and slavic languages (Ukranian, Romanian, Polish, Galician, Hungarian, Lithuanian, Bielorus) with substantial traces of romanic languages and only a few elements of Hebrew and Aramairc, and is commonly called "mother language" (*mame loshn*) while Hebrew is called "sacred language" (*loshn koydesh*), clearly very different from the mother language.

Zarathustra

We have mentioned the fact that Khasas/Sakas and Turanians, or at least a good percentage of the Khazars in general, before converting to Judaism were very close to the religion of Zarathustra or followed it directly. How can this fact be connected to the subject of Aliens presented as Gods?

A moderate amount of research will show that all the alienist-ufologist sources from the 1800s to date contain a strong abrahamic component of an esoteric-occultist character, through currents ranging from Luciferism to the Order of Melchizedek, from Kabal to gnosticism, with ties to Rusicrucians, Freemasons and so on, and at least some reference to Zarathustra, if not openly Christian (arc)angelic or demoniac. But even more significant is an aspect relatively less known to the public: the *Khshnoom*, Parsi equivalent of the Jewish Kabal, recognized by religious orthodoxy and mentioned in the *Gathas* (Yasna 48.12 and 53.2) but of a mysteric and initiatic nature. Thus it seems useful to dig a little deeper to find the roots of this ideological current, typically esoteric-occultist, with a considerable continuity of contents and orientation, apparently since very ancient times.

The first thing that immediately catches the eye is the easy parallel between Ahura Mazda (even disguised as Ormuz, that many people may mistake as the Number One but is a mere archangel) and the Yahweh of the Bible, that through the connection with the Elohim/Annunaki of Sitchin should (according to the alienists) explains the origin and the true meaning of all religions. Here the alienist theory can find some justification in claiming that the *elohim/ annunaki* were in fact superhuman individuals of a rather homogeneous category, possessing a technology that appeared to be miraculous to their primitive worshipers. Indeed, unlike Vedic tradition, Parsism remains rather confused about Asuras and Devas: in the earliest texts (the *Gathas*) Zarathustra states 19 times that the *daeva* are actually deities but they are "the wrong gods" that must be rejected (see Yasna 32.3 and 41.6 where it is said that they were worshiped by the Iranian people) or bounces them into an intermediate position subordinate to the supreme Ahura allowing a measure of worship albeit marginal and occasional (especially to Mithra, Anahita, Vrthragna, Ritis and Tistriya). On the other hand there is no scarcity of angels (Yazad, Fereshteh) and archangels (Ameshaspend, Mino), deified ancestors (Fravarti), saints (*durvesh*) and saviors (*sosyant*), devils of various types, sprites and so on - apart from the monotheistic God and the supreme Prophet Zarathustra, the scene is rather complicated and changing.

There is no doubt that Ahura Mazda is a jealous and intolerant God, who forbids the cult and veneration of other "competition" deities and orders the destruction or conversion of their temples, but whose form and true name cannot be known or depicted; the sin of "idolatry" is considered an extremely serious crime. The name Ahura Mazda simply means "Great Asura" (where *asura* is translated as "benevolent spirit") and the Parsis theology commentators explain it on the basis of *ahu*, translated as "I am" (the same theological explanation of the name YHWH in Judaic tradition). For Zarathustra, the concept of sin consists in a lack of faith towards the only true

God Ahura Mazda, disobedience towards the orders of the priests and the political, social and family authorities, and in heresy, that means the choice of believing in something else or according to a different interpretation than the official one. His religion includes a strict patriarchalism, a linear vision of the history of creation (albeit containing several long cycles) ending with a final Judgmet (*Roshan Rooz*) with the threat of eternal hell. We also find the serpent and even the name of Satan as symbols of Evil, the need for a Savior (*sosyant*, Yasna 19.88), the concept of supreme Prophet, and contempt for material Nature that is called "putrid" - a concept that will become even starker with Mani and the subsequent sects of manicheism and gnosticism, their side branching as mandeism and yazidism and the various Christians "of the origins".

The doctrine of the souls is complicated by the idea of a "splitting" of each individual soul into various components - human, animal, vegetal and mineral - that must be subsequently integrated in order to reach perfection: minerals are integrated into vegetals in the form of fertilizers, vegetals integrate into animals as feed, and animals (especially goats and lambs) integrate into humans by being eaten preferably well roasted. Finally the feminine "pieces" must find their masculine counterpart, while always keeping the maximum purity with frequent ablutions and especially with rituals and imprecations and spells of all kinds, that are also considered the best medicine for any physical problem and not just for the evil eye and sorcery, snake bites, stings of poisonous animals and so on. An expert priest (Atharvan) must have 16 different spiritual powers and the ability to hear the divine music, know the proper intonations for the spells, and so on.

The need to constantly fight contamination also extends to ordinary devotees: even after taking bath (a source of "contamination" because it could stimulate lust) one should purify oneself by smearing one's body with the urine of cattle or sheep (but it should be fresh, not beyond 72 hours of shelf life) and muttering the appropriate magic formulas. There are also complicated clothing needs (such as the obligatory *sudreh* tunic and the *kusti* rope belt) and great importance is given to talismans and protection amulets (*taviz*), pentacles, alchemy, elixirs and astrological influences, especially of the planets of the week. In regard to planets and extraterrestrials,

Zarathustra's cosmology is even more complicated than the Vedic one, and covers various dimensions with many details both about the regions and on the life species that reside there. Unfortunately the names do not correspond and are not even similar to the Vedic version and therefore it is reasonable to think that the concepts could be different as well, but also to suspect that the detailed information on the planetary systems could have been supplied by individuals and groups that had a stronger interest for space traffic around the Earth - as in fact we see in Asuras.

On the social level the original followers of Zoroasters were organized on military basis and divided into birth classes that do not correspond to the Vedic *varnas*: at the top we find the royal aristocrats all related among themselves (*kshatram* or "king", and *hvetu* or "princes" equivalent to the Celtic or Teutonic *thane*), then the clergy (the *magu*, members of a caste or ethnic tribe like the Jewish Levites but sworn to celibacy, with the functions of officiating priests, preachers and judges like the Islamic *mullah*), then the semi-free commoners (farmers and shepherds, subject to the families of aristocrats who own the land and similar to the Celtic and Teuton *thrall*) and finally slaves, who have no rights and are equated to cattle and sheep. We can remember here that in the Vedic *varnas* the highest position is occupied by the *brahmanas*, that are intellectuals, counselors and teachers, have no material power in the government and do not accumulate wealth but usually marry and have children, then there are the *kshatriyas* or kings whose role simply consists in personally protecting the subjects from all aggressions and injustice, the *vaisyas* or entrepreneurs who develop the land independently (without being subject to a vassal position) and the *sudras* or servants, who are free but engage in manual work to assist their employers or customers. In Vedic society there is no provision for the acquisition of goods or cattle through raids or invasions and there is no slavery; a king who is proven unworthy of his position is removed by a more qualified *kshatriya* supported by the people, or in case of emergency by the assembly of the *brahmanas*. The general assembly of the people (*sabha*) is presided by the king and open to debates in which everyone can participate, including women and foreigners; when there are no issues of security or practical problems to be discussed, the assembly focuses on public debates about spiritual and religious knowledge.

The aggressive and war-mongering approach of Parsism became even stronger with the increasing importance of Mithra, the god of blood vengeance, sometimes described as the companion of Ahura Mazda, or a sort of his "double". If we make a connection with ancient cults, Mithra can be compared to the destructive aspect of the Sun, that is particularly fearsome in hot and desertic or semi-desertic regions, while Ahura Mazda is the primary aspect of the Sun as the supreme power in the world.

With time, the cult of Mithra developed into a new and almost independent religion, spread all over Europe by the Roman legions: the cult of the Sol Invictus ("unconquered Sun"). Protector of soldiers of all ranks and adopted also by several emperors (with the tendency by the emperor himself to identify with the god, as we see for example in Heliogabalus), his cult became official on 25th December 274 CE, when Aurelian elevated it to the position of State religion: we find his image on coins up to the times of Constantine, when its cult opened the way to the rise of Christianity as official religion of the Empire. With the *Codex Justinianus* (3.12.2) besides the 25th December (winter solstice, the "birth day of the Sun" or *Dies Natalis Solis Invicti*) all Sundays became public festivities as *dies dominici*, "day of God". The image of the Sun God is also found in Judaism and Christianity especially in the early centuries: a mosaic floor at Hamat Tiberias shows David as Helios surrounded by a ring with the 12 zodiac signs, and similar decorations are also found in ancient synagogues such as at Beth Alpha and Husefa (Israel) and Naaran (west bank at Gaza). On the other hand, we see that Clemens of Alexandria describes the Christ as riding his chariot across the sky.

Mithraism gives special importance to the ritual called *taurobolia*, the "purificatory baptism" by which the adept is washed or bathed with the blood of the sacrificial bull, and especially in the lower social classes as in the army, it takes the place of the ancient mysteries, creating a basis for the subsequent secret societies of the esoteric-occultist type, that require a community and hierarchy bond with a strict secrecy. The cult of the Sun is easily connected to the ancient middle eastern tradition, not only in Sumer and Mesopotamia, but also in the region of Caucasus, from Scythia to the Himalayas, as we have already seen.

The dating of Zarathustra/ Zoroaster is controversial even within official academic circles. The "most conservative" indologists, such as Henning, give a precise date 258 years before Alexander the Macedonian, calculated on the basis of a current of opinion born in the late Sassanid period in Persia. Some academics openly declare that the period of 600 BCE brought a sort of "spiritual revolution" in the east placing Zarathustra together with Buddha, Lao-Tze and Confucius all within the space of half a century. Even if this "revolution" never really happened in this way, it remains useful to those who want to present the idea of a "religious evolution of the human spirit" going from "polytheistic idolatry" to "moral philosophy". On the other hand the authors of classical Greece (Aristotle, Hermodorus, Dinon, Eudoxus, Hermippus, Xanthus of Lydia, Diogenes Laertius and others, quoted by Plinius the elder) believed that Zarathustra had lived at least 6,000 years before Plato, who was considered the reincarnation of Zarathustra himself. Between these two extremes we find various other possibilities, with a popular favorite cutting the problem in half and assigning a period around 2000 or 1200 BCE.

Our contemporary Parsi religious community, that took shelter in Indian in the previous centuries and more recently in other regions of the world, strongly believes in a much earlier date, such as 6500 BCE (as declared by Dr Ervad Karkhanavala of Bombay) or 6900 BCE (magazine *Mazdaznan*, September 1957, Los Angeles, California, USA) or even 7551 BCE (according to some astrological calculations). The confusion is increased by the fact that all ancient documents were lost, burned with the repeated destruction of libraries, including the first islamization campaign of Iran by Khalifa Umar (584-644 CE), who also destroyed small private libraries. But even without this problem, western academics will hardly accept the time frames suggested by ancient writers: the earliest historical documents traditionally accepted by mainstream academics begin with Herodotus' chronicles, and any previous date is catalogued as "legendary".

The problem of the time frame of ancient civilizations is due to the fact that western academia, born as an instrument of abrahamic propaganda, was based on the idea that the first and only creation of the world had happened at 9 in the morning of 23rd October 4004

BCE and the great flood exactly in 2349 BCE (dates calculated by archbishop Usher, who died in 1656). Even after the biblical version was discarded because of the discovery of geological fossils and the growing popularity of the Darwinian evolution theory, global academic institutions have preserved the idea that until a few thousands years before Christ the entire mankind lived in a very primitive state. Still today the global calendar points the Zero year rather arbitrarily to the time of the birth of Jesus (although historical verification has shown that it is not an accurate date) and a great number of scholars in the English speaking world (including India) still use the acronym AD (*Anno Domini*, "the year of our Lord") to designate the years of the current ("Christian") era. It is therefore from the perspective of abrahamic calculations (more or less narrow-minded) that conventional academics have fixed the dates of birth for Buddha and subsequently of Adi Shankara respectively around 500 BCE and 800 CE; similarly the aryan invasion theory puts the introduction of Sanskrit and the *Rig Veda* in the Indian sub-continent around 1500 BCE, after which in the subsequent centuries a sort of "religious evolution" would have produced the other *Samhitas* (*Sama, Yajur, Atharva*), a job that according to "expert" scholars had required up to about 800 BCE. Then followed the *Brahmanas* between 900 and 600 BCE, the *Aranyakas* (700-500 BCE), then the *Upanishads* (600-400 BCE), and finally *Mahabharata* (350 BCE- 50 CE), *Ramayana* (250 BCE-200 CE), *Puranas* (200-1500 CE) and *Vedanta* (after 800 CE).

Actually these are completely arbitrary dates, based on the style of the composition and the preservation conditions of the most ancient manuscripts found - rather questionable criteria, if we consider that literary styles largely depend on the individual writer and are not necessarily homogeneous in each historical period, also because the style differences in Sanskrit works are minimal, and mainly consists in difference in subjects. In other words, in bigoted archeology the more complex and perfect artifacts are assigned to a "period of highest splendor" while the simpler and rougher items must necessarily belong to a "primitive" or "decadent" period. In other words, the *Upanishads* must necessarily be more recent because they contain complex and abstract philosophical elaborations, something that the compilers of the Vedic *suktas* could not have be able to do because they were still a bit stupid and undeveloped. Obviously for the academics that are officially recognized as "authorities in the field" there is no relevance in the fact that the Vedic scriptures themselves state they have been compiled *all together simultaneously* within a period defined by precise astronomic references around 3000 BCE, and based on a tradition transmitted orally for thousands of years more. According to the Vedic tradition, the passage from oral to written is also considered a sign of decadence and not of progress, because it indicates a decrease in the memory capacity of human beings. Official academics do not even give credence to the documents of the Tibetan tradition, according to which the historical Buddha (Siddhartha Gautama) had lived over a millennium before 539 or 544 BCE, and precisely around 1800 BCE: the historical references recorded by Buddhist sources indicate the year 1807 BCE for the attainment of enlightment by the Buddha.

On such basis, we should push back the date of the appearance of Adi Shankara, whose declared mission was to repair the damage caused by the degradation of the original Buddhism: this historical mark seems to trace back, according to the documents of his religious lineage (the Shankaracharya mathas), to 509 BCE. In regard to the dating of the texts on the basis of the most ancient available manuscripts, it is interesting to note that still today nobody has ever tried to apply the same criteria to the biblical scriptures: both Vedic and biblical scriptures contain references to previous and more ancient compilations, but because the Vedic texts (and those of other cultures, such as the Egyptian and the Sumerian) speak of "too ancient" dates, such references are labeled as unreliable or incredible.

Also, the geographical location of Zarathustra (whose family name was Spitama) remains quite controversial, even if the texts mention it with the name of Iran-vej and therefore generally identify it with the region on the border of north-west Iran, precisely on the bank of lake Urmia, south of the river Araxes and east of the lake Van in Armenia. Urmia, a city that is still quite important in Iran, is the largest in the province of west Azerbaijan; it is on the highland of the same name, along the river Shahar Chay and between the salt lake Urmia and the mountains on the border with Turkey. The etymological derivation of the name, that is explained as "city of the water", is according to Thomas Burrow (1909-1986) a fusion between the Indo-Iranian *urmi* ("wave") and the Assyrian *mia* ("water"); it is interesting to note that the local population still speaks an Assyrian dialect. However, we think it is interesting also to note that in the *Zend Avesta* (Yasna 55.1) the word *urvan* refers to the souls that descend in the material world; the etymological origin is uncertain (*Avesta dictionary*, by Ervad Kanga) but it is known that *uru* means "vast" and *an* means to "live".

According to Richard Nelson Frye (1920-2014), the name Urmia derives from Urartian language - another piece of information that surely not many of our readers have found during the school studies. Urartu is the Assyrian name of a kingdom officially dated between 880 and 590 BCE covering the Armenian highlands between Anatolia, Mesopotamia, Iran and Caucasus; the language spoken there was Urartian, written in the typical cuneiform characters. We might be excused for getting the impression of a possible association with the name of Ur, the famous Sumerian city, and the definition of "Ur of the Chaldeans" found in biblical literature: the connection could indicate that Mesopotamia extended to considerable distance from the two rivers or that between the Caucasus and the "fertile crescent" there must have been quite some movement, with migrations up and down also in extremely ancient times. We should not be confused by the relatively recent dates assigned to the kingdom of Urartu, because the name of Urartu already appears in 1400 BCE as a league of peoples (according to Boris Piotrovsky, 1908-1990) and the region had been inhabited since 6500 BCE (by the "Shulaveri culture") or even from 9000 BCE, soon after the end of the catastrophic inundation of the Altai, as demonstrated by the remains of Jarmo, an agricultural village on the Kurd hills of north Irak at the border with Iran, excavated by Robert Braidwood of the Chicago University Oriental Institute.

According to Parsi hagiography and cosmology, the Airyana Vaeja (*Vendidad* 1.1) as the birth place of Zarathustra is in the arctic region (north pole), that before 9000 BCE was not covered by ice, because being holy it could not be touched by Satan. Other names of this region were Thrishva (literally "one third", Yastha 13.3) and Khanirath Bami ("The golden bank", Yastha 10.15). The house of Pourushaspa, father of Zarathustra Spitama, was on a highland of mount Alborz or Haraiti-Barsh (*Vendidad* 19.4, 19.11), presented as the place that cannot be destroyed by recurrent deluges (one every 81,000 years) and where the Savior of the period takes shelter with a couple of each human and animal species, and from where the first human beings of the new cycle (called *maabadian*) descend to go settle in the plains, guided by the first king Gayomard.

Unfortunately it seems that no Parsi hagiographer (or commentator in that line) is aware of the fact that the arctic polar cycle has been occupied during the last 5 million years by an ocean more or less completely frozen and thus totally flat, between Canada, Groenland and Russia. Both the magnetic poles and the geographical poles shift, with a total inversion (north-south) about every 200,000 years, although according to mainstream academics and space agencies the last reversal of poles happened around 600,000 years ago. For several thousands of years, the only human inhabitants of the region have been the Eskimos (Inuit) and their ancestors the "people of Thule", who besides the temporary shelters made from hardened snow called *igloo*, lived in subterranean lairs in the winter and in tents (made with skins and whale bones) in summer, hunting reindeer, seals and whales for survival. The Inuit speak of a legendary people even more ancient, the Sivullirmiut or Tuniit, who were tall and big but very shy and easily scared, and even less advanced technologically than the Inuit.

It is true that the idea of the north pole could have been leaked from the relative position of those who recorded the legend, and therefore it would be reasonable to seek a land that was at the north, for example Siberia, where we actually find a central plateau, very rich in minerals, where a people of Ugric language lived; the name seems to have derived from the Turkish (*su*, "water", and *bir*, "wild lands") and refers to its large marshes. The considerable climate changes presently happening, that are melting the *permafrost*, could reveal a quite different place, a land where mammoths and woolly rhinos lived, together with lions and horses. But we should not discard the possibility that the legendary land of the north is the memory of some happy valley hidden between the mountains of the Caucasus or the Himalayas.

The theory of a very ancient civilization "away north" traces back to Greek mythology, according to which the divine land of Hyperborea was blessed by Apollon, who visited it regularly in the winter. Here we find some support for the alienists: the extremely advanced civilization of Hyperborea is described as having extraordinary priests and scientists, as for example Abaris, who never ate any food and used to fly on an "arrow" that he had received personally from Apollon. According to Russian researcher Valeriy Nikitich Demin that civilization would trace back to about 15,000 or 20,000 years ago, and had flying machines.

The Greek idea of the lost civilization of Hyperborea was presented again by Jean Sylvain Bailly, a French astronomer of the 1700s, and then by William Fairfield Warren (1833-1929, first director of Boston University) in several books: *Paradise found - the Cradle of the Human Race at the North Pole* (1885), *The true key of Ancient Cosmology* (1883), *The Quest for Perfect Religion* (1886), *In the footsteps of Arminius* (an ancient character symbolizing German unification, 1885), *Religions of the world and the World Religion* (1900). It is useful to note that Warren had studied theology at the seminar of Andover and later at Berlino and Halle, becoming president of the Boston University School of Theology (1866-1873). He was also a member of the Mystical Seven - an important and ancient *college fraternity* at the Wesleyan University, Middletown, Connecticut, connected with the Skull and Bones of Yale and the IKA of Trinity, that chose Jewish references instead of Greek references as fraternities generally do. Later the organization expanded to other universities creating "temples" with rather interesting denominations: Temple of the Wand (Wesleyan, 18837), Temple of the Sword (Emory, 1841), Temple of the Skull (Georgia, 1846), Temple of the Star (Mississippi, 1848), Temple of the Serpent (Cumberland, 1867) and so on.

In Warren's view, everything traced back to the north pole: Atlantis, the garden of Eden, Avalon and Hyperborea; if we want to follow this theory, the presence of the arctic ocean could be explained with the sinking of those lands only a few thousands of years ago, and it impossible to verify that. Unfortunately some Hindus, too, such as Bal Gangadhar Tilak, have embraced this theory on the basis of the interpretation of the *Zend Avesta* and western thinkers, coming to the point of indicating the north pole as the locality of mount Meru - although this mountain, described in Vedic texts as the highest peak of the entire planet should be poking out of the present arctic ocean at least of a few meters. But no: the only high points in the region are the Lovozero Massif, in the Kola peninsula in Russia, around lake Seydozero (67°50'44.88"N, 34°40'92"E). The dilemma could apparently be solved by postulating, as some Hindus have done, the locality of this mount Meru in a "subtle dimension" that is not visible for the naked eye or material senses, but this interpretation does not seem compatible with the Parsi tradition or with the descriptions of Hyperborea, so they should not be lumped up together.

We will not elaborate here on the story of the life of Zarathustra (told especially in the *Dinkard*) and his various miracles, but we can summarize briefly saying that many demons tried to kill him several times. The Prophet engaged in spiritual practices until the age of 30, after which he was visited by archangel Behman/ Vohumand and then by Ahura Mazda himself, who ordered him to go and preach the true religion, called Mazdayasni Jarthoshti Daena. The first disciple was king Vishtaspa, who initially arrested him because of the disorders caused by his preaching against the previous religion, but then the king was convinced by some miracles and obtained enlightenment. A curious episode is about a famous Hindu *brahmana* whose name is reported as Cangranghacah, who arrived at the court of Vishtaspa for a philosophical debate with Zarathustra but ended up converting, too; the most interesting point is that according to some indologists Vedic civilization, from which Hinduism descended, would simply be a later deformation of the "original" religion and culture established by Zarathustra. We should therefore ask why a *brahmana* coming from India and contemporary of Zarathustra was trying to establish the superiority of Vedic philosophy, if that had not been existing already for a very long time. According to the Parsi hagiography, this *brahmana* was the *guru* of Jamaspa, a minister of king Vishtaspa, and had arrived at court with a following of many disciples. Finally Zaruthustra was murdered, stabbed in the back by a Turk while he was offering prayers in his fire temple; in turn he threw his own rosary against his attacker, killing him on the spot. The hagiographic version presents this "Turk" as Satan himself and Zarathustra's death as the voluntary acceptance of martyrdom for the purpose of saving Earth from destruction; it seems there are no explanations about the extraordinary quality of the rosary as a lethal weapon.

We do not want to increase the size of this book inordinately by elaborating on the various subsequent ramifications of zoroastrism, such as zurvanism, but it is worth mentioning that in the zoroastrian system and later in gnosticism there are two different priest figures: one is the wise *vaedemna* ("who knows, who sees", almost parallel to the Vedic *rishi* or Jewish priest-oracle) and the other is the *zoatar* ("illuminated" or "ordinator") who is the official advisor or minister of the theocratic government. Unfortunately this does not mean that the government became free from the religious powers, but rather that the power of the clergy on society became a fundamental basis for the government to be enforced materially and without bothering to bring knowledge or vision to the people.

From the word *zoatar* derive the Greek word *soter* ("savior") and the word *soteriologic*, that applies to messianic religions. The function of such priests was taken up by the Jewish "prophets" in the so-called "period of the kings"; this is the origin of the development of the idea of messiah that carries both roles: the human character of the King of the Jews and the superhuman character of the Melchizedek of the Zaddikim sect, and later the idea of the Christ proposed by the pauline current, headed by the figure known as Paul/ Saul of Tarsus.

The priests of the zoroastrian cult have been identified historically with the Mages and the Chaldeans, custodians of mysterious astronomical and astrological knowledge, alchemy and esoterism; according to the biblic tradition, zoroastrism is superimposed to the Assyro-Babylonian or Sumerian civilization, for example about the geographical-cultural location of "Ur of Chaldea" that we have already mentioned. Some have connected the word "Chaldean" with a Sumerian word, *kasdim*, similar to the Hebrew *chesed* (designating a *sepiroth* of the Tree of Life in Jewish Kabal) and with the *chassidim* ("the pious"), the ultra-orthodox Jewish sect also known as *zaddikim*.

Even more interesting is the fact highlighted by Jean Doresse (1917-2007) in his *Livres secrets des Gnostiques d'Egypte* ("The secret books of Egyptian gnostics") where he says that on the highlands of lake Urma there is the sacred mount Hermon, also called the White Mountain of Seir and traditionally considered "the abode of the Children of Seth", a denomination that gnostic tradition ascribes to a lineage of *phoster* ("those who reveal"). This was the place of origin of two movements known as "Turan culture" and "Zurvan culture", one south towards Mesopotamia before the foundation of the earliest cities of Sumer, and another east towards the Caucasus and more precisely towards the region of the Caspian sea that later (around 700 CE) became known as Khazaria. Another branch in central Turkey was neutralized by the Hittite empire, while a dissident group (separating from the Turans and taking the name of Irans) settled in the northeast area of the Mesopotamian region, giving origin to the culture of Hajii Firuz, then to the kingdom of Elam and finally to the Persian empire.

It is possible that these Turans subsequently descended around 1200 BCE together with the other "Sea Peoples" to pillage the Mediterranean region to settle in a more fertile and wealthy territory. The Tyr or "Tyrrhenian" branch finally found a good residential solution in the Italian peninsula and became the origin of the Etruscans; we have analyzed the historical and cultural developments in the second volume of our work on the Mother Goddess (*The Awakening of the Mother Goddess: The Goddess in History*).

According to Guenther Wachsmuth (1893-1963), first secretary and treasurer of the Anthroposophic Society founded by Rudolf Steiner and author of *Werdegang der Meschheit* ("The evolution of Mankind"), the Turanians were pathologically violent: we could make here an illuminating connection with the theory of the Kurgans described by Marija Gimbutas, but considering a time frame at least 2 millennia earlier than the period proposed by Gimbutas. In other words, the Turanians or Zurvans could be the ancestors of the so-called Kurgans, responsible for imposing armored patriarchalism in the Caucasus region before "exporting" it to Ancient Europe and to the Mediterranean region.

In Parsism, the general idea of religion becomes drastically separated from the concept of *dharma-vidya* (natural ethical principles and transcendental knowledge) that characterizes the Indo-Vedic tradition. In the *Zend Avesta* and in Parsism we find the earliest form of imperialist religion that must be enforced by the government, based on political loyalty and not on the development of human potential in harmony with all beings. In other words, it enforces a strict moral and social discrimination between "faithfuls" and "infidels", where the "infidels/unfaithfuls" (those who have not accepted to convert) have no civil rights and are legitimately subjugated, robbed and enslaved because they are intrinsically "enemies" and "bad people" by definition. It is precisely this perspective that has attracted the colonial abrahamic indologists to grow a great interest and respect for the *Zend Avesta*. Abraham Hyacinthe Anquetil-Duperron (1731-1805), the first academic to specifically study Indian culture, began his work with a French translation of the *Zend Avesta*, and only later (in 1804) produced a Latin translation of the *Upanishads*. Friedrich Max Müller dedicated to the *Zend Avesta* several volumes of his large work *The sacred books of the East*, a collection of translations by various scholars in the field, including clergyman Lawrence Mills, professor of Philology of the *Zend* at Oxford (1897); some of Mill's speeches have been published under the title of *Our own religion in ancient Persia*, or *Being lectures delivered in Oxford presenting the Zend Avesta as collated with the pre-Christian exilic Pharisaism, advancing the Persian question to the foremost position in our biblical research.*

A corollary of this academic tendency has political and social aspects in India, as the small Parsi community that anciently took shelter in the region (more precisely at Bombay, present Mumbai) obtained special favors from the British colonial government, so much that it became the major financial power in the sub-continent. Still today Mumbai, that in colonial times was known as the "gate of India", constitutes the financial capital of India and the center of asuric propaganda, whose primary pillar is the cinema industry of Bollywood, controlled for many decades by the mafia of Daewood Ibrahim.

In any case mainstram academics still consider the *Zend Avesta* as one of the most ancient religious texts, contemporary if not precedent to the compilation of the *Vedas*, and equally connected to the peoples labeled as "indo-europeans" or "proto-indo-europeans", therefore the objective analysis of its contents and implications is very important if we want to understand and expose the academic myths on Vedic civilization and on Hinduism, that is its direct heir. Unfortunately the biased presentations based on the notorious aryan invasion theory and its corollaries have been absorbed not just by academics, but also by the public and by amateurs, and especially by the various esoteristic researchers and practitioners that have built their own speculations over the old false theories.

The various "modern" gnostic sects are heavily loaded with prejudice in this regard, and do not hesitate to dish out with the utmost seriousness the most absurd theories peddling them as absolute truth or mystic revelations, so much that under the umbrella of the "gnostic" ideology we find the weirdest and most disturbing characters and groups, from Helena Blavatsky (with her theosophist magazine named *Lucifer*) to the ariosophists (theoreticians of the mysticism of the "arian race"), from Freemasonry to Satanism, from the Hermetic Order of the Golden Dawn to the Ordo Templi Orientis (with its Ecclesia Gnostica Catholica) of Aleister Crowley (1875–1947), without forgetting the nazi author Miguel Serrano (1917-2009) who claimed that the "arian blood" was of extraterrestrial origin, and scholars otherwise interesting such as Hans Jonas, German-American Jew (1903-1993) famous author of *The Gnostic Religion: The message of the Alien God and the beginning of Christianity* and *The Gnostic Syndrome: Typology of its thought, imagination and mood*. Or, the friends of alienist Mauro Biglino - Giuseppe Baroetto and Ezio Albrile, who albeit less famous, are more than eager to present themselves as authorities on the meaning of Hinduism and Buddhism "in the light of gnosis".

Gnosticism

In this publication we do not intend to go deep into analyzing the ideology and the history of the gnostic movement, but we will just mention some details that appear particularly interesting for the primary subject of our work. In any case, it is not easy to find a clear definition of gnosticism: the congress of professional scholars in the field, assembled in Messina in 1966 seems to have ended in a rather less encouraging way, with the only visible result of proposing a cavillating distinction between *gnosticism* and *gnosi*.

Nonetheless, the representatives of the gnostic movement are generally convinced they know and understand very well Hinduism and especially the so-called "monism" (*advaita darshana*), *yoga* and *tantra*, mentioning them very often in their presentations, just like it is done by theosophists and other esoterists of the abrahamic persuasion. This is not a new problem: already in the times of the Greek scholars a considerable amount of confusion was created, due to the vast space of approximation and arbitrary interpretation commonly accepted in their schools. To give an example: in the first book of his dialogues on philosophy, Aristotle claims that the Mages, followers of Zarathustra, believe in Zeus and call him Oromasdes and in Hades calling him Arimanius. This very distorted idea is confirmed by Hermippus in his first book on the Mages, by Eudoxus in his travel diaries, and by Theopomp in the eighth book of his *Philippica*.

With the same imaginative arrogance and approximation, the Greeks projected their own beliefs on the iconographic depictions they saw in India: a fragment of the treatise *De Stige* by Porphyry tells about the visit of some Indians at the court of emperor Heliogabalus, in which the visitors clarified the ignorant misconception previously spread by Greek travelers who had interpreted the image of Shiva Ardhanaresvara in the Elephanta caves as the picture of an Amazon - because "she" had only one boob. Ardhanaresvara is the composite form of Shiva and Shakti, in which half of the body is masculine and the other half is feminine, while the Greek mythology on the Amazons says they were ordinary women, trained in combat and so totally dedicated to the warrying ideal that they chopped one breast off to be better able to shoot arrows. In spite of the authoritative clarification, still in 1775 the German explorer Carsten Niebuhr, in his report about travelling in the East (6 volumes, translated into French, Dutch and English by admiring contemporaries) commented on the Elephanta image according to the Greek interpretation of the Amazons; Niebuhr was worshiped as a cultural hero by Goethe (1749-1832).

Apart from their stubborn complex of cultural superiority, the Greeks and their gnostic disciples were heavily handicapped in their understanding of the Indo-Vedic tradition by another macroscopic factor: everything they could learn about Indian culture was mediated by Buddhist sources, that owned the famous great Indian universities of their times and went on missionary preaching campaigns ideologically hostile to Vedic tradition. While the filter of the Buddhist religious prejudice had no effect on presentations about mathematics, geometry, medicine and similar technologies, it is rather naive to think that Buddhist teachers could be reliable when they elaborated on the purpose of *yoga* and *tantra*, what to speak of the *advaita* perspective of Shankara, their greatest opponent - all these traditions were actually based on typically theistic principles, to which the late Buddhism of Alexandrine period was drastically opposed.

To really access Indo-Vedic knowledge, those ancient gnostic "authorities" should have converted to Hinduism through the prescribed method of *vrata, suddhi* and *prayascitta* and receive initiation (*diksha*) from a qualtied *guru* willing to take adequate responsibility for their spiritual progress. This method has always been open also to foreigners, but it requires a change of name, a permanent commitment to observing specific rules and ethical principles, and the practice of religious rituals and activities for the rest of one's life. Thus they should have ceased to be gnostics and become Hindus under all aspects, and instead we see that they remained unmistakeably Jews or Christians. The same problem also jeopardizes the credibility of academic scholars and professors who hold chairs on Indology although they personally remain on incompatible religious or ideological positions, or are even hostile to Hinduism.

The sistem of transmission of Vedic knowledge is based on the sincere personal acceptance and practical application of the teachings of the *shastra*, without which it is totally impossible to attain a level of genuine realization: at most, one can remain on the level of general information, and this certainly does not confer the required authority to teach Vedic knowledge. It is not sufficient to simply contemplate the theory or to mechanically memorize concepts or definitions, without the intention of applying the teachings sincerely and practically in one's life according to the genuine traditional perspective. The attachment to behaviors and dogmatic beliefs that are contrary to the principles of *vidya* and *dharma* prevents any student to overcome the barriers of ignorance, just like keeping one's boat tied to the moor prevents any progress in a journey along the river: mere theory cannot take us anywhere. If we want to make another simple example: nobody can become an expert swimming teacher if he always remains on dry land without ever entering the water, even though he makes a big show of gymnastic acrobatics on land illustrating the most famous olympics styles.

Because gnostic authorities have remained in the Jewish-Christian identification without truly following the prescribed method for the study of Indo-Vedic knowledge, it is clear that their pretenses of superiority in talking about the Hindu tradition - *advaita, yoga, tantra* and so on - simply remain an empty and ridiculous illusion. In their arrogant ignorance, many of these "masters" have even convinced themselves of having found a final validation of their beliefs because they were impressed by the courtesy, open-mindedness, tolerance and understanding demonstrated by many traditional Hindus especially during the colonial period, when Indians were deeply moved by any favorable interest shown by some foreigners towards Vedic tradition.

This naturally applies also to all the other currents of esoterism-orientalism built on abrahamic foundations, including theosophy, freemasonry and nazi-fascist interpretations such as that of Baron Giulio Evola (1898-1974), in whose view *Bhagavad gita* is a sacralization of sadism, demonstrating that the divine will is aimed at the destruction of the world. It is important to notice that such hallucinating distortions find ample space in contemporary alienist mythology - something that once again suggests the possibility that it has a deliberate scheme for the defamation of the Indo-Vedic tradition.

Plato uses the word *gnostikos* ("based on knowledge" or "intellectual") as opposed to *praktikos*, a definition that we can apply to the simple and direct approach of popular religiousness, that easily accepts rituals, festivals and customs as a cultural, social and ethnic bond, and mirrors a rather material view of the world. Thus *gnosis* is the constant search for the deep meaning of the existential and transcendental human experience, that is characteristic of the philosopher, literally "one who loves knowledge" (from the Greek *philos*, "love" and *sophia*, "knowledge"). To return to the rough example we mentioned before, the *praktikos* are those who jump into the river without spending much time in mental elaborations and learn to swim by instinct, while the *gnostikos* are those who prefer to read and write heavy tomes on the art of swimming.

Naturally ancient paganism left ample space of philosophical and theological elaboration for everyone and did not even condemn the attempts at synchretism, because of the fundamental concept of Natural Religion as universal and eternal, and the trust in sincere human intelligence that through personal evolution will open the doors of the deepest mysteries of the universe. The true philosophers of antiquity were perfectly aware that it is impossible for man to really damage the Divine (exactly like it is impossible for him to spit on the sky) and respected the freedom of thought and religion even for those who appeared to be confused, crazy or ignorant. They allowed Nature to "run its course" for better education, because Knowledge in itself was considered a divine principle, independent from human limitations.

In the hellenistic period, this search for knowledge expanded through the contact with oriental traditions, because the extraordinary capital of Alexandria of Egypt, under the reign of the heirs of Alexander the Macedonian, had become a center of collection and cultivation of knowledge coming from all parts of the known world. Buddhist missionary delegations had been sent regularly to Alexandria since the times of Ashoka, as we can also see confirmed in one inscription at Gimur in Gujarat. In a lesser measure, there was a more or less occasional presence of gymnosophists (adepts of *yoga*), who were particularly open to the so-called "interfaith dialogue" and willing to find common intents and similarities with other cultures, and eagerly shared some of the simpler and more superficial aspects of their science - as for example the circulation of *prana* and the centers of energy in the human body (the *chakras*).

The library and university of the Serapeum in Alexandria had a large team of copists who worked full time, collecting original manuscripts and giving back copies to contributors: it seems that at a certain point the catalogue of the library had reached the 800,000 volumes. And there were not just copists: because the academic institution was attended by students and teachers of all nationalities and languages, a group of translators and writers were engaged to produce several volumes of history and culture of their respective civilizations, as for example the famous Berossus and Manetho, who were entrusted with the task to illustrate Mesopotamic and Egyptian cultures. Alexandria also produced the first compilation of the biblical texts, the famous

Septuaginta (literally "seventy", from *versio septuaginta interpretum*, "the version of the 70 interpreters", referring to the 72 scholars who worked at it), in Greek language completed in the 2nd century BCE by the thriving local Jewish community by appointment of Ptolemy II Philadelphus. Philo and Josephus considered this version as genuine as the original Hebrew, that is now lost except a small fragment (the Blessing of Aaron, *Numbers* 6.24-26) dated 700 BCE and found quite recently in a tomb at Ketef Hinnom in Israel. All the other existing manuscripts of the Bible (including the Dead Sea scrolls) are later than the Greek *Septuaginta*.

The Jews were the main beneficiaries of this cultural exchange with "oriental" philosophies and spirituality (Indian, Egyptian, Meso-potamian): this is the precisely the origin of the Judeo-Christian gnostic movement. Initially there was no distinction between the two branches, because the earliest Christians were Jews under all aspects, as clearly indicated by the first "Fathers of the Church" in their writings against the "heresies". Gershom Scholem (1897-1982) and Gilles Quispel (1916-2006) have observed that the elaborations of the gnostic Christians amply derived from the Jewish literature of *Hekhalot*, *Maàseh Bereshit* and *Maàeh Merkabah*. Differences developed only gradually, with a major turning point when Paul/ Saul of Tarsus (a city in Cilicia, present Turkey) began to address mostly non-Jews and preach a new version of simplified Christic gnosis meant to create a larger base of popular acceptance.

With the final fall of Jerusalem and the Jewish diaspora, messianic escatological and apocalyptic hopes had taken a very serious blow: the two main Jewish currents - the orthodox and the etherodox - were forced to drastically review the perspectives and strategies for the present and the future. While the rabbinic (pharisaic) talmudism and zealot currents went "underground", focusing on the development of a commercial and financial power, the etherodox sects (especially Hessenes, Nazireans and Ebionites) turned to mysticism, moving the concept of messiah from the political to the spiritual level: these were the very first "Christians". The mysticism they adopted was precisely the hellenistic-gnostic type, still based on the Jewish matrix, with a general sentiment of renunciation towards the material world, not to overcome its illusion as we see in the genuine versions of Buddhism and Hinduism, but to condemn it as demoniac, and to align the idea of renunciation with their own destructive tendencies that we can call "catastrophist" or "escatological", from the Greek *eskhatos*, "final", as in "the end of the world".

According to the Indo-Vedic perspective, this view of the world is typical of the Asuras, as we see clearly explained in chapter 16 of *Bhagavad gita*: the *asuras* do not have a correct understanding of renunciation and engagement in the world, they do not give proper importance to truthfulness and ethics (preferring to choose loyalty to the leaders or masters and blind obedience to their orders), and they say that the world is false and temporary and not controlled by God. They do not understand the natural laws of karma and reincarnation, and believe that the only purpose of the world consists in offering sense gratification - although they reject such gratification as reprehensible. On the basis of such beliefs, they build religious systems that are impure and illusory, becoming arrogant and hypocritical, and they adopt any means to accumulate money and power, success and followers.

This is precisely the problem we are facing today: the gnostic sects and their heirs in the western esoteric-occultist trend have certainly picked up some ideas and nomenclature from oriental cultures, but in their interpretations they have strayed very far from the original positive vision and have taken a particular dark character, more asuric than divine, also because of the strong influence of Zarathustra's Parsism, which as we have already mentioned, colonial indology identified (incorrectly) as the *origin* of Vedic civilization, based on the false theory of the arian invasion. Thus it has become urgent and crucial to eliminate the misconceptions developed in the west about oriental knowledge, by applying an objective verification of the original sources.

It is easy to clearly demonstrate that the gnostic vision of the creation of the world is non-compatible with the Vedic vision: for example Brahma the demiurge-creator of Hinduism has absolutely nothing to do with the gnostic Yaldabaoth, who is more similar to the asuric Ahura mazda of Zarathustra. Brahma does not create the material world as an imitation of the spiritual universe or Pleroma, and certainly does not try to present himself as the only God to whom all human beings must pay worship and obedience - again, a typically asuric characteristic. And certainly the Archons generated by Yaldabaoth do not have anything to do with the Devas, but they are rather the Asuras we have mentioned in previous chapters. Other examples will become evident if we keep an open mind in studying the original Indo-Vedic tradition, something that we offer our readers especially in other publications.

The Vedic system based on *dharma* and *vidya* always remains very tolerant and does not try to persecute different or even offensive perspectives, but rather applies a "proactive" approach by which the persons that are less educated and intelligent can gradually elevate their understanding and realization to wider and more solid levels (see *Bhagavad gita* 3.26). However, this process requires a favorable environment, where the individual search for knowledge is facilitated by society and government, so that truly qualified teachers have the opportunity of speaking freely also in public, something that enables intelligent and sincere listeners to make conscious and informed choices and attain a clear and genuine vision.

In the western world in the first three centuries of the present era it was still possible to keep a certain plurality of perspectives, but when Roman Christianity (developed from the ideological line of Paul of Tarsus and inheriting his gnostic sect of zoroastrian inspiration) became the official religion of the empire, it started to actively persecute "heresies" (from the Greek *hairesis*, "choice") meaning the personal beliefs in the fields of religion and spirituality that were somehow different from the dogma officially imposed by the government. This veritable war against free information and free thought attained levels of incredible intolerance and cruelty, destroying even the roots of the rich cultural and religious tradition of ancient civilizations, razing temples, libraries and universities to the ground to build churches and even brothels on their sites, and even erasing the memory of the previous glories or distorting it with slandering and offensive depictions. And eliminating in the process any positive aspect that may have been contained in the gnostic current from which it had sprouted.

This negative development also had a very deep impact on the western psyche, so much more damaging because the process and the result cannot be clearly separated as toxic superimpositions but instead appear to be the norm, the only possibility and the automatic view of the nature of reality or normality, that distorts any further perception - as we see for example in the perspective of atheists towards all religions and towards the very idea of religion, which for them is not distinguishable from the typical characteristics of abrahamic religion.

An important turning point in this scenario, that opened a direct window on the past beyond the wall of cultural superimpositions accumulated in the centuries, came with the discovery of the manuscripts of Nag Hammadi and the Dead Sea scrolls, found respectively in 1945 and between 1947 and 1956, shedding new light on the cultural situation of that particular historical period.

The manuscripts of the Dead Sea, also known as Qumran texts, are certainly the most substantial and wide collection of surviving writings from that period, and include copies of almost all the books of the canonical Jewish Bible (Old Testament, masoretic version) besides various theological commentaries, calendars, apocalyptic texts, psalms, prophecies, prayers and ritualistic rules, and even administrative, financial, legal, military and personal documents, for a total of over 15,000 fragments, from about 870 rolls. They are almost all in ancient Hebrew and Aramaic, with very few Greek texts, and the period of their burial has been evaluated between 132 and 135 CE, at the times of the revolt led by Bar Kokhba just before the final diaspora. The caves of Kirbet Qumran, in the desert of Judea, about 20 kms from Jerusalem towards the *West Bank* of the Jordan river, are not far from the ruins of an ancient Hessene community, a Jewish sect to which Jesus is believed to have been affiliated: strangely enough, however, neither Jesus nor his direct companions (apostles-disciples) are *ever* mentioned in any of the numerous texts in the collection.

According to Flavius Josephus (*De bello judaico*, "The Jewish war", and *Antiquitates judaicae*, "Jewish antiquity", written in Greek and then translated into Latin, and survived only as quotes in Christian texts) the Hessenes were heterodox (non-rabbinical and non-talmudic), but strictly observed the Torah, they were messianic, apocalyptic and baptist, and called themselves "the Children of the Light", something that certainly seems to indicate gnostic or mysteric tendencies. They abstained from blood sacrifices, did not eat meat, rejected slavery and did not engage in commerce or professional activities meant for profit, they practiced asceticism and voluntary poverty, kept an extremely strong sense of community (almost as a monastic order) and had a very peculiar approach towards marriage, couple relationships, and the social and religious position of women: all this put them in direct opposition to the talmudic rabbinism of Pharisees, and shows a strong Buddhist influence.

As also recognized in the canonical texts (*Numbers*, 6.1-27, *Judges* 13.5,7, 16.17, *Amos* 2.11-12, *Levitic* 22.2, *Deuteronom* 33.16, *Lamentations* 3.7, *Acts* 23.5), nazireanism (from *nazir*, "separate", and *netzar*, "to separate or distinguish oneself" and also "branch" in the sense of "sect") was a particular vow of strict religious observance, with modalities that are found in paleo-Christian movements and in the Mandean tradition still surviving today.

In this regard, we need to observe that in all the region of Palestine there was not even one village named Nazareth at least until the year 221 CE, when its existence is documented by Sextus Julius Africanus. There is no trace of any Nazareth in the Old Testament, although the *Book of Joshua* mentions 12 cities in the area, and the *Talmud* lists 63. In his chronicles, Josephus mentions 45 cities and villages of Galilee but has no notion about Nazareth, that is found only in the gospels that apparently were not written before the second half of the 2nd century, because the early "Fathers of the Church" seem to have never heard about them. The writings of Justin Martyr, for example, contain over 300 quotes from Old Testament and almost 100 apocriphal books of the New Testament (apocriphal gospels) but makes no mention whatsoever of the 4 canonical evangelists that are presented by the later Christian doctrine. Theophilus, who was writing around 275 CE, only mentions one gospel of John (which could even be the one that today is considered apocriphal), while Ireneus, only a few years later, names all the 4 canonical gospels and gives ample quotes from them. However, we need to notice that Ireneus also mentions as genuine several other texts that the Church later labeled as apocriphal, such as for example the gospel of John found in Nag Hammadi.

The Nag Hammadi texts are quite different from the canonical gospels as well as from the Dead Sea texts. Among others, they contain the following texts: *The gospel of Thomas* (the head of the Syrian community), *The gospel of James* (Jesus' brother), *The gospel of Philip*, *The gospel of John* (the apocriphal one), *The gospel of Truth* (by the famous Valentinus), *The dialogue of the Savior*, *The Sophia of Jesus Christ*, *Prayer of the apostle Paul*, *Apocalypse of Paul*, *Apocalypse of James* (first and second), *Apocalypse of Peter*, *Apocalypse of Adam*, *Acts of Peter and the 12 apostles*, *Teachings of Sylvan*, *Melchizedek*, *Hypsiphrone*, *The thought of Norea*, *The blessed Eugnost*, *Exegesis of the soul*, and even a modified version of *The Republic* by Plato. All these texts are written in Coptic, a language that gave its name to the peculiar type of Christianity originated in Egypt; it was invented by the local priests of the Egyptian god Seth to prepare amulets that could seem familiar to the Greek or hellenized devotees of the period, while maintaining the sound of the original Egyptian spells. There are also other texts recovered at different times, such as *The gospel of Mary* in Coptic language (found by Karl Reinhardt in Cairo in 1896 and dated 5th century) and the books preserved by the various "heretical sects" that survived longer, such as the Cathars, but we do not want to stray too far from our main subject, even if all this would make a truly fascinating story.

Nag Hammadi is on the bank of the Nile, at a short distance from the Ptolemaic temple known as Dendera (that was also the center of the mysteric cult of Hathor), on the perimeter of an area with a radius of about 55 kms, where we can still find the ruins of an extraordinary concentration of religious monuments around the center of Luxor, and only 30 km from the temple of the female pharaoh Hatshepsut, a place where islamists slaughtered 54 tourists in November 1997. Another interesting detail is that the ancient name of the place was Sheniseth, "the acacias of Seth", something that inexorably leads us to make a connection with the "Sons of Seth (who) were considered the first teachers of the science of astronomy" (*Jewish antiquities*, 1.2-3, Josephus). Here we could make some extremely interesting connections with the other middle-eastern cultures, but this would increase too much the size of this publication.

Among the manuscripts of Nag Hammadi we find the *Second Treatise of the Great Seth* (*Codex VII*), although this text does not speak about Seth but about the *irrelevance* of personalities such as Adam, Abraham,

Isaac, Jacob, David, Solomon, the prophets and Moses, and about the fact that the Yahweh of the Bible is certainly *not* the "true God". This elaboration is presented as a speech personally from Jesus. Always in the same collection we have the *Three steles of Seth, The sacred book of the great invisible spirit* (also known as *The Coptic gospels of Egyptians*), *The Zostrian, The Allogenes* (literally, "the aliens") and *The reality of the rulers* (also known as *The hypostasis of the Archons*). The sethians (in Latin *sethoitae*) are recognized as one of the major Jewish-Christian gnostic sects of the 2nd and 3rd century, together with the valentinians, the ophites and the cainites (*Catalogue of heresies* by Philasterus); according to tradition this Seth was the son of Adam, and according to the sethians he had appeared again as Jesus. The sethians are associated with other Christian gnostic sects such as barbeloites, archontics, audians, borborites and phibionites, all eliminated during the middle ages by the persecutions against heretics. In modern times (since the 1800s with esoterism-occultism) we see a revival of the "Temples of Seth" but with a strongly luciferine character, often with references to Egyptian mysticism.

Thus we believe that we should add a note on the Egyptian deity called Seth (also written as Set), who is one of the four primary deities born from Geb (earth) and Nut (sky): the couples Osiris-Isis and Seth-Nephthys. The other deities descend from these two couples. It seems that initially (3150-2613 BCE) Seth was considered a benevolent figure, who helped the passage of the dead into the afterlife and also favored unhappy lovers; in some stories he even assists Ra (the Sun God) fighting against Apophis/ Apep, the Serpent of Chaos. There are two versions of the myth of Seth: in the more famous, Seth is the rival brother of Osiris and is defeated by Horus, while in the other version Seth and Horus are the rival brothers. In any case Seth is always described as jealous and revengeful; his hostility against Osiris begins because Nephthys had taken the form of Isis to get a child (Anubis) from Osiris. Then Seth devises a plan to shut Osiris in a coffin and throws him into the river, where he floats down to distant lands and is entangled into a tree. Isis goes to retrieve the body of her brother-husband but Seth comes to know about it and rushes to cut the body into pieces, then we see a fight for the right to succession. Seth sexually attacks Horus and is finally defeated in battle, with the approval of the assembly of the Gods.

In the second intermediate period of Egyptian history (1650-1550 BCE) pharaohs known as *hykshos* (literally "from foreign lands") chose Seth as their patron Deity, at least in one case as their exclusive Deity, as we see from Papyre Sallier 1 by king Apophis (extremely interesting name). Ramesses I came from a military family that was strictly connected with the cult to Seth, and many pharaohs of his dynasty took Seth names such as Seti I and Seti II ("man of Seth") and Setnakht ("Seth is powerful"). Ramesses II established the Steles of the Four Hundred Years at Pi-Ramesses to commemorate the 400th anniversary of the cult of Seth in the Nile Delta. The main temples of Seth were at Ombos (Nubt) and Oxyrhynchus, and in the cities of Sepermeru ("the door to the desert") and Avaris in high Egypyt (in the south).

The association with the invader rulers and the imperialist military dynasty of Ramesses developed the figure of Seth as the god of the foreigners, associated with foreign female deities such as Anat (Ugarit, Syria) and Astarte (Canaan) besides the Egyptian Teshub (in the form of female hyppopotamus, governing fertility and birth) whose name (Teshub) is identical to the main Deity of the Hittites. Because of this association, Seth is sometimes pictured as a donkey or with a donkey head (like the Hittite Teshub). Because he is a desert god, Seth is worshiped alone and his female companions are housed separately at a distance. Seth is depicted of red color, often in a canine form, with tall rectangular ears and a long forked tail, but he is also associated with poisonous or dangerous animals (boar, crocodile, hyppopotamus). His dominion is on wars, invasions, destruction, chaos, storms, deserts, mountains, drought and famine, death and impurity, so much that at a certain point during the 20th dynasty he gradually became demonized and Egyptians started to show intolerance and hatred against people with red hair and animals with red fur.

The Coptic texts show Seth as an enlightened (*illuminatus*) who went to live on mount Seir with his consort Norea; the mandeist tradition (in the original language, *manda* means "knowledge" and is therefore the exact synonym of *gnosis*) in the marshy region of Irak has a parallel legend speaking of one Anosh-uthra and his wife Yohanna who went to live on the White Mountain, beginning a lineage of Illuminati. The Mandeans are an important gnostic movement originally from Mesopotamia and have their own semitic language derived from Aramaic; according to some they are connected to the Jewish sect of Nazoreans (Nazireans) or Hessenes, and therefore hostile to Babylonian talmudism.

The God of the mandeans is the "King of Light" (Melka d Nhura) indicated by an impersonal plural (*elohim*), assisted by many angels or spirits of light; he is also called Hayii or "Life", identified with flowing water, an essential element for the rituals, so that mandeans traditionally live on the banks of rivers. Any river that is suitable for baptism is called Yardana (Jordan). During their prayers mandeans face the polar star in homage to the benevolent spirits who live in the skies and who rule the universe (but there is no mention whatsoever of extraterrestrials "descending" to Earth); the prayers are different for the different days of the week but are always performed at dawn, midday and dusk. The *mandi* or *mashkhana* is the temple, a simple and small structure (about 3.5 meters x less than 5 meters) made of reeds and bricks, built along the bank of the river next to the pool for the ablutions. Each member of the community has two names: an ordinary one and another religious name based on astrology and meant for protection. Marriage is encouraged (including polygamy) and the procreation of children is considered a religious duty, while celibacy is condemned as an impious choice. The practice of circumcision is rejected as abominable.

The most interesting concept in mandeism is that the God of the Bible is considered an evil deity and no authority is attributed to Abraham, Moses and Jesus Christ: in this sense, the mandeans are not exactly "abrahamics". Instead they venerate Adam, Abel, Seth, Enosh, Noah, Shem, Aram and especially John the Baptist, and in fact baptism is one of the most important ceremonies in their tradition. According to mandean theology, the earthly world was created by a demiurge named Ptahil (reminding us of the Egyptian Ptah) with the help of "dark powers" defined respectively as Ruha (a demoniac representation of the Goddess as material Nature), her consort Ur (a sort of "dragon") and their children called the Seven (planets) and the Twelve (zodiac signs). The body of the first human (Adam) was created by the evil powers, while his soul was created by the good powers, thus attachment towards the body must be condemned and destroyed by ascetic practices, ablutions before prayers and a generally vegetarian diet. The *ganzivri* (priests or bishops) must only eat uncooked fruits and vegetables, bread cooked by themselves and water, totally abstaining from alcohol, coffee, tobacco, and even spices and mushrooms. The ritual dress or *rasta* is similar to the dress of Parsis - always and only white. The boys who are trained to become *ganzivri* must never cut their hair or shave their beard (as in the nazirean vow) and during the three passages of consecration they must observe long purification periods in total isolation.

Religion and science fiction

We will now elaborate on our contemporary alienists and on their theory by which all religions have developed from the invasion of Earth by a specific group of aliens called Annunaki, originally from the extraordinary gigantic planet Nibiru and interested in exploiting the minerary resources of Earth and specifically gold. Contrarily to what one may think, Sitchin did not take the idea from the sacred scriptures of Sumer (where academic researchers never found it), but from American science fiction. A very similar scenario had already been created by the famous Lafayette Ronald Hubbard in his thrilling futuristic novel *Battlefield Earth* (in 3 volumes, 6 million copies declared) and subsequent *Mission Earth* (in 10 volumes, 7 million copies declared).

In that story, Ron Hubbard projects a future (rather than a past) where a race of aliens, called Psychlos, decide to invade Earth and establish industrial installations in various regions with the purpose of extracting minerals for the profit of their galactic empire, where the central planet, that is much bigger in size than Earth, has been already exploited to the core and is always hungry for resources. The Earthlings, reduced to a small group of refugees hiding on inaccessible mountains, have fallen into ignorant barbarism, so much that the memory of their ancient cities has become simply a legend or superstition. Terl, one of the main leaders of the Psychlos in the central Earth colony, decides to capture a human specimen, Johnnie Goodboy Tyler, and train him as a first experiment to create a work force of human slaves to engage in the difficult extraction of a gold mine on the mountains. The story continues with a war between different groups of aliens and the final liberation of Earth.

Ron Hubbard (1911-1986), founder of the Church of Scientology (also known as Dianetics) was a prolific science fiction and fantasy writer (with 1084 titles translated into 70 languages, as noted by the *Guinness Book of Records*, the most widely known publication on curious world records) published on pulp fiction magazines since the 1930s, when Sitchin (born in 1920) was still a schoolboy. It is very interesting to notice that in turn, Hubbard had found important inspiration for his work from the séances of "esoteric" demoniac occultism together with his mentor John "Jack" Whiteside Parsons, a space researcher at the California Institute of Technology and founder of the Jet Propulsion Laboratory of Pasadena. Parsons was a faithful Thelemite, a follower of the famous Aleister Crowley and even head of the lodge of Crowley's Ordo Templi Orientis; he rented rooms to persons who wanted to get deeper into his teachings. Ron Hubbard moved in with Parsons in August 1945, probably also because he was attracted by Parsons' girlfriend (Sara "Betty" Northrup), and became his closest associate; together Hubbard and Parsons organized a ritual of "sex magic" to evoke an entity they called Babalon and considered the "Supreme Goddess" of Thelema. The ritual was rather simple: Parsons the High Priest masturbated "creating energy vortexes with his magic wand" (his penis) while Hubbard the Scribe "explored the astral plane searching for signs and visions". According to their evaluation, the ritual was shown as effective by the arrival, a few days later, of the "incarnation of Babalon" in the person of a new female adept, Marjorie Cameron.

Soon afterwards Hubbard convinced Parsons to invest all his money in a financial venture called "Allied Enterprises" to build a navy fleet, the "Sea Org", of which Hubbard appointed himself "commodore", maybe to overcome the delusion suffered as navy officer during the WW2, when he had been removed from the position of captain of the USS YP-422 and later of USS PC-815 because deemed "unsuitable for command posts". Without wasting time, Hubbard unilaterally dissolved the "Allied Enterprises" and sailed to sea with Sara Betty leaving Parsons in total bankruptcy, so much that Parsons had to sell his house to recover from the disaster. People both in the esoteric-occultist milieu (including Crowley himself) and in the science fiction fraternity (including Asimov) were flabbergasted by the scandal and betrayal, and made several explicit comments about it.

In 1950 the idyll with Sara was over, and after replacing her with a 20-year-old secretary, Hubbard secretly denounced to the police as "communists" both Sara and "her lover" Miles Hollister, who was working in his organization as facilitator of sessions of psyonic therapy; the FBI investigator archived the case with the brief note "*appears mental*". About 3 weeks later, Hubbard and two minions kidnapped Sara (and her child Alexis, one year old) with the purpose of forcing some doctor to declare her mentally ill; this scheme failed and he had to let Sara go, but he kept the little girl, taking her to Cuba for several months. He agreed to let her go only when her mother had signed a document glorifying Hubbard and declaring that any accusation against him was to be considered false and unfounded. In that same year Hubbard convinced the billionaire Don Purcell to support him by financing a new "Wichita Foundation" in Kansas; in 1952 Hubbard declared bankruptcy and accused Purcell of having been paid by the American Medical Association to destroy his work.

Another venture of Hubbard's was the "Guardian's Office", a spy agency that became famous for the "Snow White Program", a plan to infiltrate organizations and "take action" against anyone who dared to criticize Hubbard and the rising Church of Scientology. Scientology charged hefty fees for courses such as the OT3 or "Wall of Fire", teaching that 73 millions of years ago one Xenu, supreme chief of the Galactic Confederation composed by 75 planets, had sent billions of aliens to Earth to exterminate them with hydrogen bombs. The confused spirits of these alien victims had been collected in "implant stations" to receive new artificial memories and be "inserted" into human beings. Hubbard announced that the discovery of this valuable information had costed him dearly physically, causing fractures to the knee, the arm and the back - although it is not clear how exactly, maybe someone had beaten him but no details are mentioned. His conclusion was that all human beings are in fact powerful aliens, the *thetans*, who after creating the universe have forgotten their own divine powers; through the techniques offered by Dianetics they could "cleanse themselves from psyonic enneagrams" and return to full operational status, also thanks to technological devices he had created such as the E-meter, a tool that "could read hidden thoughts". Of course this theory is quite different from the story of *Battlefield Earth*, but not all science fiction stories must necessarily have the same details - otherwise Hubbard would not have been able to write over 1000 of them, different enough to be accepted as original stories.

Compared to the other science fiction writers of his time, Ron Hubbard is quite noteworthy for the disturbing character that connects alienism with occultism: together with Parsons he had gone to the Mojave desert in the period between 1945 and 1946 for a series of black magic rituals specifically designed by Aleister Crowley with the purpose of opening an inter-dimensional portal to bring the "Ancients" into our dimension. The ceremonies seem to have been performed successfully, because the participants witnessed they had "established extra-terrestrial contacts", specifically with Lam or dark entities they called "Secret Leaders".

Hubbard's seminal work was written in 1939 under the title *The Dark Sword Excalibur, the Science of the Mind*. According to him, the book would be the cure for all types of nervous stress and would have a greater impact on human history than the Bible, and it seems to have contained revelations on the "fundamental principles of human existence based on 20 years of research on 21 races and cultures" (which he does not give details about). We cannot know for certain, because the text is not available to the public. According to the statements of Hubbard himself (quoted by his literary agent, Forrest J Ackerman), all those who had read the manuscripts had gone crazy or had committed suicide - one of these, the editor working in a publishing house in New York had jumped from the window during a meeting with the owner and with Hubbard himself. Maybe due to stress?

We know that the techniques of Dianetics/ Scientology, from *auditing* to *clearing*, were developed from the material contained in that book;

however the presentation of their practical results in a lecture at the Shrine Auditorium in Los Angeles in August 1950 proved a colossal fiasco: the "highest psyonic potential" attained by the chosen subject, a woman named Sonya Bianca, proved insufficient to make her remember even one single formula of the entire doctorate course in physics that she had recently attended at the university, or even just the color of Hubbard's tie when he turned his back around for one moment.

Excalibur was printed at the beginning of the 1950s by Scientology and sold at the price of 1,500 dollars per copy (equivalent to about 15,000 dollars in 2016) exclusively to the most faithful followers, with the recommendation not to divulge its contents to other people. At a Convention of science fiction fans in 1948, Hubbard declared (as reported by Arthur J Cox, who worked for John W Campbell's *Astounding Science Fiction magazine*) that the inspiration for that work had come to him during a surgical operation when he had died for 8 minutes; the archivist of Hubbard's diaries, Gerry Armstrong, clarifies that it was actually the removal of a tooth under the anesthetic and hallucinogenic effect of nitrous oxide (chemical formula NO).

The biographers of Hubbard, as well as his diaries and almost all his acquaintances (including Isaac Asimov, Robert Heinlein, Theodore Sturgeon, L Sprague de Camp, AE van Vogt and other famous science fiction writers, as well as publishers Winter and Art Ceppos and John W Campbell) tell different stories from the official version of the representatives of the Church of Scientology, that turned Hubbard into a messianic figure, the revealer of supreme esoteric truths that would be the faith for the "new age".

However, his influence should not be underestimated, as in 2014 the magazine *Smithsonian* mentioned him as one of the 100 most notable Americans in history, and more precisely as one of the 11 religious leaders of its list. Certainly Hubbard had a lot of personal charisma and had incorporated perfectly reasonable and sensible concepts side to side with completely absurd ideas (as noted by an article in *New Republic*) as well as interesting pieces of knowledge copied from the writings of other researchers (as for example Sylvan Muldoon and Hereward Carrington, authors of the famous *Phenomena of Astral*

Projection) or tested practices of psychology (such as the recovery of repressed memories through hypnotic regression, already popular in the previous century). But he distorted and trivialized them in the quasi science-fiction mosaic he sold at a high price to his followers and even to franchisers, with a 10% commission on first level courses, while the second level therapies were solely managed by the headquarters. His "Spiritual Guidance Centers" charged 500 dollars (of his times) for a cycle of *auditing* of 24 hours, and sold mysterious pills presented as "anti-radiation treatment".

In this light we can better evaluate the vision of the alienists by which the human race would simply be a puppet created by extraterrestrials that are almost omnipotent and more or less ill-intentioned, and all forms of spirituality or religion should be traced back to the mythological indoctrination planned by these aliens to control their "human cattle". This certainly does not exclude the possibility that there are actually persons or groups of persons who are working or scheming, more or less openly, to materialize such ideological projections, but this does not mean that their plans should be considered intrinsically valid or characteristic of "all Gods and all religions".

While it is certainly possible that Hubbard, Crowley and several other "esoterists" have actually had some contacts with powerful malevolent entities, extraterrestrial or not, it is certainly not acceptable and reasonable to try to peddle as absolute factual truths all the "historical" reconstructions and the ideological constructions based on their theories, especially when such elaborations deliberately ignore or distort the knowledge of the ancient, of which we can find more direct and consistent evidence in the original texts. And it is not by chance that the same mistake (more or less deliberate) is also found in the publications of the alienists just like in the compilations of the Bible and the other abrahamic texts: the dynamic is identical. We should not forget that practically all alienists keep the Bible in great consideration, even when they use it to explain that the God of the Bible is merely an alien. It is therefore necessary to take the approach of the alienists in the correct manner - instead of despising it *a priori* as done by conventional academics, or embracing it on faith as done by the fanatical followers of alienism. Each concept, each story, each expectation must be carefully evaluated through intelligence, good sense, ethical conscience and practical usefulness for the good of the individuals and of the planet - in other words, we must contemplate the stars but while keeping our feet solidly on the ground, otherwise we risk dangerous accidents.

Ron Hubbard was not the only one to theorize about a race of superhuman aliens interested to enslave earthlings, but he is certainly the most famous. In spite of his pseudo-religious tendencies, however, he had the good sense (and the humility) not to try to demolish the very concept of genuine spirituality by denying the existence of an original natural religion or genuine religious traditions. For example, it does not seem like he ever tried to demolish or distort the Indo-Vedic tradition or to misappropriate it.

On the other hand, Zecharia Sitchin started his career by stating that "the Bible was right", postulating that the biblical stories had a valid historic foundation, more or less covered by a mythological language developed in a later period. With this theory he probably hoped to emulate Heinrich Schliemann (1822-1890), who was able to raise the story of the siege of Troy from the mythological and literary mists of *Iliad* and *Odyssey*, and bring them to the attention of official archeology after 2,000 years of oblivion, or Arthur Evans (1851-1941) who had excavated the minoan civilization of Crete by following the thread of Theseus' legend. He was certainly also inspired by the excavations that between the 1800s and the 1900s had revealed the existence of the ancient civilization of Sumer, of which all memories have been lost except in some Babylonian legends.

Building on his own Jewish roots, Sitchin created a thrilling story that contains more fiction than history and finds no confirmation in Sumerian texts proper - rather it exploits their name as a basis to elaborate his theories. Sometimes he completely invents such texts, as for *The lost book of Enki* that many Sitchin followers see as a genuine scripture of Sumerian tradition; we should stop a moment to wonder why it is called "lost" and who precisely found it, when, how and where. But if he had merely stuck to the Bible as a slightly distorted echo of previous traditions, and presented his elaborations as picturesque science fiction without trying to "explain all religions", probably Sitchin would have sold less books and made less money.

It does not take much to upgrade from distorting Sumerian and Egyptian cultures to projecting elaborations and adaptations of the Indo-Vedic culture, and as we have already seen, the road had already been traced and traveled by other ideologists. This is how Sitchin and followers ventured into the mysterious Indies for a safari of "confirmations" to support their theories and bring back trophies that are heavily doctored or totally manufactured - but who has ever seen a real lion?

In the same alienist religious-science-fiction trend (falsely presented as "New Age philosophy") we find groups such as Raëlism, Urantia (Unarius) and other similar ones, that have created a following of believers by peddling a mixture of abrahamic concepts and nomenclature with strong tendencies towards a sort of utopian global dictatorship - one global government, one single religion, one language, a new monetary system, elimination of elections and of military service. The whole thing, justified and embellished by some pseudo-science and futuristic technological images (especially about genetic engineering) and a pinch of orientalism here and there, just like spices are used in cooking.

For example we are reminded of a curry rice (or maybe chicken curry) when we watch the amusing interview of "Raël" in which the picturesque character declares that the "Buddhist Vedas" confirm that the first human beings were created in laboratory by the aliens. To begin with, Buddhism does not accept the authority of Hindu Vedas and does not have any type of "Vedas" of its own, and no other Buddhist or Hindu text contains statements of this kind. The extraordinary declaration by Raël is accompanied by revelations on his own birth presented by the same alienist prophet (born Claude Maurice Marcel Vorilhon), whose mother was allegedly abducted by extraterrestrials and inseminated "exactly like Mary the mother of Jesus", and on his close encounters with the same aliens and particularly with Yahweh (apparently on 13th Deceember 1973), who had renamed him Raël, which is supposed to mean "messenger of the Elohim" - but we are not told precisely in what language. In the same interview, however, Raël merrily switches Latin with Greek, claiming that *angelos* or "messenger" is a Latin word (maybe he meant "Latino" as in Spanish for Los Angeles).

But who does not like some exotic seasoning? We see that almost all the alienist religious groups proclaim the extraterrestrial origin of the "great masters members of the supreme secret organization" with a clear predominance of Jesus Christ but with mentions of Mohammed and the "oriental masters" such as Krishna, Buddha, Mahavira (and for someone, even Gandhi). Some adventurous minds add, on the same level of alien deities, also Zoroaster (not really unexpected), Moses, Akhenaton, Manicheus (probably they mean Mani), Tammuz, Lao Tze, Confucius, Horus, Zeus, Hermes, Orpheus, Mithra, Apollon, Dionysus, Apollonius of Tiana, and even Merlin the magician, king Arthur and queen Genevieve.

To the famous faces of the "great oriental masters and prophets", these authors add imaginative distortions of concepts (especially reincarnation, *tantra*, *yoga*, *chakra* etc) or fragments of history such as the war of the *Mahabharata*, that according to the Urantia channelers was a "racial war" fought in north India, that ended with the survival of 100 families of superior race (all the others were eliminated in a campaign of genetic cleansing). Some sources that speak of sex orgies practiced by the gnostic Christians of the origins also quote Alain Danielou who commented, "it is an idea very close to shivaism and therefore to dyonisiac mysteries".

In this current we can comfortably classify also some groups that became famous for mass suicides, such as the Order of the Solar Temple (Canada, Switzerland, France, Spain, Australia etc) that claimed to be a part of the Templar tradition and wanted to unify all Christian and Islamic sects with the second advent of Christ as the Sun King, and Heaven's Gate (San Diego, USA) where the leader, Marshal Applewhite, claimed to be the reincarnation of Jesus, ready to transfer his followers to another planet through a mass suicide, taking as a "heavenly sign" the appearance of the Hale Bopp comet. We should also mention the Aetherius Society that offers "a new type of yoga" (King Yoga, maybe to lump it up with Raja Yoga or suggest the idea of royalty) invented by its founder George King (1919-1997), and the Italian group Nonsiamosoli by Giorgio Bongiovanni "the stigmatized" (not to be confused with other organizations with a similar name but very different finalities) that has toned down in 2012 after the failed fulfillment of the millenaristic prophecy dictated by the usual aliens.

This development of alienist or science-fictional religions, that remix Christian-based ingredients with oriental ingredients, has been supported also by the immense production of literature, movies and TV shows increasingly successful since the 1930s. But while early science fiction often carried positive messages, encouraging the public to become more open-minded, tolerate diversity without prejudice, explore the external and inner universe, become aware of the problems and dangers of the so-called technological progress that is not controlled by ethical principles, be more creative in imagining possible alternative solutions, and so on, the more recent entertainment products convey a general impression of defeat, depression, confusion, darkness, pessimism, irrelevance, when it is not degrading or idiotizing or aimed at de-sensitizing critical sense and compassion in the viewers with ever increasing horrors, terrors and violence. They blur the line between the alienist science fiction scene and the "*supernatural horror*" of evil monsters, predators, multi-dimensional beings, vampires, zombies and the like, or even just human beings that are mentally and emotionally imbalanced but increasingly presented as positive "heroes" and behavior models, if not as religious saviors.

On a parallel line we find the opinion trend (that is apparently opposite) known as "*new age*" - full of "good vibes" and angels, excessively and superficially optimistic, promoted by some "psychic channelers" and "spiritologists" who claim they are speaking in the name of "higher entities" that usually have strong Christian traits - archangels, Entity A, Melchizedech, "New Apostles" and a long list of characters, prophets and messengers as already mentioned. These "voices from the ascended masters" paint a rosy and glorious future, where suddenly thanks to "positive thinking" there will be a general enlightenment for everyone, a sort of automatic genetic transformation or spontaneous mutation of the present human beings into superior beings, worthy of being accepted in the Galactic Alliance of the evolved consciousness in the universe. In both cases, the trend encourages the public to develop a precise ideological orientation meant to establish a "new world order" under one single *new* religion or rather *non-religion* that denies the existence of a transcendent God but worships superhuman entities of great power and intelloigence, that can be malevolent or benevolent, but are always superior to human beings.

The characteristics of this new "alien religion" are the need for total obedience, a sort of social utopia that promises perfection through a dictatorial structure of complete control and abolition of individual freedom, the dominion by a genetically superior class, the unification of a world government and globalization of culture, a much higher technological and scientific level that is not necessarily ethical and increases the gap between *élite* and general population also at the level of the quality and value of life, racial and "eugenetic" discriminations and control over the emotional and sexual lives of people through repression and manipulation.

Sitchin on the Annunaki

According to the calculations of Sitchin, 4 billion years ago there was a gravitational cosmic clash (albeit not necessarily a collision with physical contact) between the planet Nibiru and Earth (called Tiamat); at that point Earth lost a considerable amount of mass that went to form the Moon and the Asteroids (and even some comets) while the "seed of life" (apparently, alien micro-organisms) was passed from Nibiru to Earth giving origin to the evolution of the species - of *all* species, those still present today and those that have become extinct.

Nibiru is supposed to have a very large orbit around our sun: a journey requiring 3,600 years and going in the opposite direction in respect to the planets of the solar system; every 3,600 years therefore Nibiru should come back towards Earth (but it seems it does not bang into it every time) and if the calculations of Sitchin are correct, its return would seem imminent, and this time it will bring the end of the world - a series of disasters of extreme gravity that will wipe out human civilization or even cause a mass extinction phenomenon, and we will be saved only by a return of the aliens. This "second coming" of Nibiru, that is practically an article of faith for the followers of Sitchin, certainly tastes like the appearance of the awaited Messiah or the "second coming" of Jesus Christ and the Last Judgment, which in turn could represent the traces of an ancient original awareness of a return of more general planetary alignments and a passage in the astronomic-astrological cycle, as suggested by Giorgio de Santillana in his famous book *Hamlet's Mill, An Essay on Myth and the Frame of Time*.

It is possible that the changes of this "New Age" could be less dramatic and spectacular, without fleets of alien spaceships like in movies and TV shows, and could happen not externally but rather inside the awareness of human beings on the planet, something that could have global effects anyway. In this perspective it is clear that we should stop "waiting for the messiah" and we should rather roll our sleeves up individually and collectively to fix the damage, as it appears to be urgent and inevitable at this point. A very practical idea, that we can see reflected in the pragmatic observations of some Jewish commentators, who have concluded that the messiah they expected should be recognized as the Jewish people itself and in the resurgence of the nation of Israel, with the building of the new temple in Jerusalem.

Around Nibiru there have been lots of speculations, to try to explain how a planet of such gigantic dimensions as suggested by sitchinians and with such an eccentric orbit around the Sun could be able to support life and even disseminate it spontaneously in the universe and on Earth. Should we conclude that the issue of the beginning of life on Earth must be explained with the accidental falling of garbage from Nibiru, some waste ejected into space because the Annunaki were unable to recycle their resources or too lazy to worry about it? This is a bit depressing scenario, albeit not more absurd than those presented by mainstream academics, for which the development of life on Earth was merely due to chance after innumerable "attempts" of atoms and cells to aggregate in a stable and useful manner. According to Eugene Ricks, who claims he worked as a scientist at NASA, Nibiru is nothing less than a solar system consisting of a brown dwarf star with 7 planets, of which the third, often called "planet X", has a mass 10 times bigger than Earth. Rumors say that according to another researcher connected to NASA, one Shimschuck, the USA government created an investigation committee on Nibiru in 1985, prohibiting everyone to discuss the issue in public. According to the alienists, Robert Sutton Harrington, who had denounced the problem in a 1993 lecture, connecting it with the issue of chemtrails, died 4 days later in circumstances that are considered mysterious.

Sitchin's theory is that due to the immensely advanced technological knowledge of its inhabitants, Nibiru has an artificial system for heating and cooling itself; some even suggested that it is an entirely artificial planet, a sort of spaceship larger than Earth itself, built by the Annunakis before the geological formation of our solar system, probably to escape the natural or artificial destruction of their original planet. Sitchin speaks of heat generated by nuclear radiation and a very dense atmosphere that prevents the dispersion of heat, but it seems rather unlikely that organisms adapted to such conditions could easily live on Earth or even find it pleasurable.

Obviously we cannot verify this scenario either negatively or positively, but the grain of interesting logic contained in Sitchin's theory is the idea that the so-called "civilization of technological progress" developed on Earth with the help of the Annunaki traces the roots of its destructive tendency against Nature precisely from the fundamental ideology that had supposedly caused irreparable damages to the ecological system of the original planet of the Annunaki themselves. This is reinforced by Sitchin's idea that the Annunaki had arrived on Earth searching for gold they needed to "fix" the ecology of their planet - probably after destroying their natural planet of origin (to the point of losing even the memory of it) they were also destroying their artificial one! This is a disturbing observation, but a potentially very valuable one to deflate the rosy and sugary expectations of alienists and highlight the negative effect of their fantasies.

Sitchin claims that 445,000 years ago a contingent of 50 Annunaki inhabitants of Nibiru, led by one Enki, established a colony named Eridu (according to Sitchin, "home of a distant world") in the region of the Arabian gulf, fleeing from a political upheaval on their planet and searching for gold to save its ecology. We see the saga beginning with ecological disasters and political struggles for absolute power, with implications of wars and violence. There are also deceit and betrayal: the first Annunaki to "discover" Earth was one Alalu, the former king who fled from Nibiru after being overthrown by his cupbearer Anu (therefore the position of "father of the Gods" is simply a political one). After landing in the Persian gulf, Alalu found the gold and proposed an agreement to the new ruler on Nibiru, asking to be re-instated on the throne in exchange for the precious metal that would save the ecology of their dying planet. It seems that Anu decided to ignore him, because Alalu did not obtain what he wished for, and he even disappears from the story at that point (we could say *desaparecido* - maybe secretly assassinated?), as the usurper remained on the throne although he organized anyway a mining expedition to Earth to get the gold.

Anu sent his son Ea, who was married with Alalu's daughter Damkina, and who traveled with "water chariots and not fire chariots", something that Sitchin's followers connected with a prototype of engine working on laser-heated water in an aluminum container (*New Scientists* magazine, 15th June 2002) and with the experiments of D Cirillo, A Dattilo and E Iorio in Grottammare, AP, 18th April 2004, on the "Transmutation of metals at low energy through plasma confined in water" (with a potassium carbonate solution).

That is an excellent example of second-level elaboration by imaginative speculation based on a previous fantasy, both without any confirmation in the Sumerian texts, and where the only connection to reality is an experiment made by persons who never made any reference to the story of the Annunaki and who probably never read any of Sitchin's books. From the point of view of known human technology, the "water chariots and not fire chariots" mentioned by Sitchin could be anything from steam engines to hydrogen-based nuclear engines using heavy water as fuel, because the definition is really too vague.

After the expedition of Ea/ Enki another wave of 550 colonizers, led by Enlil, who founded the city of Nippur ("point of crossing") and built a sort of portal or space corridor called Duranki ("sky-earth connection") and subsequently the centers of Larsa, Larak, Sippar, Shruruppal and Lagash, for a total of 7 settlements. Enki's sister, Ninhursag, was part of this second contingent and medical officer of the expedition. Then Enki was given the task to develop new mines in Africa, assisted by his sons Marduk, Dumuzi and Nergal. Other

300 Annunaki remained in orbital stations and the general command on the planet was taken up by Enlil (son of Anu, the king of Nibiru), whose sons were Ninurta, Nannar (also called Sin) and Adad. These would be the (only) Gods of the ancient world, that according to Sitchin and his followers are the original deities of all cultures and religions at global level, because not just all forms of civilization but also the creation of the first human beings at global level are to be ascribed directly and exclusively to the Annunaki.

According to Sitchin's reconstruction, around 380,000 years BCE the political problems of the Nibiru immigrants exploded into a war for the control of the Earth mines, and Enlil came out winning. This is another impressive indication: Sitchin's theory continues to explicitly demonstrate that the Annunaki mentality is at the origin of our present troubles - after the ecologic disaster caused on their worlds (both the natural and the artificial) these sublime creators of mankind continue to show their colors as violent, quarrelsome, cruel and power-thirsty war-mongers, obsessed with selfishness and control. It does not seem that the original Sumerian texts actually contain explicit material in regard, but there is no doubt that such a theory will seem perfectly reasonable for a person with an abrahamic background, aiming at demonstrating the historical value of the Bible as the basis of Earth civilization.

Let us continue with Sitchin's reconstruction: 300,000 years BCE the lower-rank Annunaki (called Igigi, practically a caste of divine slaves) who worked in the south African mines went on strike in protest against the hard work and asked to be replaced by some other type of slaves, possibly not divine. It is interesting to note that in the south African region the Annunaki do not seem to have built even one single city but just mines - probably the Igigi lived in temporary mud shelters or in the mine shafts without ever seeing the light of the sun. And it is difficult to understand what they were eating, because without a trace of any surface settlement, agriculture and animal farming seem to be rather problematic. It is no wonder they were feeling rebellious.

At this point Enki and his sister Ninhursag made some genetic experiments on local apes, creating a certain number of specimens of *Homo erectus* or *habilis* ("the Black Heads"), who were still unable to reproduce by themselves because they were sterile hybrids. It ensues that all the specimens of hominids different from the *Homo sapiens* whose remains have been found on the planet were born from artificial insemination of ape ova, genetically manipulated and delivered (as in birth) exclusively by a small number of "breeders" chosen among the low caste Annunaki females - probably the wives and daughters of the Igigi who were working as slaves in the mines. We do not find it unlikely that such female breeder slaves may have complained and strongly requested a better system, by which the humans could independently take care of their own fertilization, pregnancy and birth process. In fact it hardly seems practical to have all the new humanoid slaves be incubated in the uterus of a small number of Annunaki females, with all the physical problems involved - anyone who has given birth just once will understand this point easily - to ensure a convenient production of workers to replace the Igigi. This introduces the idea of the various genetic experiments of the Annunaki who, after repeated failures along a period between 230,000 and 100,000 years ago produced the actual *Homo sapiens*, starting from two individuals who finally became independently fertile: one single Eve and one single Adam, presented as the first real humans.

The issue carries a certain measure of controversy even among alienists: some, who better know the Jewish commentaries, have noted that according to tradition there were some other human groups (pre-adamitic), such as the one joined by Cain (Kain) after killing his brother Abel. This detail seems to have been eliminated from the canonic texts in the first centuries of the Christian era because it carried a certain measure of confusion into the picture of the Genesis, where simplistically Yahweh had manufactured the universe and the first human beings in 6 days of a week (keeping the *shabbath* as a resting day), creating Adam from the mud as the lord of animals and Nature, and separating from him the ideal companion called Eve. A careful examination of the first chapter of the Bible will still show some remaining crumbles of alternative versions of the story, but generally the study of scriptures was forbidden to potential critics, therefore the editors were not particularly careful.

According to Sitchin and his most faithful followers, before 300,000 years ago there were even no primitive hominid species but merely primates or anthropomorphic apes, while the *Homo sapiens* that is the origin of all subsequent humans did not exist in any place of the planet before 100,000 BCE; obviously such "historical" dates have been written down before official academics reviewed the conventional timeline. This theory has already been shown as obsolete and mistaken by many pieces of evidence even recognized by official academics, who have accepted the existence of independent evolutionary lines, especially the Neanderthals and Denisovans (but more are in the ideological "waiting hall") also in other geographical regions, but generally more ancient. We will speak of these pre-historic human beings in the second volume of our work on *The Awakening of the Mother Goddess*.

According to Sitchin the semi-human beings depicted in Sumerian iconography were not symbolic representations of archetypal qualities, but gross recordings of the results of "failed experiments" of the Annunaki geneticists, evidently groping in the complete darkness of ignorance and making blind attempts worse than their modern colleagues. Although it is not really clear why they should try to cross humans with scorpions, birds, lions, ordinary horses or cattle, when the relatively easier step from ape to man had proven to be problematic. Like the authors of the Old Testament, Sitchin claims that *Homo sapiens* would not have come to exist without the deliberate act of creation performed by the Annunaki/ Elohim; the difference is that for Sitchin instead of the famous "Eve", the original maternity of all human beings is ascribed to a small group of Annunaki females who were made pregnant with the clones of ape-like hominids, genetically modified with Annunaki DNA. In the geneticists' mythology these would be the "7 mytocondrial Eves" that seem to have replaced the one Eve of abrahamic mythology. It is not that much of an improvement and we are not very surprised, considering that according to geneticists at least 70% of human DNA is nothing but incomprehensible and useless garbage, and their elegant theories of the original evolution of the human species, presented as objective, absolute and undisputable evidence, are based on a meager 30% of understanding of man's nature. Sitchin's theory represents a rather lame effort to melt the biblical creationist theory with the academic darwinian theory, but the resulting scenario ends up leaving everybody dissatisfied.

According to Sitchin and his followers, these Annunaki women were the only exclusive origin of all the "Mother Goddesses myths" in all the cultures of the planet, including those of the the Neanderthals, Australian aborigines and north American natives, who do not seem to have ever had any contact with the Annunaki. This conclusion simplistically sends to the garbage bin the immense amount of iconographic, literary and mythological evidence that describes the Mother Goddess as the natural, ontological and universal archetype of Earth and Life. It paints a truly depressing image of the respect and understanding that Sitchin and companions demonstrate towards the sacred feminine, ontological archetypes and Nature. Because no one among the main Annunaki females is mentioned with reference to the group of anonymous breeders producing slaves, it ensues that the ontological "Mother Goddess" worshiped by the universal natural religion was even lower in rank than the submissive and raped goddesses who were the wives or nurses of the high caste Annunaki.

Let us continue with Sitchin's theories: after 100,000 BCE, at the end of a glacial period on Earth, some Annunaki in Mesopotamia started to mate with human women and their descendents received a special position by Enki: these are supposed to be the descendents of the Nefilim mentioned in the Bible (*Genesis* 6.1-4), also identified with the Anakim or "sons of Anak" (*Numbers* 13.22, 29-33), that the scouts sent by Moses described as a race of giants with long necks who lived in the Ebron region.

Enlil was quite displeased by this "contamination of the pure race" (a particularly disturbing concept in someone who had first promoted genetic manipulation with alien and animal DNA with the specific purpose of creating humans) and so he decided to terminate the experiment and destroy all humans (that in the meantime had multiplied ominously) taking advantage of a new passage of Nibiru that was nearer to the Earth orbit in 11000 BCE and that caused a serious disaster, called "Great Flood" in the Bible.

Sitchin's construction seems to postulate that in the entire history of our planet there has been one single big Flood and therefore one single post-glacial period, that wiped the almost totality of the human beings from the whole planet, and forced the Annunaki to flee quite suddenly. This is a seriously incorrect supposition, as we can see from the geological data we can even find on internet. To justify the story of the Bible, Sitchin explains that Enki decided to help one of the earthlings, Ziusudra (the Sumerian name of the character that Sitchin identifies with the Biblical Noah) to build a submarine and save a small group of human beings from the imminent global disaster, and later he supplied them with seeds of many new plants, agricultural tools and farm animals.

In the subsequent period (from 10000 to 8000 BCE) Enki moved to the Nile valley, while the main son of Enlil, Ninurta, worked in the marshy region of Mesopotamia, draining it to make it inhabitable again and established a new control center at mount Moria, the future site of Jerusalem. Enki's son Marduk installed his two sons Osiris and Seth in Egypt (a major turn in the story!) but there was a fight and the defeated Seth moved to Sinai, where he probably became Yahweh. Subsequently there were the so-called "pyramid wars", that Sitchin "reconstructs" without the least scriptural or historical scrap of evidence, then the control over Egypt passed to Thoth and a second spaceport was built at Baalbek (Heliopolis), together with new cities such as Jericho. Until now, human beings are supposed to have had only a very marginal role as low-rank laborers in the mines, while both kings and "normal" subjects consisted in the various castes of Annunaki.

Actually the Egyptian religious view was rather different, not just from the scenario created by Sitchin but also from the Sumerian-Babylonian approach; its representatives speak of Gods, gods or demi-gods "who came from outside", but from the south and on the river from the fabled "land of Punt", that several scholars identify with Somalia or Yemen or even with India. Certainly Osiris and Seth are never presented as sons of Marduk or grandsons of Enki. Furthermore, Egyptian texts never speak of a Great Flood or actual wars opposing different factions of Gods (except for the personal fight between Seth and Osiris-Horus): although there have been mythological superimpositions in later periods due to commercial and cultural exchanges in the region, the ancient texts do not show the correspondences that Sitchin takes (or gives) for granted. And because there is no evidence that the original Sumerian texts ever even slightly mentioned Egypt, we must conclude that Sitchin has allowed himself to be swept away by enthusiasm and largely spilled out into fiction, inventing most of the information he gives in his books.

Again according to Sitchin's theory, from 7000 to 3800 BCE the contigent of slaves (this time, human slaves) consisting in the *Homo sapiens* species continued to multiply, gradually forming a population of "very low caste" (practically outcaste or untouchables, an idea that should make us stop and think a little about the origins of social birth prejudice) compared to the Annunaki social system, and for whom the Annunaki of all levels, including the Igigi miners and their breeder females, were a pantheon of deities and superhuman beings of various types. And it would seem that many of such untouchable slaves sneaked off unnoticed and created independent colonies without any contact with the Annunaki, because otherwise nobody could explain the evidence of human settlements spread all over the world and traced back before 7000 BCE, and in whose documents and stories there is never any reference to the Annunaki as their supposed creators and owners.

The continued genetic mixing between humans and aliens, initially considered as racial contamination and then happening normally in various measures and on different occasions through direct mating, produced an "intermediate caste" of "*demigods*" that are supposed to be the first great heroes and kings of history, later deified. We notice how Sitchin's theories are firmly based on the strong birth prejudice about race and caste that we find in all abrahamic and post-abrahamic ideologies, and that caused so much suffering, injustice and tragedy in these last 3 or 4 millennia of bloody history, from the time when patriarchalism replaced the original natural culture that sitchinism obviously does not believe ever existed.

It seems that according to Sitchin, the Annunaki were the ones who built all the most famous ancient monuments assigned by official academics to "compatible" historical periods: the pyramids are supposed to have been merely "beacons" or geographical references to guide the ships towards the "spaceport" in Baalbek, while Stonehenge and Machu Picchu were their "solar-lunar calendars" because evidently they were unable to make them in Mesopotamia or Egypt, but they had to go to England or south America to find out the dates of equinoxes and solstices. Since in his time archeology had not yet discovered Gobekli Tepe and the Visoko pyramids, Sitchin does not find them mentioned in his "Sumerian sources", but he gives lots of references from the Bible: according to Sitchin, the cities of Sodom and Gomorrh were destroyed by nuclear bombs during the civil war among Annunaki factions, while Jerusalem was a spaceport and its three hills (called "mountains") had names such as Zophim or "mountain of the watchers", Zion or "mountain of the signal" and Moriah or "mountain of the indication" as translated by Sitchin himself.

The sitchinian saga continues: in 3760 BCE the first human Kings of mixed descendence (part alien and part human) were appointed under the protection of Ninurta and with the approval of Anu, who went to Earth on official visit for the occasion. Also Eridu and Nippur were rebuilt and a new city was founded, Uruk (Erech) dedicated to Anu's grand-daughter Inanna (Ishtar). In 3450 BCE Nannar (Sin) took over Sumer, while Marduk founded Babel (Babylon) and in 3100 BCE the first half-human pharaoh was installed in Memphis (where he suddenly developed a language that was totally different from the Sumerian-Babylonian, nobody knows why). In 2900 BCE Inanna went (alone, apparently) to establish a center in the very empty Indus valley, implanting the first human beings there, but then dumped them to return to the middle east to join in matrimony with the human Sharrukin (Sargon/ Shah Ruh Khan), the founder of the akkadian empire. Abandoned to themselves, the "Indian orphans of Inanna" are supposed to have fallen into a position of weakness that made them easy victims of the aryan invasions. And speaking of the notorious aryans, it remains to be explained what is their origin exactly according to Sitchin's view: since they were not "black heads", whose descendents would they be exactly? Maybe Inanna or other Annunaki had gone to the Caucasus, too, to secretly make some more genetic experiments? On the subject Sitchin does not say anything, so we shall not discuss it here.

At that point various factions of Annunaki began again to fight against each other for the control over the regions holding the most important settlements (something that does not surprise us much) and there seems to be appearing a human character named Abraham who is sent to Jerusalem with the garrison that protected the large spaceport, and who luckily survives a nuclear attack ordered by the leaders of the Annunaki to put an end to the constant warrying of the factions. It seems that according to Sitchin, Enlil had sent Ninurta with an army of Gutes from the Zagros mountains against Inanna and Naram Sin: if this was true, the traditions of the Goths or even simply some legend of the Caucasus should contain some trace of important facts or characters from Sitchin's "reconstruction", but the only connection is reduced to a generic "Sun worship" that is totally natural and spontaneous for any human being and in all cultures as an universal ontological archetype.

We see that Sitchin does not elaborate on the ancient cities of Canaan either: he briefly mentions Baalbek in Lebanon as "spaceport" but he totally ignores the very important Ugarit and Mari that were contemporaries of the nearby cities of Sumer and worshiped the same deities, but as they were excavated in relatively recent times, they did not show up in conventional academic literature in the period when Sitchin was writing his books. This means that sitchinism does not "take information directly from original Sumerian texts that are ignored or underestimated by mainstream academics" as convenient for the romantic and authoritative image it wants to project, but depends in all cases on the more or less correct versions produced by official academics, on which it proceeds to build fictional stories to demonstrate its fundamental theory, that is still based on the authority of the Bible.

The most important part of Sitchin's theory is the idea that the Annunaki left Earth between 610 and 560 BCE: his followers claim that this explains why all the gods, beginning with Yahweh, have remained completely inactive and "*incommunicado*" (silent and non-reachable) in the last 2,500 years, and so prayers and religions are useless. The logic conclusion of these elaborations is that all the religions in the world are not only false because they were invented around a small group of mere aliens, but totally useless as well because "the gods have gone away" a long time ago, and the only God that exists is the one we invent for ourselves. But the Bible remains trustworthy, because it speaks authoritatively of our alien creators.

Different perspectives

Zecharia Sitchin (1920-2010), a Russian Jew who moved to the USA in 1952, published his first book in 1976 (*Genesis revisited*) and the second in 1978 (*The 12th Planet*), followed by *The Stairway to Heaven* (1980), *The Wars of Gods and Men* (1985), *The Lost Realms* (1990), *When Time began* (1993), *Divine encounters: A Guide to visions, angels and other emissaries* (1995), *The Cosmic Code* (1998), *The Earth Chronicles expeditions* (2004), *The End of Days: Armageddon and Prophecies of the Return* (2007), *There were Giants upon the Earth: Gods, Demigods, and human ancestry: The evidence of Alien DNA* (2010), and *The King who refused to die: The Anunnaki and the Search for Immortality* (2013).

A book elaborating the cosmological theory by which our solar system was considerably modified by a planetary crash had already been published in 1950: *Worlds in Collision* by Immanuel Velikovsky (1895-1979), a Russian Jew who openly declared himself a Zionist, and was one of the founders of the Hebrew University of Jerusalem in Israel. Psychiatrist and psycho-analyst by trade, Velikovsky decided to refute the theory presented by CG Jung in *Moses and Monotheism* (1939) and to demonstrate the historical truth of the stories of the Bible especially concerning the exodus of the Jewish people from the Egyptian slavery: he published in 1960 a book entitled *Oedipus and Akhenaton*, a psychiatric elaboration interpreting Greek and Egyptian mythologies, used by Velikovsky as a basis to build his own personal and arbitrary chronology of ancient civilizations, according to which the Egyptian queen Hatshepsut was actually the queen of Saba, contemporary of the legendary Solomon in 950 BCE.

The basis of such elaborations, that is supposed to explain the entire expanse of all ancient history, consists in a parallel between Oedipus and Akhenaton, that Velikovsky identifies as the same person, because: 1. in Greek language *oedipus* means "swollen feet" and

Akhenaton is portrayed with large thighs, 2. Oedipus had married his own mother Jocasta and Akhenaton had married his own mother Tiya (no mention of such fact in the entire world collection of papyres and inscriptions), 3. Akhenaton had become blind (when?) just like Oedipus, and just like Oedipus's daughter Antigone, Akhenaton's daughter Meritaten had died in disgrace, buried alive (!), 4. Jocasta had committed suicide and Tiya also had killed herself after Akhenaton's wife Nefertiti had left him (here too, there is absolutely no historical evidence), 5. both Oedipus and Akhenaton had children from their own mothers (!) ... well, we got the picture. In Israel, Velikovsky published *The dark age of Greece* (no date mentioned). Among his other titles, *Peoples of the Sea* (1977), *Ramses II and his time* 1978) and *Mankind in amnesia* 1982). Another successful author was Keller (1909-1980) who in 1955 published *The Bible as history*, a book that won the Bancarella prize in Italy and was translated in Hebrew and distributed for free in Israel.

In 1957 Peter Kolosimo (1922-1984) published his first book, *Il pianeta sconosciuto* ("The unknown planet") followed by *Terra senza tempo* ("Earth outside Time"), *Ombre sulle stelle* ("Shadows on the stars"), *Non è terrestre* ("It is not from Earth"), *Astronavi sulla preistoria* ("Spaceships in pre-history"), *Odissea stellare* ("Star Odyssey"), *Fratelli dell'infinito* ("Brothers of infinity"), *Italia mistero cosmico* ("Italy as cosmic mystery"), *Civiltà del silenzio* ("The civilizations of silence"), *Viaggiatori del tempo* ("Time travellers") and *I misteri dell'universo* ("The mysteries of the universe", 1982) - all these books were translated and became popular also in the USA. Kolosimo does not build on the biblical paradigm but continues to present the theory of ancient alien astronauts, just like Robert Kyle Grenville Temple in 1976 with his *The Sirius Mystery: New scientific evidence of Alien contact 5,000 years ago*. In 1959 another famous book was published - *The Morning of the Magicians* by Jacques Bergier and Louis Pauwels, not particularly tied to the Bible and abrahamic interpretations either, but closer to the trend established by Charles Hoy Fort (*The Book of the Damned*, 1919) that had created quite a stir with its impressive collection of apparently inexplicable events.

Attention turns back to the Bible and alien deities with *UFOs and the Bible* (by Morris K. Jessup, 1956), *The four-faced visitors of Ezekiel* (by Arthur W Orton, 1961, elaborating on the story of prophet Ezekiel,

1.26-28), *Les Extraterrestres* (the popular English version was entitled *Flying Saucers through the ages*, written by Paul Misraki *alias* Paul Thomas, 1962, and presenting the angels of the Bible as extraterrestrials), *Gods or Spacemen?* (by W Raymond Drake, 1964), *The Bible and Flying Saucers* (by Barry Downing, 1968, claiming that the idea of hell was originated from photos of planet Venus shown by aliens to earthlings in ancient times), *God Drives a Flying Saucer* (by Robert Dione, 1969), *The Legend of the Sons of God: A Fantasy?* (by TC Lethbridge, 1972), *The Spaceships of Ezekiel* (by Josef F Blumrich, 1974) and *Los astronautas de Yavé* ("The astronauts of Yavé", JJ Benítez, 1980). Even more important, this period saw the earliest development of the new alienist religious sects with abrahamic basis, such as Raëlism, Aetherius Society, Heaven's Gate, Urantia, and the others we have mentioned before.

One of the most famous names since 1968 is Erich von Däniken (born in 1935), generally considered the "spiritual father" of alienists, or those who consider the aliens as gods and the gods as aliens, and hope in their "return". Among von Däniken's books, the most famous are *Erinnerungen an die Zukumft* ("Memories from the future", 1967) and *Chariots of the Gods?* (1968). Von Däniken does not insist on the value of the Bible and was probably the first to expand his theory beyond the borders of the Mediterranean and middle eastern region, explicitly stating that ancient alien astronauts were the founders of the great cilizations in India and pre-colombian Americas (besides the ones in Mesopotamia, Egypt and Greece), leaving evidence of extraordinary technology, and that they would return at the end of the millennium. In the same year (1968) W Raymond Drake published his book *Gods and spacemen in the ancient East*.

We remember that 1968 was also the year of the release of the famous film *2001: A Space Odyssey* (from a cycle of novels by Arthur A Clarke), with the famous alien monolith-spaceship Tycho, of a very modest size, that descends in pre-historic times among quarrelsome carnivorous apes; then we are shown a futuristic (for 1968) scene with a second identical monolith that appears on the Moon and sends a signal to Jupiter. The USA spaceship *Discovery* is sent to investigate but the ship's computer, Hal 9000, becomes paranoid, kills the astronauts and must be disconnected by the last survivor, who disappears without giving any more news.

The famous film had a millenarist sequel, *2010, The year we made contact*, with a new team of astronauts who go to investigate about the *Discovery* and find a huge third monolith, 2 km long, and signs of organic plant life on Europa (Jupiter's satellite); the astronauts are contacted by the aliens and witness the birth of a new Sun right inside our solar system, something that eventually convinces the two Earth superpowers (United States and Soviet Union) to give up war and finally live in peace and harmony. In 1984 David Hatcher Childress (born in1957) started the Adventures Unlimited Press, a publishing house dedicated to "ancient mysteries" that has produced over 200 titles, of which about a dozen written by Childress himself, such as *Vimana aircraft of ancient India and Atlantis, Vimana: Flying machines of the Ancients, Technology of the Gods, The incredible science of the Ancients* and *The Enigma of Cranial Deformation: Elongated skulls of the Ancients*.

The first book studying the issue of *vimanas* from the Indo-Vedic perspective appears in 1989: *Vedic Cosmography and Astronomy*, written by Richard L Thompson (1947-2008), an American who officially converted to Hinduism with the name of Sadaputa Dasa. Later, Sadaputa published *Alien Identities: Ancient insights into modern UFO phenomena* (1994) and *Forbidden Archeology* 1993) in cooperation with Michael Cremo (Drutakarma Dasa), another American author who officially converted to Hinduism. Both are disciples of Bhaktivedanta Swami, the founder of the Hare Krishna movement (ISKCon). More recently, in 2010, one of their godbrothers named Satyaraja Dasa (Steven J Rosen) published *The Jedi in the Lotus: Star Wars and the Hindu Tradition*.

In the 1990s Graham Hancock (born in 1950) began to produce documentaries especially on submerged civilizations and books such as *Fingerprints of the Gods: The evidence of Earth's lost civilisation* (1995), *The message of the Sphinx: A quest for the hidden legacy of mankind* (with Robert Bauval, 1996), *The Mars mystery: A tale of the end of two worlds* (1998), *Heaven's Mirror: Quest for the lost civilisation* (1998), *Underworld: The mysterious origins of civilisation* (2002), *Talisman: Sacred cities, sacred faith* (2004), *Supernatural: Meeting with the ancient teachers of mankind* (2005), *Entangled: The eater of souls* (2010), *War God: Nights of the witch* (2013) and *Magicians of the Gods* (2015). Other interesting books are *Gods of the New Millennium* (1996) by former sitchinist Alan F Ford, who also wrote *The Phoenix Solution* (1998), *When the Gods came down* (2000), *The Atlantis Secret* (2001), *Pyramid of Secrets* (2003) and *The Midnight Sun* (2004).

David Vaughan Icke (born in 1952) speaks of the Annunaki as a humanoid reptilian race probably coming from the constellation of Draco (but maybe also from the lower level of the "fourth dimension") and so evil in nature that they can be called satanic. In Icke's view, these reptilians created the human beings and built for them a sort of olographic experience (similar to the idea in the film *Matrix*, released in 1999) and are still controlling the governments and finance at global level through an occult system of secret societies that Icke calls Babylonian Brotherhood, largely based on genetic considerations and therefore similar to what others call "black aristocracy" - a definition that does not refer to the color of the skin but rather to dark motivations and intentions.

For Icke, another superhuman race of alien dominators related with the reptilians is the "nordics" (blond, with blue eyes) whose descendents are the semi-human hybrids called "arians", that are supposedly at the origin of racism, fascism, cruelties of various types, sexual abuse especially on children, obsession for blood rituals, and a strong hunger for power and control over the world. Icke accepts Sitchin's theory by which the Annunaki had originally come to Earth to get "monoatomic gold", which is supposed to have also considerable effects on the nervous system, increasing its power thousands of times.

To his credit, we must say that Icke has never dared to give reductive, false and baseless interpretations of the Vedic tradition, but on the contrary is quite open to consider the concept of reincarnation and thinks that the DNA can be consciously or unconsciously modified through experiences and "awareness reprogramming" techniques that actually exist and have been found useful by psychologists. He also believes that great damage comes from negative emotions such as fear, guilt and aggressiveness, and especially from violent acts such as "ethnic cleansing" and the killing of innocent civilians, the slaughtering of animals especially at industrial level, and sexual perversions.

Among Icke's books we may mention *The Robot's Rebellion* (1994), *And the Truth shall set you free* (1995), *The biggest secret: The book that will change the world* (1999), *Children of the Matrix* (2001), *The David Icke Guide to the Global Conspiracy (and how to end it)* (2007), *Human Race get off your knees: The Lion sleeps no more* (2010), and *Remember who you are: Remember 'where' you are and where you 'come' from* (2012).

In 1984 the idea of evil reptilians became popular through the TV series *Visitors*, although it was not completely unknown before that; the "snake men" had appeared in the story *The Shadow Kingdom* by Robert E Howard published in 1929 in the magazine *Weird Tales*, probably inspired by the theory of Helena Blavatsky (1831-1891) on the "dragon men" who had supposedly developed a very advanced civilization in the continent of Lemuria. Howard describes these beings as shape-shifters who live underground and are interested in infiltrating human society. Another science fiction magazine, *Amazing Stories* (1945) published the story *I remember Lemuria!* under the name of Richard Shape Shaver but apparently written by the magazine editor, Ray Palmer, based on a letter actually sent by Shaver. The story, presented as a report on actual events, created a strong controversy and led to the development of many "Shaver Mystery Clubs" and a huge success for the magazine, especially until 1948 when the actual facts became known and the readers revolted against Palmer, who was sacked.

Another proponent of the reptilian theory was Maurice Doreal (born Claude Doggins in Oklahoma, USA, 1902-1963) who in 1929 founded the Brotherhood of the White Temple; Doreal claimed he had gone to Tibet at the end of WW1 and studied with the Dalai Lama there for 8 years, coming in contact with the *Great White Lodge of Masters* "75 miles under the Himalaya" and receiving occult knowledge. We note that the word *master* has the double meaning of "teacher" and "owner". In the subsequent years Doreal produced a series of booklets, called *The Little Temple Library* as well as the book *The Emerald Tablets of Thoth the Atlantean*, that should not be confused with the classical Alexandrine text.

Doreal stated he had been sent by the *Ascended Masters* to announce the imminent advent of the "new *avatar*" who in 1956 was expected to start the 7th cycle of the Golden Age by establishing the "Christ

Kingdom". By mixing theosophy (that was already a concoction of ideas "freely" borrowed from various religions and even from fantasy novels of Victorian style) with similar elements picked from Christianity, Kabala, Buddhism and Hinduism (or better, from what passed as Hinduism among western occultists), Doreal added concepts fished from the writings of Nostradamus, Edward Buliwer-Lytton, Jules Verne, Frederick Oliver ("Phylo the Tibetan") and H Rider Haggard.

The popularity and success of Doreal started to decline towards the end of 1953 because of the failure of his well-advertised prophecy on the "end of the world" by atomic holocaust, expected for the period between May and September of that year. The village Shamballa Ashrama that he had founded in Colorado as "center of the occult knowledge in the west" and that was meant to be a nuclear shelter for his followers, also lost much of its appeal. However, his ideas have been carried on by several ufologists and alienists, especially in regard to the extraordinary technology of extraterrestrials (according to him, they come from "Antares in the Pleiades", although Antares is not really in the constellation of the Pleiades) who presently live "under the Shasta mountain" in the Rocky Mountains, USA, but also for topics such as the *Polar Paradise*, the *Mysteries of the Gobi* and similar stories.

Recently there has been an increase in popularity in another trend connected to the issue of the so-called "Black Aristocracy" of occultism, but *to support it* rather than denouncing it as done by David Icke, Arizona Wilder and other researchers in the field of conspiracy theories. Nicholas de Vere von Drakenberg (1957-2013), author of *From Transylvania to Tunbridge Wells* and *The Dragon legacy: The secret history of an Ancient Bloodline*, introduces himself personally and openly as "royal prince of the Dragon Blood" as well as Sovereign and Grand Master of the organization called The Dragon Court, strictly organized on "genetic" basis.

De Vere claims that aliens (reptilians or dragons) are the creators and dominators of all the civilizations of the planet, including the Ubaid (pre-Sumerian), the Sumerian, the Hebrew, the Hittite, the Egyptian and the Indian, and that the descendence of the Annunaki is the origin of the story of the Graal, now advertised separately by his former follower Laurence Gardner as a connection between the seminal descendence of Jesus Christ, the Cathars, the Templars and the Illuminati movement.

Laurence Gardner is the author of *The Origin of God* (2011) and *Revelation of the Devil* (2012); according to Gardner, Kain (Cain) had been created directly by Enki and Kâva, therefore his blood was 3/4 Annunaki, while his brothers Hevel and Satânael (Abel and Seth) were less than 1/2 Annunaki because they were sons of Atâbba and Kâva (Adam and Eve), therefore the "mark of Cain" mentioned by the Bible is supposed to be the insignia of the sacred Graal created in Sumer, later known as Rosi-Crucis ("the cup of dew", from Latin *ros*, "dew" or "spray") depicted as a red cross inside a circle. Later Cain had married princess Luluwa, daughter of Enki and Lilith, and had a son named Atûn (king Etâna of Kish) and another son named Enoch (Henôch). Gardner does not miss the opportunity to slide into the soup also the Hindu Goddess Kalì, describing her as "red and black" and originally from Sumer, where she was known as Kalimâth, sister of Luluwa the wife of Cain and princess of the House of the Dragon.

It is interesting to see how this particular current merrily makes a nice bunch of the Annunaki-Elohim-Nephilim (that are the "elves") with the descendents of Jesus Christ, the "code of the Graal" and the Merovingians, the Templars, archangel Raphael (that is the Sumerian Enki), the Black Mass (that is the original teaching of the Christ), Chem Zoroaster and the Sabbath Goat, the Skull & Bones fraternity, the reptilian shape-shifters, cybernetics, the Kirlian camera, genetic engineering, endocrinology and the components of blood, Dracula and the vampires, witchcraft and Wicca, alchemy and the philosophers' stone, the New Age, the Scyths, the Druids, the fairies, the Mages, the Bacchantes, the caste system preserved in the British royal lineage, and the "aryans" who "developed the Tantra in Sumer".

For the same simmetry we have already mentioned earlier, there has been a development of "debunking" internet websites created by "super-skeptics" who equally throw ridicule on reptilian shape-shifters, drilling of the skull to cure epilepsy, close encounters with UFOs, racist measurements of the skull, the idea that GMO are not exactly very good for health, the Yeti and Bigfoot, climate changes, the Bermuda Triangle, chemtrails, the Celestine Prophecy, natural medicine, the spam mails searching for volunteers to utilize millions of dollars sitting idly in some bank, crop circles, sexual feticism, fairies, druids, the prophecies on the end of the world, the qualities of crystals, the Ordo Templis Orientis of Aleister Crowley, psychotherapy, the evil eye, clairvoyance, ectoplasms, Atlantis, the objection against compulsory inoculation, satanism, *tao chi, feng shui,* the *devadasis, yoga,* the *chakras* and the *avataras.*

It is interesting to see how the "skeptical" opponents of von Däniken have criticized him for speaking of the famous "iron pillar" of Delhi as an extraordinary archeological artefact because after 1,700 years of exposure to the elements it is still rust-free; the pillar, about 7 meters tall and about 6 tons of weight, was erected according to the original inscription in the 3rd century BCE and is still in Delhi near the Qtub Minar. To discredit von Däniken, the "skeptical debunkers" quote a 1974 interview in which "he was reminded" that the above mentioned pillar was actually rusty, and say that from that time, von Däniken stopped talking about it. Actually the story of the pillar and its resistance to oxydation is perfectly genuine and verifiable as we can see from the photos including a Wikipedia entry, that also supplies the scientific explanation of the mystery: a superficial crystalline layer with a high content of phosphorus, that produces an automatic galvanization process utilizing the exposure to atmospheric agents. For those who want more details, we recommend *Story of the Delhi Iron Pillar* by R Balasubramaniam, published in 2005.

We cannot list here all the titles of literature and films published on the subject of Gods and Aliens, because they are far too many. However, we can see from the examples we mentioned that the originality of Sitchin's work does not consist in the idea that the God of the Bible was simply an extraterrestrial with some advanced technology, or in the idea that the Deities of some ancient cultures could have been some kind of aliens, but in the absolute identification of the Elohim with the Annunaki (that has no solid confirmation in ancient texts or chronicles) and in the unsettling certainty expressed by Sitchin that all the cultures and religions of the world should be traced back to this particular group of individuals.

As we have already mentioned, the problem we are examining is not the possibility that the universe could contain various non-human intelligent species capable of space travel, or that in ancient times Earth has been visited by space travelers, or that in the past there have been civilizations even more advanced that the present one. All this is certainly possible - also because all the "mysteries" presented by alienists can very well be explained simply with the presence in very ancient times of advanced civilizations that were HUMAN AND TERRESTRIAL, as already explicitly recognized by the ancients, including Herodotus the father of western history.

It is also possible that some extraterrestrials may have made some genetic experiments on groups of earthlings and have tried to employ them as servants, and/ or that have taught them some technology, and that some mythological stories that developed later have beeen inspired by historically true events. All this may have happened in some specific region of the planet, and if the ancient scriptures or popular traditions speak seriously about these things we should at least give them the benefit of the doubt and respect their beliefs - as long as they do not cause any damage to mankind in general or to the planet.

Rather, the problem is the attempt to trace back everything to the Bible or to the characters of the Bible, maybe presented under different names but always connected to the abrahamic religions or anyway to reduce all the Deities of the various world cultures to the same level (by identification or imitation) or even a lower level than the Bible, creating a scenario where evil and dark entities (like the Archons of the gnostic stories, who are offensively identified with the Devas of Hinduism) naturally and legitimately possess the supreme power in the world and the right to enslave and torture the innocent. It is not our intention to deny the existence of evil or ill-motivated entities, that may possess occult or technological powers superior to those of the present human society. But we can certainly not accept the idea that they can be presented as Devas.

Speculations and fragments of truth

There are certainly many fragments of truth in the mass of intellectual products (books, movies, documentaries etc) about "ancient aliens" and "lost civilizations", and certainly many archeological finds justify the need to review the certainties of conventional history.

The arguments proposed by "non-conventional" researchers are interesting and contain a certain measure of objective information, but presentations are often spoiled by ideological exaggerations or unjustified speculations that start from fragments of truths - a limited amount of iconographic and literary material, often scattered and subject to different and often contrasting interpretations, because we have lost the personal method of transmission of knowledge and several serious gaps in comprehension have been created. Alienists use these questionable data to build scenarios that are nothing but science fiction, but they give lists of "historical events" detailed and pinpointed to precise years of which no concrete proof exists, presented arbitrarily as solid facts or truths that must be accepted by faith. Indeed, it is interesting to see that we are asked if "we believe in ancient aliens" or not, and that depending on our answers we can be treated as atheists or heretics.

To separate substance from fiction, the only solution is to locate and isolate the conclusions that seem to jump out suddenly and are given for granted without precisely quoting data that can be verified at the source. Of course verification can be difficult in the majority of cases, because the actual data remain exclusive monopoly of a small number of specialized academics, who are expert in obscure ancient languages that are incomprehensible for the vast public. But a sincere interest and the application of good sense and intelligence, that support a research work that is as accurate as possible, enable us to make discoveries of huge value even if our professional and academic competence may be limited in some fields.

In regard to the theories of Sitchin and other major alienists, we can find several authors, including Michael S Heiser, Ian Lawton, Chris Siren, Bernard Ortiz de Montellano, Rob Hafernik, Robert T Carroll and Stefano Panizza, who have analyzed the stories on the Anunnaki (also written as Annunaki), highlighting the weak points and comparing them with the Sumerian literature that is actually available, and also using the dictionaries compiled by the same Sumerian scribes and published already since the 1930s by Benno Landsberger, that can be consulted even on internet as "lexical lists" - for example the *Chicago Assyrian Dictionary Project*, or the *Electronic Text Corpus of Sumerian Literature* (ETCSL) by the Oxford University. There are even Sumerian grammars, for example *A Manual of Sumerian Grammar*, by John L Hayes.

To begin with, according to the experts in semitic and middle-eastern languages, the word Anunnaki does not contain any reference to a landing of spaceships; Sitchin's translation "*those who descended from heaven and came to earth*" can at most be connected to a "divine descent" as the word literally means "born from Anu and Ki", respectively the Sky God and the Earth Goddess. Sitchin makes quite a bold jump by identifying the Sumerian Anunnaki with the Nephilim of the Bible, and adding that the word *nephilim* should be translated as "*those who came down from above*", "*those who descended to earth*", and "*people of the fiery rockets*". His reasoning is that *nephilim* derives from *naphal*, "to fall", but according to academics, the correct grammatical form of "those who fall/ descend" should be *nophelim*, or if "fallen", it should be *nephulim*. On the other hand, the word *nephilim* mentioned in the Bible (*Genesis* 6.4 and *Numbers* 13.33) is the plural form of *naphil*, that means "giant" and was translated as *gigantes* in the Septuaginta version.

For further details and in-depth analysis we have been recommended to read *A Grammar of Biblical Hebrew* (by P Jouon and T Muraoka), but this sits rather outside our field of interest. What we want to point out is that there is no scriptural connection between the Anunnaki (or Annunaki if you prefer) and the Nephilim, or between these two categories and the "fallen angels" that in the occultist-esoterist tradition are called the *Watchers*. There is also a lot of criticism by academics about Sitchin's translations and explanations about the nomenclature of the "rockets" ot the Anunnaki, that seem to be devoid of any grammatical or lexical foundation; specifically Michael S Heiser in his website totally dedicated to the issue brings ample bibliographic references that appear quite competent.

It is very difficult to apply the personalities of the Anunnaki to Sitchin's characters, because Sumerian and Babylonian mythology actually speaks of planets in regard to Gods, but not to indicate their demographic origin, but rather to identify their ontological and astrological aspects. While the Anunnaki themselves are described as the "seven spheres of the abyss" and the "protective Deities of the Earth", Inanna-Ishtar is the planet Venus, and Apsu is the personification of the primeval waters - which we could connect to space but certainly not to the Sun. Marduk is never mentioned in Sumerian literature, but only appears in the Babylonian period, and has nothing to do with the Anunnaki.

In Sumerian texts there is not even one connection between Anunnaki and Nibiru, because they are never mentioned together. Some of the images presented as Anunnaki by Sitchin and the alienists are actually the winged Sun disc, an image of Shamash and not of Nibiru and certainly not the picture of a spaceship. The winged people holding a pine cone and wearing "rosette watches" actually belong to the Akkadian and not Sumerian culture, and are identified by the accompanying inscriptions as "genies of the wind". The rosette has no connection with time measuring but represents a very frequent symbol in the iconography of that culture; if it was a watch, there would be no need to wear one on each wrist and a third one on the forehead, as seen clearly in the pictures.

The idea that the Anunnaki needed gold, or that they had come to Earth searching for gold, is totally absent in Sumerian texts; the word "gold" is mentioned rarely and never with reference to mining. The name Bel Nimiki, attributed by Sitchin to the god Ea as "lord of the mines", is not found in any Sumerian dictionary. About the "labor of the Igigi" quoted by Sitchin with reference to the famous epic poem *Atra hasis*, beginning with the words *inuma ilu awilum*, "When the gods like men bore the work and suffered the toil, the toil of the gods was great, the work was heavy, the distress was much", the context was not about minerary work - the text mentions the creation of a land suitable for settlements, specifically by the digging of rivers.

In the Sumerian texts Nibiru is not described as a planet in the solar system farther than Pluto: it is rather a name used for Jupiter and Mercury, in all the 20 times it is mentioned in the inscriptions known to academics. The cycle of 3,600 years, or "great year" or "divine year" has nothing to do with the orbit of Nibiru, but rather with the movements of the constellations and planets that can be observed from Earth. In any case there is not much precision about the time schedules proposed for Nibiru for the last 10,000 years and for the future: alienists remain quite vague indicating a period from 2010 to 2020, but if the last passage was 4,343 years ago, it ensues that the arrival expected 3,600 years ago failed to happen, or it happened and nobody noticed, and the next passage should be in 2,875 years. Maybe. Or not.

Contrarily to the recurrent rumors, it seems that in fact there is no evidence of the existence of Nibiru or the mysterious "Planet X" or "12th planet" or even of the hypothetical binary star that is said to be the distant companion of our Sun, called Nemesis, that according to some (such as Marshall Masters) is not clearly visible because very tiny (twice the mass of Jupiter, although according to astro-phycisists the minimum mass for a star to function as such is at least 13 times the mass of Jupiter) but whose existence has always been based exclusively on statistic projections, that is, on the idea that many stars in the universe are binary systems.

The popular idea of the "Planet X" started in the 19th century when astronomers were making calculations on the Kepler's law of planetary movements and discovered a "gravitational perturbance" in the orbit of Uranus, something that indicated the presence of another and more distant planet. In this way they found Neptune and then Pluto, but still the calculations did not tally and so they suspected the existence of another mysterious planet; in 1989 *Voyager 2* sailed closer to Neptune and the collected data showed a difference of mass compared to previous information, therefore in 1992 astronomers made the required corrections to the calculations without any need to include other planets. Here, too, we need to rely on the specialists' word, because we do not have the instruments and mathematical knowledge required to personally verify the facts, but if we cannot believe the professional astronomers on such matters, we are generally in trouble and Sitchin cannot help us.

What is certain is that the passage of the "Planet X", also identified as Nibiru or Hercolobus, had been forecast by Masters for November 2017 (after the perielion announced for 20 March 2017 and the dates previously supplied by various other sources for 2016, 2013 and 2012), but it seems the appointments have been canceled again and again, and the mass extinction with sudden reversal of Earth poles did not happen. If this cosmic failure is a symptom of the scientific credibility of the persons supporting the theory and of the theory itself, it does not seem necessary to make a leap of faith to respect the information given the "regular" astro-physicists. Some interesting indication that we found on one of such alienist websites is a list of the "various other names under which Nibiru is known", such as the comet Elenin, the "Blue Kachina, "*a star*" (unidentified) and a "Chinese Guest Star" sighted in 1054. Well, *something* will have to pass near our solar system, sooner or later.

Among the mass of bold speculations in the theories of Sitchin and his followers, the one that annoys us the most is the arbitrary date of 2900 BCE fixed as the beginning of the first human civilization in the Indian sub-continent, where in fact for several thousands of years there had been cities of considerable cultural complexity, not unlike the ones described in the Vedic texts, such as Mehrgarh (in present day Baluchistan) that mainstream academics officially trace back to 8500 BCE, Bhirrana (same antiquity) or Harappa (presently estimated around 3800 BCE but some artefacts appear to be over 2,000 years older) as well as Lothal, Dholavira and Kalibangan. Another site found quite recently (in 2002) at sea in the Gulf of Cambay, near Dvaraka, contains artefacts officially dated 5500 BCE. Other sites are still unexplored, such as those submerged in the Bay of Bengal, or out the coast of Tamil Nadu and towards Lanka, that many believe to be the remnants of the semi-submerged continent of Kumari kandam, one of the lost civilizations generally catalogued as legendary together with Atlantis and Mu or Lemuria.

We shall not elaborate on the issue here because we want to keep this book within a reasonable size, but we can mention as an indication of the antiquity of Vedic civilization some of the astronomical references in Vedic scriptures: Konrad Elst has calculated that the references in *Rig Veda* indicate a period tracing back to 6000 BCE, while the analysis by P Gokhale on *Brahmanas* (*Taittiriya* and *Aitareya*) supplied a date in 4650 BCE and another in 6000 BCE; NS Rajaram found several reference in other texts suggesting a period between 3000 and 10000 BCE. It is therefore absurd to give credit, like Sitchin and his followers do, to the retarded theory for which the earliest Indian civilization - defined as the Indus valley culture - started only in 2900 BCE and was totally destroyed in 2350 BCE because it had been abandoned by the "supreme goddess" Inanna, leaving a complete void that was filled only in 1450 BCE by the Vedic culture introduced by the "aryan invasions" that went to build settlements further inland.

As we have already mentioned in previous chapters, some alienist authors who write on the "fall of the Indian gods" have stated, on the basis of Davenport's obsolete nuclear theory, that Mohenjo Daro was destroyed by a "rain of fire" during "a war among gods" in which "many spaceships" were used - all ideas that we have already shown as grossly mistaken. The same presentations claim that "for millennia" the city of Mohenjo Daro has been "known by all as the island of Lanka" in the middle of the ocean "formed by the Indus river during the rainy season" while before 1972 nobody had ever called the island of Ceylon with the name of Lanka: it ensues that the Ramasetu ("bridge of Rama") and the temple of Ramesvaram (established by Rama for the worship of Shiva) would have been built after 1972 CE or they would not have any connection with the story of Valmiki's *Ramayana*, that according to Vedic tradition it is even more ancient than the present compilation of the *Vedas*, written about 5,000 years ago.

The same authors claim that Hinduism started in 1200 CE (while before that, nobody in India had ever spoken about Gods but only about aliens and human beings) with a "dogmatic and sectarian crystalization" that engaged in persecuting and prohibiting the original and genuine interpretations, with the purpose of enforcing the political deification of a group of mortal alien individuals coming from the constellation of Orion, called "transcendent" just because they were "searching for transcendence" while they constantly engaged in killing one another in bloody wars. The name of the *Padma Purana* is thrown on the table to support the idea that these aliens discovered Earth by chance, and because they found it more beautiful than their own planets they decided to establish some colonies; when they arrived on Earth, they involved the earthlings in their "heavenly wars" among gods by conscripting armies composed of human beings. Finally, "according to the Indian sacred texts" these "gods" had physically left their colonies on Earth but promised to return in the future to take back what they considered their property. Nothing of this has any confirmation in Indo-Vedic tradition.

It is possible that western authors have found some Indians who were ready to work with them (it would not be the first time) also because the simple fact of having been born in India does not constitute a guarantee for authoritativeness or even simply for a proper understanding of the Vedic culture. It is not impossible to find Indians who have only a vague or incomplete knowledge, or even a distorted knowledge, of Vedic scriptures and Hindu religious tradition, also because the ideological structure of Hinduism is very tolerant and open-minded, and does not persecute even those who are ignorant enough to actually compromise and damage the general image of Hinduism. The traditional method to oppose false and distorted versions consists in public philosophical debates, where the defective presentations are defeated by better presentations. Unfortunately in our days the picture is complicated by vested interests, political and financial pressures, and especially by a general tendency for institutionalized ignorance and by the difficulties of access to the information sources by the public. We are working to remedy the situation, both among the western public and among Indians, and we hope that other people will join in this dutiful effort.

Always according to the false elaborations of the alienists, the concept of *avataras* (such as Krishna for example) should be reduced simply to the birth and death of a limited individual alien that was later "deified" by a class of priests who used religion to "exploit society". We have already seen how actually in the Indo-Vedic religious and social system the priestly class totally abstained from political and material power, and was expected to demonstrate a great simplicity and modesty in their life style.

No Deva has even given commandments or appointed a caste of priests to enforce their will on the entire human society; as we have already seen, *dharma* is simply the natural and universal law of ethics, that each human being is instinctively able to recognize thanks to the "voice of the conscience", and the Hindu system is based on a vast concept of religious freedom.

It is worth noting that devotion to the Supreme and his *avataras*, and even to the Devas separately (as *ista devata*) has always been characteristically "self-managed" by individuals even among the people in general, and due to its popular and simple nature had no need for the intermediary of priests or even for specific rituals or complicated *mantras*. For example, we read in *Bhagavad gita* (9.26), a fundamental text that has been valid for at least 2,000 years (according to the *Mahabharata* for more than 5,000) that worship to Krishna just requires a little water, a fruit, a flower or a leaf, directly offered by the devotee; in a tropical region covered by forests and where the climate and the soil support agricultural harvests all year long, obtaining such ingredients for offerings is certainly affordable for everyone, without any need for priests or money.

Participation to religious functions has always been individual, personal and free in Hinduism: the only ceremony we could call "collective" is the *arati*, that is the offering of pleasurable things to the Deities at certain times of the day and especially during some festivals, in temples that are open to the public and sometimes on the street, but the attendance of the public has never been compulsory even as a general social norm. Actually it may be exactly the opposite, as that many temples are not open to the public and therefore the ceremonies are strictly private, exclusively financed by the legal owner of the building and attended only by family members and servants.

In the Vedic system, the function of the *brahmanas* (besides teaching) had a ritual aspect that simply concerned the correct recitation of the hymns of Vedic *samhitas* and precision in procedures, and only in the public "State" ceremonies in honor of the entire assembly of the Devas (the "administrators" of the universe) in which the king distributed food and gifts to the people. For private ceremonies (marriages etc) normally compulsory only for the three higher classes (*brahmanas, kshatriyas, vaisyas*), each individual relied on his personal relationship with the *guru* who was directly responsible for his education and only occasionally, because the vast majority of rituals were, and still are, performed directly by each individual. Today, if someone wants to obtain the service of a brahmin for some ritual, it is with the same approach by which one would call an architect, a carpenter or a plumber to have some guarantee of better performance of the proceedings, by reducing the risk of the "do it yourself" mess.

Also strictly individual are *yoga* and *tantra*, that are practiced directly under the guidance of a personal teacher who is chosen freely, and who does not (or should not) have any political or material power on the lives of his disciples. We cannot elaborate much on the issue here, so we invite our readers to consult our specific publications on the subject.

Some authors have used, arbitrarily and falsely, the name of the *Shiva Purana* to claim that Shiva was an alien from Orion who landed 40,000 years ago on mount Kailasa with an egg-shaped spacecraft, then later attained enlightenment ("*nirvana*") and met the Sapta Rishis (as Earth residents); for 80 years he refused to give them knowledge, but then he ordered them to go and fill the Earth with people by making children and recreating human civilization by teaching their descendents to grow agricultural products, read and write and do maths. These are nothing but ignorant speculations.

Actually Shiva, as the direct manifestation of Vishnu, does not have to "attain" enlightenment but is eternally and ontologically enlightened; traditionally he is depicted as immersed in meditation to show this state of awareness that is implicitly natural in him, and that he demonstrates for the benefit of human beings. The idea of the egg is probably a distortion of the concept of *brahmanda*, literally "the egg of Brahman", but this refers to the entire universe as the product of transcendental Existence, and it certainly does not apply to any spacecraft, also because no *vimana* has always been described in this form. The Sapta Rishis (seven *rishis*) normally reside in the constellation of Ursa major (Big Dipper) and have always been endowed with full knowledge and enlightenment since "birth", as direct sons who appeared from the mind of Brahma at the beginning of the creation of the universe, therefore their position is much higher that the position of ordinary human beings "seeking transcendence". True, they descend to Earth at the end of each *manvantara* to inaugurate a new golden age, but it is a recurrent task -

according to the *Surya siddhanta*, every 306,720,000 Earth years or 852,000 heavenly years, that is every 71 cycles of four ages (*maha yuga*), which in the present creation of the universe have already happened 14 times in each single day of Brahma, who has recently turned 51 years of age. It is not difficult to understand that such mission has nothing to do with the story of Noah, with the reconstructions of Sitchin and the alienists (that indicate a period between 8000 or 11000 BCE), or with local alluvional sediments that geologists and archeologists have traced to many different times in the history of the planet.

Among the other imaginative speculations of alienists on Hinduism, we find the Kumaras described as "naughty children or short hairless aliens" who bring war to various planets, and Narada Muni as a God/god who used to go to various planets to civilize wild aboriginals. It is not clear where they got the idea that the Vajra is Shiva's weapon (and not Indra's) and Duryodhana and his 99 brothers were removed from their mother in the form of 100 ova produced simultaneously from her ovaries, and not as one single fetus already developed but damaged. Another extraordinary interpretation is the one offered on the famous statue of the Buddha "all skin and bones" that for some alienist is supposed to illustrate the idea that the Buddhist monks are expected to practice severe austerities by abstaining from food for weeks altogether - rather than the ascetic phase of the meditation entered by the historical Buddha, who had to overcome and reject it in order to achieve enlightenment.

Nonsense like that is on the same level of the theory (peddled as historical fact by the same authors) that Micenean culture (that was aggressively patriarchal) worshiped "one Inanna-type goddess"; probably they are confusing the Micenean culture with the Minoan culture, that was actually centered on the worship of the Mother Goddess Earth, the primary ontological archetype of the natural universal religion, and certainly not something that can be explained away by the romantic fables about one Annunaki female.

We will not elaborate on the preposterous "crypto-philology" claims by Sitchin and followers, as for example the one assimilating Uranus with Varuna - merrily ignoring the fact that Varuna is one of the 12 Adityas and not their father (and certainly not the father of ther

Asuras or Titans) and personifies the element of water. These superficial parallels based on similarities in sound have already been condemned by many serious researchers, but anyone can become aware of their lack of substance simply with a quick verification of actual parallels.

This does not mean that the sitchinists are the only ones who spread garbage on Vedic civilization and other cultures. One Gene D Matlock, particularly anxious to prove the theory of the north pole as the earthly paradise, claims that "the Indian god Krishna" was the King of Jerusalem, the Tara ("protective father") of Abraham (Brahma), Sara (Sarasvati) and Moses (Mahesvara). Matlock imaginatively presents a name of Krishna as Malika sadhaka, that he imaginatively translates as "King of the Magicians", and that "obviously must" be identified with the name Melchisedec. Not all readers bother to consult the Vedic texts or even just a Sanskrit dictionary to find out that *malika sadhaka* is a totally invented name, built with the arbitrary coupling of *malika* (literally "garland, necklace") and *sadhaka* (meaning "a person who engages in *sadhana* or spiritual discipline") that makes no sense, applied to Krishna or anybody else. What does it mean, "someone who practices the spiritual method of the necklace"? Certainly there is no connection with kings or magicians.

Matlock continues claiming that "Hindus believe" that the first men came from other planets because they were called Navalin ("the people of the space ships", a translation offered by Matlock for a name he totally invented himself) and Anunaka ("those who come from the sky", another translation by Matlock of a name he invented). Nothing of all this is mentioned even slightly in any scripture or Indo-Vedic (Hindu) tradition. The Sanskrit word that comes nearest to "Navalin" is *nanaphalamaya*, which means "of noble mind", while *anunaka* means "non minor", as the opposite of *unaka*, meaning "insufficient". However, *anunaka* means "ours" in the language of the Australian aborigines (nothing to do with Sanskrit), and has given its name to an agricultural settlement about 130 km from Canberra in New South Wales. Let us examine some more ramblings offered by Matlock: according to him, those "first men" landed not in India, but in Israel, "as demonstrated by the fact" that still today the Druze worship Krishna and read the *Vedas*, and have the same DNA of Indians - all totally baseless statements. Those divine men - that Matlock identifies without any doubt with Shiva, Zeus, Apollonius, Apollon and so on - created the descendence of Japhet/Yayati (quoting a non-existent *jyapeti* to imitate the Bible's name of the Caucasian race) corresponding to Yadu, Yadava, Yahuda and "*jews*" - as Matlock seems to believe that the earliest Jews, just like the ancient Indians, spoke English as their first language. Actually "Yadava" was the dynasty where Krishna appeared about 5,000 years ago, a name derived from Yadu who was one of the most famous ancestors in that line: no Indo-Vedic source shows a global or regional predominance of this dynasty or its descending from Devas administrators of the universe of from aliens, or even any relevance or connection with Zeus, Apollon or Apollonius of Tiana. Or with Jews.

The line of reasoning presented by Matlock is similar to the one proposed by Russian writer Murad Adji who writes very seriously in his book *The Kipchaks - An ancient History of the Turkic People and the Great Steppe* thanking the Hindus for having preserved the history of the ancient origin of the Turkish and Siberian people, although they (the Hindus) seem to be convinced that it was their own origin (the Hindus' or Indians'). In his view, such origin must be traced back to about "two thousand years ago, or even slightly earlier"; at those times the "antediluvian aryans" were afraid of venturing south because they thought they would fall into the void (because Earth was flat) and they would find an intolerably hot climate. And because the *Mahabharata* says that the Pandavas went to the mount Mandara/ Meru, obviously they went to the north pole (!).

Other authors circulate similar nonsense, for example like the idea that Shiva was "the Queen of the Fairies", that the "Sactis" (*sic!*) are sylphids or guardian angels, and that the mission of the *avatara* Kalki is about destroying the Goddess Kali to put an end to Kali-yuga. Browsing through the available literature we have read with consternation that the name Buddha is supposed to derive from the name of Ptah, the Egyptian deity who represents the Sky, and *therefore* the name of Pythagoras is a compound derived from "*buddha guru*". Compared to these extraordinary statements, we can even be less shocked by those who mention the "Hindi religion" or the "Bengali Sanskrit government".

It is amusing (but with a touch of the tragicomic) to read that according to the "tradition of the bramins" (which ones?) precisely in 18,617,837 BCE a "group of aliens called Kumaras coming from Venus" had landed on an island in the present Gobi desert (which at the time was an ocean) or that Alexander the Great ended up conquering India ("from the Himalaya to the ocean"), that the *Mahabharata* is a "confused story of wars and battles that happened in some vague legendary antiquity along the Indus valley", and that the *Ramayana* speaks of "a battle among *vimanas* or *vailix* or flying vehicles that happened on the Moon", where the *asvin* (or *vailix*, it is not clear) was a typical spaceship in Atlantis. According to this imaginative view of the *Ramayana*, "Rama" was not a prince of the Suryavamsa, but an empire of seven cities smack in the middle of the Atlantic ocean (where obviously north India and Pakistan were), ruled about 15,000 years ago by "enlightened King-Priests"; the same commentator reveals that "Ramayana, Mahabharata and other texts speak of the terrible war that happened about 10,000 or 12,000 years ago between Atlantis and the Rama empire, that used weapons of destruction so terrible that nobody could imagine them until the second half of this century". Others claim that according to the *Ramayana* the first people of India were Mayans emigrated from Lemuria.

On the same level, there are also those who present the *Oahspe* (the "New Bible" compiled in 1882 by American dentist John Ballou Newbrough) as the genuine "secret doctrine of the ancient" or the writings of Madame Blavatsky (*Books of Dzyan*) as the origin of the knowledge contained in the sacred scriptures of India, China, Egypt and Israel - originally composed in a non-existent "lost" language called *senzar*, and later translated into Chinese, Tibetan and Sanskrit, and according to which the ancestors of all human beings had come from the Moon. Again according to Blavatsky (*The Secret Doctrine*), the *Mahabharata* is about the war between two races of extraterrestrials - the Suryavamsa who worshiped the Sun and the Indavamsa who worshiped the Moon.

The Christian-based academic doctrines, elaborated mostly by Jesuits and carried on officially until the post-colonial period, taught (and still teach) that the various non-abrahamic cultures and especially Hinduism and Buddhism developed after the beginning of the Christian era or at least after the beginning of the Mosaic era, and therefore had "borrowed" ideological, theological, iconographical and hagiographic ideas from the Bible.

Thus several authors (including "non-conventional" ones and even atheists) have claimed that Krishna was born on 25th December and from a virgin in a cave of mount Meru, was adopted by a carpenter, then went to preach to the poor, was persecuted by the priests of his times, accepted 12 disciples and finally died crucified between two robbers to pay for the sins of mankind and then rose again from death ascending to heaven. They also mention other "similarities" of the same type with the figure of Jesus Christ, but we are not so interested to make a full list.

What we want to point out is that Krishna's birth has always been celebrated on the 8th day of the waning moon of the month of Sravana, that covers the period between the middle of July and the middle of August (and at most it can slide to the first days of September), that Devaki had 6 sons and a miscarriage before Krishna's birth, that his birth was in the palace of Kamsa in Mathura (on the bank of the Yamuna river, near present Delhi) and that after his birth his father Vasudeva went to hide him in the village of Vrindavana in the house of the chief of the cowherd men (*gopas*), a man who was completely engaged in cow farming and certainly was not known as a carpenter. At the age of 16, Krishna and his brother Balarama returned to the city of Mathura in their family of *kshatriyas* of the royal order. As we see from *Mahabharata (Bhagavad gita)* and *Bhagavata Purana* the "preaching" of Krishna was limited to the transmission of teachings to two of his relatives and close friends, Arjuna and Uddhava, who could be considered as his "disciples" although they were never asked to go around to spread his teachings.

Apart from a few comments offered during his childhood to friends in the village of Vrindavana, we do not see any situation where Krishna had gone to preach to people and certainly not to the poor; also there is not even one indication that there was any "persecution" by priests. The disappearance of Krishna, described especially in the *Bhagavata Purana*, was due to an arrow wound to the foot, and has no reference to atonement of sins or thieves or robbers, to crucifixion or some form of resurrection.

We could continue for several pages quoting also other monumental blunders (such as the eucharesty of brahmins with "rice bread") but we will stop here, inviting the interested readers to get proper information about the Indo-Vedic tradition from suitable sources.

Ufology as a cultural trend

We should remember here the necessary distinction between the "alienist" current for which the aliens are the only possible Gods, and the movement called "ufology" concerned with collecting data and reports about the phenomenon of UFOs or *Unidentified Flying Objects*, which technically could also be of human origin. It is possible that many ufologists believe in extraterrestrial theories on the identity and motivations of the persons behind such objects. Some of these ufologists could be contactees, claiming they had close encounters with such UFO people, and some may have become alienists, but the choice of implicitly superimposing the two beliefs can unnecessarily increase confusion, leading to baseless and dangerous conclusions.

We should also not exclude the possibility that such confusion could be deliberately engineered, because we see that the general trend supported or created by propaganda favors a very specific attitude towards the issue: when we see some unidentified object we are supposed to believe it is alien - good or evil, but superhuman - otherwise we need to deny the very existence of the object in itself, because such existence contradicts the official dogma. This approach is very dangerous, as it reinforces the effects of the propaganda campaigns against the individual cultivation of a divine awareness, the concept of a transcendent God as ontological reality (as we have already explained) and a healthy sense of dignity and respect for the true nature of the individual soul and for the potential of the human race as well. While trying to destroy these fundamental principles of the Natural Religion, the dangerous propaganda circulated about Gods=Aliens reinforces a superstitious fear of "the unknown", discourages the use of intelligence and verification in the search for actual knowledge, and shapes the collective mind into abject submission and worship when faced with oppression.

The fact that UFOs are "unidentified" simply means that their origin is not known by the observers. In 1969 physicist Edward Condon, presenting the famous Condon Report, modified the distinction with the definition ETH (*Extra Terrestrial Hypothesis*) to refer more precisely to a possible extraterrestrial origin of such objects; the theory still remains rather neutral, without attributing specific motivations, good or evil, to any aliens, or offering detailed historical reconstructions of their interventions in the history of mankind. Later the scenario was expanded to consider the IDH or IH (*Inter Dimensional Hypothesis*), that according to some researchers is strictly connected to realities specific of our planet.

This is also the opinion of Jacques Fabrice Vallée (born in 1939), who became interested in the subject in 1961, when he was working as computer consultant at the Space Committee of the French government and saw the people in charge of the project destroying recordings because they showed a non-identified object orbiting around Earth. Vallée wrote several books, including *Anatomy of a Phenomenon: Unidentified Objects in Space, a scientific appraisal* (1965), *Challenge to science: the UFO enigma* (1966), *Passport to Magonia: From Folklore to Flying Saucers* (1969), *The Invisible College: What a group of scientists has discovered about UFO influences on the human race* (1975), *The edge of reality: A progress report on unidentified flying objects* (with J Allen Hynek, 1975), *Messengers of deception: UFO contacts and cults* (1979), *Dimensions: A casebook of Alien Contact* (1988), *Confrontations: A scientist's search for alien contact* (1990), *Revelations: Alien contact and human deception* (1991), *UFO Chronicles of the Soviet Union: A Cosmic Samizdat* (1992), *Forbidden Science: Journals, 1957-1969* (published in 1992), *Wonders in the Sky: Unexplained aerial objects from antiquity to modern times* (2010).

This ufology that is free from religious projections is now quite accepted culturally, with a growing percentage of the world population in industrialized countries that have come to believe in the likely existence of other sentient species in the universe and in the possibility that extraterrestrials have sometimes come in contact with human beings or could do so. According to current calculations, it is supposed that 1 on 500 planetary system could support life of a terrestrial type (for planetary size, distance from its sun, composition of elements etc); because about 200 billion stars have been detected in our galaxy, the number of possibilities comes up to 400 millions, of which at least 50% could be suitable for the development of a technology based on metals, due to minerary deposits on the surface.

It seems that astronomer Claudio Maccone has recently reinterpreted the famous mathematical formula known as "Drake equation", proposed by Frank Drake in 1961 to calculate the number of intelligent civilizations with which it would be possible to communicate in the universe, and this has now reached the number of 4,590. It is obviously pure speculation simply based on the number of stars visible in the Milky Way, the percentage of stars that have planets, and the percentage of planets that are potentially inhabitable (according to human parameters of course) from which the theorician arbitrarily extrapolated the percentage of probabilities for development of intelligent life of human type, evolved enough to send electro-magnetic signals. But the theory seems to be acceptable to many convential scientists, although not to everyone.

A famous book (one of the earliest) published in 1966 on the issue is *Intelligent Life in the Universe* by American astronomer Carl Sagan, probably inspired by the work of the Soviet astronomer Iosif Shklovsky (*Universe, Life, Intelligence,* published in 1962); other writers who have discussed the issue to popularize it from a scientific perspective are Isaac Asimov, Fred Hoyle, Robert T Rood and James S Trefil. Unfortunately Carl Sagan and others such as William Marcowitz have addressed the problem only to "solve" it in a negative sense, offering quick conclusions based on the arbitrary premise that the only possible form of technology in the universe is the one of the 20th century Earth, and the only possible form of sentient life in the universe is the human form according to the darwinian line of reasoning.

For these critics, interstellar space travel is not practical and therefore it must be impossible, and exobiology can be nothing but pure speculation because the expeditions of NASA have never brought back any specimen of extraterrestrial living beings, no matter how little evolved. So they conclude that UFOs cannot exist, because if they existed they should work according to the Earth technological modalities, and nobody else in the universe has yet developed a technology that can be compared to ours.

The USA government has started to study the issue of UFOs in 1947 with the "Project Sign" (then renamed Grudge), that was followed by "Project Blue Book", both bogged down by public controversies and much disinformation and counter-information. Arthur Lundahl, ex director of PIC (Photographic Interpretation Center) of CIA, has stated publicly that he examined a great number of film recordings for the government, and found them genuine. In the 1950s Elmer Green (from Topeka, Kansas) was at the head of a group of engineers under government contract for photographic measure-ments in experimenting new weapons; one day during a test for V2 missiles they filmed some UFOs that were following the missiles, and for such a long time that they had to go get more film to complete the work. The American James Edward McDonald (1920-1971) was professor at the faculty of Metereology at the University of Arizona, Tucson, and head at the Institute for Atmospheric Physics, but he became famous for his rigorous research on UFOs during the 1960s: he personally examined over 500 reports, brought many important government documents to light and in 1968 he presented an official report to the USA parliament (Congress) on the issue.

Among the persons who have made public declarations about UFOs there are the minister of Canadian Defense Paul Hellyer (25th September 2005, video published on *youtube*), scientist Boyd Bushman (who worked at the Lockheed department of so-called Area 51), NASA astronaut Brian O'Leary who is professor of physics at Princetown, astronaut Edgar Mitchell (Apollo 14), professor of oceanography of the University of New Hampshire Ted Loder, and some officers of the USA army as for example colonel Philip Corso, who said he had studied the artifacts of the Roswell case, from which many important technological inventions may have derived in the last decades. It seems that in 1973 USA president Jimmy Carter and his son Jeff publicly declared they had seen an UFO. All these references are rather widely known, and from our research it does not seem they are considered as controversial, and because our ideological position does not depend on the truthfulness of those sources and the actual historicity of the events they speak about, we consider our research sufficient to give a general picture that is quite realistic on the situation in the field of ufology.

There is a record of official declarations by president Ronald Reagan, such as the one during the 42nd general assembly of the United Nations on 21st September 1987: "how quickly our differences would vanish if we were facing an alien threat from outside this world. And yet, I ask you, is not an alience force already among us?" It is true that this declaration could be interpreted in different ways, from the alienist or conspiracy theorist to the simple anti-communist or anti-immigration paranoia, but there is no doubt that it contains a disquieting message from a person who had access to information that was not available to the public. However, USA magistrature has given quite a clear pronunciation in a court case on 18th May 1982: "Public interest in disclosure is far outweighed by the sensitive nature of the materials and the obvious effect on national security their release may entail" (US District Court Opinion in the case of Citizens Against UFO Secrecy vs the National Security Agency). A declaration of this kind should at least arouse our attention.

In 1997 journalist Sarah McClendon (corrispondent at the White House) published an article based on the declarations of a group among the hundreds of scientists and technicians engaged in government projects "with extraterrestrials". Bill Cooper, ex marine officer, published on internet in 1989 a very detailed document on the so-called "Operation Majority" and "Project Grudge" (*Blue Book Report 13*); an interesting detail in regard is that according the declarations of "Ebe" and "Krill" (aliens with whom the USA government is supposed to be in contact), the RH negative factor and the blood group O present in about 20% of the global population are connected to genetic manipulations performed by aliens on the human species.

Another famous official document (published in 1992) is the report of the British army concerning the base of Bonnybridge, Scotland, where there have been regularly an average of 300 sightings every year. In 2009 the British Ministry of Defense announced that because after 50 years the government has not found any damage from such phenomena, the report service has been interrupted. It is certainly not possible to mention even a part of the official and non-official reports from radar installations, military and civilian pilots, astronomical observatories and so on, because there are thousands of them. The "National Aviation Reporting Center on Anomalous Phenomena" (NARCAP, that at some point moved from USA to Canada) has a catalogue of about 3,400 cases of anomalous sightings reported by air pilots from government and from private companies. Some people connect extraterrestrials also to the famous *crop circles*, that have been found in very different places, not only in various cultivated fields but also on sandy deserts and even on the frozen surface of lakes.

Another famous issue in the field is about the so-called mutilations, targeting mostly large animals such as cattle and horses but also sheep, pigs, chickens and occasionally also human beings. The phenomenon started in 1974 in USA, with over 700 cases reported within 18 months in 15 States, then over 180 cases in Colorado in 1975, and more cases in Canada in 1976 and in France in 1977. According to some ufologists, the victims were taken for the purpose of bio-genetic analysis, probably to monitor the levels of pollution of the planet. The case reports are very precise and consistent: the corpses are totally exanguated but there is no trace of vascular collapse, and the dissection is surgically precise, removing rectus, genitalia, eyes, tongue, ears or viscera, without causing any damage to the adjacent areas. Other characteristics are the total lack of blood or prints (from predators, humans, vehicles etc) in the place where they have been found, and the absolute silence during the event.

These events and cases of biological implants and post-traumatic stress in many subjects who reported being kidnapped by aliens, have convinced many people that the "aliens" are not benevolent gods as believed by some. Brad Steiger and Joan Whritenour, in their book *Flying saucers are hostile* (1967), are very explicit in regard and denounce the danger of the new type of evangelism in which the alien messiahs are soon expected to bring peace and well-being to our poor tormented planet. Like Vallée, Steiger makes a connection between the aliens of the contactees and the disquieting malevolent personalities of terrestrial occultism and so-called parallel dimensions, such as orcs, werewolves, ghosts and the like. Naturally even simpe ufology still finds quite some resistance among intellectuals and academics, with reactions of emotional denial, contempt and ridicule, but we should not be very surprised. For many "scientists" that are still rigidly attached to the cartesian-newtonian paradigm, anything that cannot be measured by official academic authorities must be labeled as foolish superstitions. Even although the limits of knowledge continue to be moved by genuine research and in many cases with the validation of official academics.

In 1926 professor AW Bickerton declared that the idea of sending a rocket to the moon was stupid and impossible. In 1935 the famous astronomer FR Moulton wrote that man shall never travel into space. In 1958 (just 8 months before the launching of the *Sputnik I*) doctor Richard van der Riet Wooley (Royal Astronomer) defined the idea of space travel as *utter bilge*. We will not quote the numerous evidence of incredulity by intellectuals and scientists of the past in regard to the origin of meteorites, of the possibility of building an airplane that could fly or a metal ship that could float, and so on.

Some scientists launch into the opposite attitude, fostering the dream of the "modernist" movement that started with the industrial age in the 1800s, by which artificial and mechanistic progress can be the only solution to save mankind and the planet from poverty, malnutrition, wars, illiteracy, and even muscular and mental fatigue. Why walking when one can drive a car? While climb stairs when one can ride an elevator? Why make calculations mentally or with pen and paper when one can use a calculator? Unfortunately the increase in health problems due to sedentary life and the loss of autonomous mental abilities in the mass of the population are aggravated by an acceleration in artificial tendencies imposed by a wrong artificial lifestyle, with alienating jobs, idiotization in entertainment, boundless consumerism, huge increase in the minimum cost of life, burocratic and fiscal hypertrophy, and unattainable "success" models.

The myth of the "modern solution" has taken deep roots in the fields of medicine (pills and injections, synthetic medication especially antibiotics, painkillers, synthetic implants for cosmetic surgery), nutrition (industrial, pre-cooked, freeze-dried, refined, synthetic foods with chemical additives), agriculture (monocultures with hybrids, genetically modified organisms, pesticides, herbicides, chemical fertilizers, hydroponics, etc) and clothing (synthetic fibers, plastic, etc). These products are imposed by the system especially by eliminating or restricting the natural alternatives, and then blaming consumers for the ensuing damage and presenting "solutions" that are often worse than the problems themselves.

It is in this perspective that we must observe the fantasies of technological progress still dished out by the mass media as the stuff of dreams (or nightmares) of alienists: this does not mean that all innovations must be rejected *a priori*, but rather that it is essential to carefully consider all the consequences in the middle and long term and the sustainability of the proposed applications, especially in regard to the laws of nature and universal harmony. Renewable energy, soft and clean technologies, permaculture, self-managed practices for the development of human potential, the recycling of waste are excellent examples of innovations that are sustainable and intrinsically positive, unlike the nuclear proliferation for the production of electricity, the compulsory application of electronics especially for the personal lives of individuals and so on.

Hopeful fantasies on the possible future developments of human technology already started in the times of Jules Verne (1828-1905) and have become increasingly bolder; at a certain point people have started to imagine that if human beings were capable of high technology, somewhere in the universe there could be other intelligent species similar to humans, and as aggressive and dangerous if not more. But to claim of having directly met such aliens and to perfectly understand their intention, it is a very big step.

Once again, we want to clarify that we do not intend to deny the possibility of actually having contacts with some non-human or even superhuman intelligent species. As we have already mentioned in regard to the equivalence Gods=Aliens, what we do not accept is the blind faith perspective we call alienism, that asks us to believe in the statements of some new prophet who claims to have received some new supernatural revelation that is substantially different from the ancient and healthy natural human traditions. We should not let ourselves be confused by persons who say they have been abducted or had "close encounters" with aliens, especially if their "messages" support racism, dark occultism, messianism, contempt for human beings, and catastrophism painted as inevitable and cathartic (as in millenarism). The need to believe in a new "scientific" revealed religion is extremely dangerous and can easily be a trap cleverly devised by people who may have sinister motivations.

This very important distinction has been stressed by many reseachers, such as Jacques Vallée and Jean-Bruno Renard, and we should not underestimate it. We also want to clearly state that the vast evidence of Indo-Vedic tradition is perfectly aligned with this *caveat* because it explicitly warns the earthlings against the ignorant illusion that could lead them to worship superhuman Asuras, with disastrous results both for the individuals and for the general community. If we examine the available data on alienists and contactees, certainly we can notice many points that appear at least suspicious.

The first modern "contactee", George Adamski (1891-1965), was an occultist that many even call "theosophist". An American citizen of Polish origin born in Germany and with a primary school degree, in 1930 he started to teach his own religion where he mixed Christianity with "the oriental religions". He founded the Royal Order of Tibet that had meetings at the Temple of Scientific Philosophy and obtained from the government a special licence to produce wine "for religious purposes", that he sold with excellent profits to a vast public. The end of the prohibition period stopped the thriving business; according to Curtis Peebles in his book *Watch the Skies: A Chronicle of the Flying Saucer Myth*, Adamski told to two friends that at that point "*he had to get into this flying saucer crap*". In 1940 Adamski purchased a small piece of land near mount Palomar, in California, where he put up a diner, a camping site and an "observatory" in a wooden shack, equipped with a 6 inch telescope, letting his correspondents and readers believe he was an astronomer of the famous Palomar Observatory of Caltech (California Institute of Technology), where the telescopes are a bit larger: Oschin is 48 inches and Halle is 200 inches.

On 24th June 1947 a pilot named Kenneth Arnold (1915-1984) reported having seen a row of 9 non-identified flying objects over mount Rainer; according to his evaluation their minimum speed was 1,200 miles per hour (1,932 km/h). The story obtained vast coverage on newspapers and stimulated the interest of Adamski, who declared in the August of that year (1947) that he had seen no less than 184 UFOs fly over his own farm during one single night, and that previously he had seen a large cigar-shaped "mother ship" in the same area. In 1949 Adamski started to give paid lectures on UFOs, claiming that the goverment had detected the existence of an alien spaceship 700 feet long (almost 214 meters) on the dark side of the Moon, and recognized that all the planets of the solar system are inhabited.

In 1952 Adamski claimed he had met a Venusian astronaut named Orthon, with whom he had a conversation through telepathy and hand gestures, and who left him an imprint of his own shoes, containing a message written in mysterious symbols. One year later Adamski published his first book, *Flying saucers have landed* (1953), followed by *Inside the space ships* (1955), *Flying Saucers farewell* (1961) and *Cosmic philosophy* (1961). In 1949 he had already published *Pioneers of Space: A trip to the Moon, Mars and Venus*. Adamski's declarations sold at least 200,000 copies, but were heavily criticized by researchers of all groups, even by ufologists. In his science fiction novel *3001: The final Odyssey*, Arthur C Clarke calls the ufologists as people who suffer from *Adamski's disease*.

Adamski's lack of credibility is due mostly to the fact that the composition of the atmosphere and soil, the gravity and other characteristics of the planets in our solar system were already well known in his times. Venus in particular, as confirmed by *Mariner 2* in 1967 and *Venera 7* in 1970, only shares with Earth an approximation of mass and distance from the Sun; the atmosphere is very dense, with 96% carbon dioxide and clouds made mostly by sulphuric acid with traces of iron chloride, iron sulphate and phosporic dioxide, and it has 167 volcanoes with a crater of over 100 km diameter each. Atmospheric pressure is 92 times the one on Earth and the average surface temperature is 462 C degrees (863 F), and there are winds of about 300 km/h that regularly sweep the planet at a speed 60 times (6,000%) its rotation, while the fastest winds on Earth are just 10% of its rotational speed. In short, a journey to Venus would hardly be a pleasure trip, unless of course one remained in orbit in a beautiful and comfortable space ship, and without even attempting to land.

CG Jung commented favorably, in his *Flying saucers: A modern myth of things seen in the sky* (published in 1979 after his death), on the work of an Italian American, Orfeo Angelucci (1912-1993), entitled *The secret of the saucers* (1955) and apparently according to Jung, "soaked in gnosticism". Angelucci claimed he had been renamed "Neptune" (discovering his original alien identity) during one of his space travels, when he had found out that actually the human race was originally from a lost planet named Lucifer, once orbiting between Mars and Jupiter, and had been created as a penal colony for rebellious criminals originally from that planet; the non-criminal survivors of that planet are the aliens who visit Earth periodically. Other similar authors of the same period are Truman Bethurum (1898-1969), Daniel William Fry (1908-1992) and George Van Tassel (1910-1978). From the 1930s to the beginning of the 1960s the topic of space travels and aliens remained mostly within the community of science fiction buffs, that has grown larger also thanks to the increasing number of sightings and other extraterrestrial-connected phenomena, that have been taken more seriously by the public and are better documented.

One famous event was the radio show (Columbia Broadcasting System) on 30th October 1938, known as *The War of the Worlds* (adaptation from the novel by HG Wells), a fiction piece presented as real newscast, that according to the media created a lot of panic. During the broadcast hour there were increasingly more alarming news bulletins about a supposed invasion of Earth; the first announcement spoke of explosions on Mars, the second said that unidentified objects had fallen over a farm at Grover's Mill, New Jersey (USA). According to the third "interruption for special updates" Martians armed with infrared ray weapons had come out from the crash, then there was a quick series of announcements about hostile actions by the invaders in the United States and in the rest of the world. The broadcast had been explicitly announced as a theater piece within the series *Mercury Theatre on the Air*, but more than one million listeners were scared or upset, according to a study by a Princeton professor, Hadley Cantril (*The Invasion from Mars*, 1940). The details are controversial, but the episode made history.

Public interest has been roused by films such as *The Day the Earth Stood Still* (1951), *The War of the Worlds*, *Earth vs. the Flying Saucers* (1956), *Forbidden Planet* (1956), and *I Married a Monster From Outer Space* (1958). In the 1960s writers started to examine the issue beyond fiction and fantasy. The year 1966 saw the debut of the famous TV series *Star Trek*, in which the United Federation of Planets, imagined by Roddenberry on the basis of the United Nations established after WW2, had solved all the problems of Earth and developed good contacts with other species in the universe. In 1967 the University of Colorado sanctioned over half a million dollars for a study in cooperation with the Pentagon (Air Force); in 1969 the director of the project, professor Edward Condon, simplistically concluded in his report that there was no evidence for the reality of UFOs, but the only result was to further enflame controversy.

The public discussion on UFOs and aliens started in 1978, when Canadian citizen Stanton Terry Friedman, after a career as nuclear physicist in cooperation with the USA government, started to investigate the famous "Roswell case". According to a press release originally issued by colonel William Blanchard, commander of the Roswell Army Air Field (New Mexico, Homey Airport, Groom Lake, about 134 km north-west of Las Vegas, Nevada), on 8th July 1947 an alien space ship was recovered from a desert crash. An official denial followed but too late, because the news had already been published by local newspapers. A few years later rumors started about a secret USA army base, popularly called "Area 51" (officially Restricted Area 4808 North or R-4808N) where the government had moved the remnants of the Roswell incident and other cases, including some dead aliens and even some alive aliens. Official spokespersons have stated that the UFO hypotesis is simply a myth, and that the air force bases in the area - Nellis, Edwards and Nevada Test and Training Range - simply engage in designing and testing of airplanes that are advanced but terrestrial technology.

Some believe that many "new technologies" including advances in aereonautics were borrowed from aliens with whom the US government is supposed to have been in contact for decades. Rumors speak of an official committee called MJ-12 (Majestic 12) formed in 1947 by USA president Harry Truman to study extraterrestrials and conduct projects in cooperation between the USA government and some aliens; many researchers connect the famous *Protocols of the Elders of Zion*, the *men in black* (unofficial secret agency), the classified top secret documents on inexplicable phenomena (*X files*, that inspired the famous TV series), the manipulation of climate and ionosphere with the HAARP project (High-frequency Active Auroral

Research Program) and the notorious *chem-trails*, the Bilderberg Group and the Bavarian Illuminati, multinationals and intelligence and counter-intelligence agencies of various governments. Of course Hollywood jumped on these stories, but most of all, for the purpose of pushing them into the field of science fiction.

Another episode that became famous is the sightings at Phoenix, Arizona ("Phoenix Lights"), on 13th March 1997, with thousands (some say tens of thousands) of witnesses who filmed the event, not just in Phoenix but for 300 miles (480 km) above Arizona and Messico, with a great number of luminous objects that moved in formation. Some people (such as Damont T Berry) comment that between 1930 and 1970 similar sightings have been reported with many photos and videos, but from 2009 they have become even more numerous and better documented, and that by studying these recordings one can see that the flying saucers are trying to communicate with terrestrials through a symbolic language based on the astronomical knowledge of constellations.

The issue of contacts with aliens and the message they are trying to give us has become popular especially through films such as *Close Encounters of the Third Kind* (1977), *First Contact* (1996, from the *Star Trek* franchising) and *Contact* (1997). After 2000, the perspective became increasingly darker and pessimistic, down to *The Fourth Kind* (2009) in which the alien entity is clearly demoniac and speaks Sumerian, and the new *Arrival* (2016) that underlines the invalicable difference of perspective and mentality of the aliens compared to earthlings - although it gives the impression that the director does not have the faintest idea even of what is happening in the film. We cannot give a list of all the entertainment productions that present invasions by aliens with more or less evil motivations, or with good motivations but ended badly, because such list would require one entire chapter.

The SETI initiative (Search for ExtraTerrestrial Intelligence), already proposed in 1959, covers a series of installations for the search of electro-magnetic radiation from space, especially for possible transmissions by alien intelligences. The inspiration had started from Nikola Tesla and was carried on by Guglielmo Marconi; both stated they had observed anomalous radio signals, respectively in 1899 and

1920. The first project of the SETI series, named Ozma, was implemented by Frank Drake of Cornwell University in 1960 (installation at Green Bank, West Virginia, oriented towards Epsilon Eridani and Tau Ceti); the next one was in 1968 at the State University of Gorky (Soviet Union). Followed the Ohio State University Radio Observatory telescope (Ozma II, also called "Big Ear") in Delaware, financed by the National Science Foundation, and then in 1971 the "project Cyclops" (1,500 antennae and 10 billion dollars, under the direction of Drake and Bernard M Oliver of Hewlett-Packard Corporation) that was not completed. The organizers turned to a smaller version (budget of "only" 25 million dollars) that was named "Allen Telescope Array", implemented by the Radio Astronomy Laboratory of the University of California, Berkeley; it seems that out of the 350 parabolic antennae planned, only 42 have been installed, at the Hat Creek Radio Observatory.

In 1974 the Arecibo Observatory sent the famous message towards the globular mass M13, at 25,000 light years from Earth, that seems to have received a reply in the form of a very complex and explicit "crop circle" that appeared in a nearby field; other messages have followed also from the Eupatoria Planetary Radar in 1999, 2001, 2003 and 2008. In 1977 (15th August) the Big Ear telescope picked up a rather strong signal coming from space; one of the project members, Jerry Ehman, commented on the report writing a big "*wow*", that became the moniker for the event.

With the financement of the National Commission for reform and development, the National Academy of Sciences in China has built a spherical telescope with an opening of 500 meters (the largest telescope in the world) with the declared purpose to pick up interstellar communications from extraterrestrial intelligences. It is not a mystery that the directors of the Vatican astronomical observatories (one at Castel Gandolfo, Rome, and one at Mount Graham, Arizona, USA) have repeatedly declared they seriously consider the possibility of the existence of extraterrestrial humanoid species. It seems that mons Balducci has given declarations in this regard during a TV show in Italy, and the Protestants have not lagged much behind: Evangelist Billy Graham has declared that UFOs could actually be angels, and Presbiterian Carl McIntire has organized an "UFO Bureau" at Collingswood, New Jersey, to study the connection between UFOs and angels. Even atheist preacher Richard Dawkins has made statements in favor of alienism, suggesting that the human DNA could be of alien or diabolical origin. In Vienna there is even an office called UNOOSA, or United Nations Office for Outer Space Affairs (present director, Simonetta di Pippo), with the declared task of coordinating the cooperation among space agencies of the various nations and monitor the use of technologies, but because the declaration of intents has been modified several times, we can suspect that the program for "*disaster risk management and emergency response, resolution* 61/110" could include the authority to welcome possible extraterrestrial envoys to our planet. If the matter is not taken up first by the Pentagon military as we see in the vast majority of the science fiction films.

The debate rages on various fronts with representatives of many different perspectives, some of which aggressively try to ridicule the subject even in front of objective facts that cannot be explained otherwise. Many admit the possibility of contacts with beings from other planets or other dimensions, and even of human civilizations that were lost and forgotten after having probably attained high technological levels.

About this whole thing, our opinion is that we should take the various pieces of information carefully, without rejecting anything *a priori* but without putting all the questions and answers in the same ideological container, with one single sectarian theory that claims to explain everything without bothering to reconcile apparent contradictions. Of course, everyone has the right to develop his/ her own view of the world that is consistent and sensible, especially if such vision is confirmed by sufficiently authoritative sources. But we should not turn it into a mere "matter of faith": also in regard to the information offered by the Indo-Vedic tradition, nobody should just blindly believe out of loyalty (often mispresented as "consistency"). Each source should be quoted and analyzed independently, for its actual contents and in the correct context, and each individual should take responsibility for what s/he chooses to accept or not.

The real problem is that people are confused and desperately seeking "absolute truths", ready-made, from "new religions" and extra-ordinary revelations, and undisputable "scientific dogma" that could be more solid and beneficial than those that have created so much suffering and disappointment in the last 2,000 years. Many perceive intuitively that the answer could be "somewhere else", in the past or in the future or on some other planet, and project abrahamic fantasies of paradises on earth or in heaven on "alternative" scenarios hoping they are soon going to materialize after the imminent disastrous "end of the world".

But no "new religion" can prove better than the previous ones, if we do not solve the fundamental ideological mistake that is at the root of our conflict against Nature and human conscience. Even the study of ancient religions and cultures cannot bring the desired results if we do not abandon our "eyeglasses" of cultural prejudice through which we observe them, and if we do not try to deeply understand the original meanings they contain instead of trying to superimpose them mechanically to the attachments and conditionings that are rooted in our conscious or subconscious mind, individually and collectively.

Specifically, as suggested by the French scientist Jacques Vallée, we should avoid supporting the dangerous concepts presented by the alienist "religious" movements: for example, the idea that the human species is incapable of creating advanced civilizations without the repeated assistance of aliens, or the idea that the aliens who created mankind (and a particular descendence of "nobler blood") are blond and tall - the typical "arian" race but originally from other planets, like the Venusians described by Adamski. Another disquieting detail is that one of the major alienist groups contacted by Vallée, the Order of Melchizedek (a denomination used in biblical tradition to refer to a higher caste of clergy) uses the "star of David" as insignia, believes in a kabalistic (Jewish mysticism) cosmology, and pursues a program for unified world government, with the elimination of religions and cash currencies. The Order includes a series of organizations called Christian Liberation Front, Jesus People Europe, Jesus Revolution, Charismatic Christians, Christian socialist party, and even Islamic and Zionist groups.

Aliens and technology in ancient cultures

As we have already mentioned, the theories of the "non-conventional" researchers generally despised by conventional academics are often as imaginary as the "historical reconstructions" of many credited university archeologists, who categorically refuse to acknowledge the so-called "controversial finds" and often even stop them from being examined by other researchers or independent scientists. Because rarely the iconographic depictions of ancient cultures are accompanied by inscriptions, the vast majority of the "explanations" of such iconography are based on fragmentary knowledge if not on the wild imagination of the people who write catalogues and add their personal comments according to their own beliefs. Until a few years ago any ancient female image was called "Venus" (for example, those from the so-called stone age) although obviously they had nothing to do with ancient Romans.

Unfortunately the popular texts, especially those written for the masses, such as history school books and encyclopedias including the multimedial ones, still present succintly as established facts the imaginative speculations of generations of historians and archeo-logists, starting with Herodotus and Plinius, who were (by their explicit declaration) almost as ignorant as our contemporaries. Luckily there is the Web, where with a bit of skill and lots of intelligence one can retrieve interesting information, sometimes even offered by some brave members of official academia to their perplexed colleagues within the "field", and where a number of "non-official" researchers are ready to catch the ball on the hop and throw it again to a section of the public that is greedy for this type of news.

A famous case was the "Baghdad battery" (found at Khujut Rabua and dated about 500 BCE), previously classified as "vessel for religious rituals" that an engineer visiting the museum recognized as perfectly capable of producing by electrolysis those magnificent ancient works of very fine plating in gold and other precious metals on which archeologists continue to declare their perplexity, because the layers are 10 times thinner than those made presently at industrial level. Since then, several similar batteries have been found, 4 at Seleucia (same area) and 10 at Ctesiphon; they are all about 15 cm high, with electrodes in iron and copper, and electrical insulation made with asphalt.

Nothing supports the idea that electricity must have been gifted to human civilization by some alien visitors, because the observation of electrical phenomena is not difficult even for an ordinary human being. The scientific discoveries of the modern world have started precisely with the study of electricity, even performed with very simple devices that intelligent individuals could well have devised by themselves also in ancient times, but without a technological approach that was hostile to Nature like the one developed in the last 3 centuries.

Many ancient human cultures actually speak of alien races, also inter-dimensional ones, some benevolent, other malevolent, still others dangerous but not necessarily evil, generally characterized by powers that are greater than ordinary humans', that have come in contact with groups of human beings.

Literary and iconographic evidence of Sumerian civilization (the most ancient recognized by official historiography and media) seem to indicate that some "heavenly beings" may have helped the humans of the region to develop a deep astronomical knowledge of the universe - a knowledge that still survives here and there, for example in the Dogon culture in Africa (along the river Niger), who have been preserving for many centuries precise information on the solar system of Sirius and its planets, that have only recently been studied by contemporary mainstream academics. The same Dogon indicate as the source of their ancient knowledge a race of fish-men that correspond to the Sumerian descriptions of Oannes or Johannes, and whose typical depiction could be connected with the origin of the strange shape of the Catholic bishop's hat. Or maybe not - but this detail is not particularly relevant.

Researchers in the fields of ufology and alienism have collected an impressive amount of similar examples, often supported by verifiable cases, from which we can easily see that ancient cultures at global level knew advanced technologies and beings that were not really human, and that such evidence could go far back in time, even several thousands and in some cases *millions* of years ago. Many of the most extraordinary and mysterious monuments are in stone and because they do not contain organic materials (Carbon-based) their datation with Carbon 14 is not very effective. Other finds that can actually be dated are too controversial to be acknowleged officially and therefore remain hidden, something that demonstrates the sore lack of intellectual honesty in the management of museums and conventional academic institutes: hiding or destroying uncomfortable historical relics cannot certainly be considered a scientific behavior.

We have discussed about these mysteries of ancient history specifically in the second volume of our work on *The Awakening of the Mother Goddess*, presenting data that can be somehow verified with the material available to the public, but all this does not lead to solid conclusions on the actual identity of the extraordinary or superhuman figures that are described in traditional stories. As we have already said, our preoccupation is primarily with the Gods of the Indo-Vedic tradition and the data offered by the scriptures recognized as genuine.

We cannot elaborate in this book about the pre-colombian civilizations in America and the pre-/proto-imperial cultures in China and Japan, or even about the Sumerian or Egyptian civilizations, or other cultures that are more or less known or legendary (Atlantis etc), therefore we will limit our discussion in that direction to the brief mentions already offered in connection to the general issue, especially because (unlike Indo-Vedic culture) those cultures have totally lost a living tradition and detailed scriptures that are authoritative enough to supply credible clarifications. The evidence given by occultists is obviously useless.

As we are not expert in the ancient languages of those cultures, we need to depend on translations offered by others - as a consequence, we do not have sufficiently valid instruments to verify, confirm or reject the speculations of academics and conventional and non-conventional researchers in regard to those fields. What we can actually do, is to highlight possible connections with the Indo-Vedic material that we have verified directly.

Of course, similarities can be genuine connections or derivations, but they should not be accepted blindly: we must separate the various concepts to understand them clearly, and then join them again in a logical time sequence that can be useful for human evolution and learning. Let us make a very practical example: a photographic report that documents a mountain range, producing a number of images in the form of transparencies for slide shows. Trying to simply and mechanically superimpose all the transparencies to obtain one single "complete image" is going to be a failure, especially if the technicians who work at the project have never seen a real mountain directly. At best, the result could be a good Photoshop or fiction job, with a purely artistic value.

The process required to establish reality requires separating all images individually, understanding them well (preferably with the help of some expert mountaineer who knows the territory in practice because he has been there) and then mount them in a sequence to obtain a film or video that can give a more correct and sensible impression of the mountain range in which we are interested - something that will be essential for tracing a traveling course for those who want to go and verify personally.

We have already said that in ancient times various cultures have spoken about ancestor figures or gods arriving on "flying chariots" or clouds, or generally descending from the sky. The concept of "god/God" or "deity" in various cultures can take different meanings that we cannot simply superimpose to the ontological universal perspective (that is transcendental and spiritual). Besides, one can "descend from the sky" simply because he has been traveling in an airplane from a point on Earth to another point on Earth. It is certainly possible that some of such extraordinary travelers were coming (and/ or are still coming) from other planets, but also that, being originally from Earth, they were (and/or still are) able to travel between planets on space vehicles.

The idea of air or space travel does not appear particularly extraordinary to the Vedic tradition of ancient India, but not because Indian civilization was founded or composed by extraterrestrials: we rather see from many Sanskrit texts, originals or copies compiled in the course of the centuries (something that makes datation quite relative), that in human civilization it is totally normal to know *vimanas* (flying vehicles for air and space travel), drive them and even build them, as we will see in the next chapters. This technological knowledge and the deep metaphysical knowledge of philosophy and theology distinctly separate Vedic tradition from other ancient cultures in connection with the central issue of our book, in the sense that Vedic tradition does not confuse gods and aliens more than a computer engineer can confuse a software program with a magic ritual - even in the case of a computer engineer who personally follows a spiritual and religious path in the shamanic or wicca tradition.

On the other hand, it is understandable that less educated and less informed people, who experience "magic" as a superhuman and transcendent force that animates Nature and all beings, but hardly know how to use metals to make primitive tools, will be pervaded by a sense of religious wonder when they witness events they cannot explain, and will not have the cultural and intellectual instruments to distinguish a technological creation from a natural phenomenon. We take the opportunity to clarify that in our opinion the category of natural phenomena also includes those manifestations that are sometimes called "supernatural" simply because the people who observe them do not have sufficient knowledge of the physical laws of Nature. Phenomena such as levitation, telekinesis, telepathy, materialization and de-materialization, storing information in a subtle form (as energy) and similar marvels are actually in perfect accord with the laws of Nature, and the basic equipment supplied by the human body enables one to access levels of knowledge and functionality on which one can operate in different dimensions. Unfortunately, centuries of repression have make such abilities almost incredible and impossible to manifest not only for the mass of less evolved people, but even for those who have developed or could easily develop the adequate level of preliminary awareness.

It is necessary to clarify that we do not intend to minimize the value of any culture or to express negative moral judgments on this or that human tradition, especially in regard to the concept of "progress", that can have different meanings from different perspectives. For us, real progress is that which brings true well-being to everyone (not just to a limited number of people) and can be sustained for a long time, or in other words, enables us to easily preserve or rebuild natural resources. In this sense, the present super-technological and mechanistic culture entails many disadvantages because it is based on consumerism, obsolescence and exploitment that are non-sustainable and non-balanced, not because it is technologically advanced, but because its technology is not supported by solid ethical considerations. On the other side, the cultures that are presently considered "primitive" often contain precious values of respect for Nature, that we should rediscover and apply with humility and gratitude, while still recognizing the limits that exist, where they exist.

The reaction of awe and wonder in front of more sophisticated technology is found especially among nomadic populations, whose lifestyle forces them to keep to a very primitive and elementary level of technology because the transportation of books and machinery would require a considerable extra effort on top of the hardships of normal survival and also creates greater risk of damage, when it is impossible to obtain spare parts for repairs. Nomadic technologies are in fact based on the utilization of primary materials that are easily found in nature (sticks, wood, stones etc) or derived from animals through hunting or breeding (skins, leather, bones, horns, ligaments etc). Besides, a very small number of individuals among the members of nomadic tribes can afford to dedicate time and energy to the search of theoretical knowledge or specialized technology, because the life of a nomad is very hard work: apart from the requirements of packing and unpacking, setting up and taking down, the scouting expeditions and the journeys proper that involve the entire community, the sense of uprooting and the insecurity implicit in moving one's residence are compared as stress factor to a divorce or the death of a family member, as observed by modern psychology.

In all nomadic communities therefore we find only one shaman, with one or at most two or three young apprentices who must still continue to perform some measure of personal and communal duties for survival, such as hunting or herding. Of course this does not mean that nomadic cultures should be despised or forced to convert to so-called "civilization"; their specific cultural contribution could be extremely valuable at individual and collective level because it develops other aspects of human potential, such as precisely the "magic vision", meant as the ability to perceive and utilize the existence of subtle dimensions and the animistic connections among all beings and things.

However, these are generally contacts that remain on the material (if subtle) level, and therefore they are still limited; the "spirits" one can find on this level can prove benevolent or malevolent but are generally non-trascendent, something that easily explains the misunderstandings on the definition of deity or god/ God. Still there can be exceptions, especially in the case where the perception of the sacredness of Nature attains an ontological level, where one worships the very principles of Existence, and thus some religious person that is particularly sensitive and evolved becomes able to directly communicate with God as immanent, eternal, universal and unchangeable, as we have already mentioned; this individual ability does not necessarily depend on the cultural parameters of the group, although it can be facilitated or obstructed by them.

Nomadic cultures are typically shamanic and by necessity very attentive to the natural cycles and events, because they strongly depend on the movements of the seasons and atmospheric weather, as well on the reproductive instincts of animals and on the diverse conditions of the territory in regard to the opportunities for pasturing and migration, on the prowling of predators and so on. Originally the observation of terrestrial phenomena was complemented by the observation of the heavenly phenomena, of which our distant ancestors of the stone age were already well aware, as we can see from numerous studies presented in the last years in the academic world, and on which we have elaborated in the second volume of our work on *The Awakening of the Mother Goddess*.

Without any need to produce judgements on superiority or inferiority, we simply want to note that the less technological peoples, especially those who are nomadic by long tradition, have a particularly "simple" perspective for the observation of complex phenomena, complex philosophies or complex cultures. For a "primitive" of any time and any ethnic or national identification, all the manifestations and figures that appear to be unusual, extraordinary, wonderful, powerful, are automatically catalogued as "superhuman" and therefore "divine". Or "demoniac".

The border between "divine" and "demoniac" can become rather blurred for the simpler minds, and is exclusively based on the rather selfish question "will it give me benefits?" although the category of "beneficiaries" is not limited at individual level but extends to the group, tribe, community, nation etc: it is still selfish. Thus we see the development of the concept of a tribal superhuman entity ("good" or "evil" in general does not matter much) that *gives special benefits* to the "faithful" in exchange for offerings, worship and obedience managed by a priestly caste that can be hereditary or elective but is always powerful politically. This concept does not exist in the *arya* system of Indo-Vedic tradition, but as we have already mentioned, it can appear in ancient Indian societies that are *anarya* (defined as "non-civilized") in connection with the Asuras and especially with Yakshas and Rakshasas; on the other hand in *arya* Hindu tradition the concept of *ista deva* does not contain any type of pact, covenant or alliance but simply expresses an individual attraction of the devotee toward one form of God rather than another, and the form of the Divine remains in a non-exclusive attitude, that is impartial and benevolent towards all beings.

Many cultures in the world recognize the existence of powerful wizards able to change their form at will, hungry for blood and flesh, who consider human beings as inferiors to be enslaved and exploited. Among this human cattle, some ruthless individuals who desire greater wealth and power over their own kind may accept to worship the Asuras and therefore obtain places of supervisors or foremen, with considerable privileges compared to other humans. Sometimes they offer their own women to be impregnated in order to reinforce their own position with relations and alliances with a hybrid descendence that is considered very powerful both physically and mentally. In this category of Asura worship we can also include the service that materialistic persons offer to powerful humans (kings, politicians, etc) with the intention of obtaining selfish advantages.

The worship to Asuras such as Rakshasas and Yakshas, mentioned by some scriptures with reference to the forms of religion influenced by ignorance, remains generally individual or private or even secret, because it requires the worshiper to cause pain, fear and despair to innocent creatures. Fear, blind submission, madness, cruelty, masochism and self-destruction are connected to the dark presence of these terrifying Asuras, who are able to take human forms or any form they wish, or to remain hidden in a subtle form. This shape shifting ability could be at the origin of the prohibition to make cult images.

The most serious confusion between divine and demoniac seems to have begun with the doctrine of Zarathustra/ Zoroaster, of which we have already discussed. Here and now, we simply want to mark these fundamental cultural and ideological tendencies that clearly distinguish the perspective of nomadic and tribal peoples from the perspective of Vedic civilization, that is openly inclusive of other traditions but not bound by the superstitious fear created by simple ignorance. Thus we affirm that it is useful to make a deep study of Vedic knowledge, to clarify all misconceptions in regard to Gods and Aliens, but also to discover a very interesting perspective on the cultural, social, and historical problems that we are facing today.

We have already mentioned the superhuman beings described by Sumerians, saying that they were not the only "humanoids" known in ancient cultures. The traditions of China, pre-colombian America and India speak about serpents or winged dragons of almost human appearance but with superhuman powers, these humanoids (genetically and sexually compatible with humans) have a deep scientific knowledge that enables them to transform the appearance of their bodies, live under water, fly in the sky, use mysterious weapons and have a very long life.

Some Mesopotamic deities are connected with the image of the snake, for example Ningizzida, the "Lord of the Tree of Life", but there are also several "serpent" characters famous in other cultures, such as Cecrops (the founder of Athens), Fu Xi and Nuwa (founders of semi-divine dynasties in China), Typhon and his wife Echidna (origin of all monsters in Greek mythology) and the Gorgones. Many traditions speak of a people of gnomes, elves and fairies that are not always benevolent, prefer to live in underground tunnels and caves sometimes quite vast in expanse, and where they often guard treasures, especially golden objects; they also have the faculty of changing their shape at will, to appear and disappear mysteriously, manipulate time and make weapons, strange objects and large buildings.

It is said that sometimes they capture human beings, children or adults, to keep them and less frequently even to establish conjugal relationships, but they do not mistreat them and they could be very generous, if they are not offended or annoyed. Another humanoid race that is famous in many cultures is much more terrifying and has originated the folk tales of orcs, vampires and demons: these beings have a great power in manipulating matter at the subtle and gross levels, travel between dimensions, consider human beings as prey and cattle, and feed on blood and flesh and especially on the negative emotions of their victims, such as fear, horror, despair, sense of impotence and so on.

These figures have become real cultural and popular archetypes, and as such they have taken roots in the human subconscious, becoming sub-personalities with whom some even try to identify, in the desperate search of an ideological and mythological connection with Nature or with the manifestations of the universe that seem to be incomprehensible or fearsome.

The study of the evidence of UFO sightings in ancient times has been named "clipeology" in 1964 by the magazine *Clypeus,* of the Centro Studi Clipeologici (in Turin, Italy); the etymological origin of this neologism is explained with the description of the *clypei ardentes* ("shields of fire") mentioned by Roman authors also in reference to the mysterious objects that scared the soldiers of Alexander the Macedonian during their military encounters at the border of India. Another quote is given from the Papyrus Tulli (the name is from Alberto Tulli, director of the Pontificio Museo Egizio in Vatican city), allegedly containing a passage about 3 flying objects that appeared at the time of Tutmosis III.

Sightings in Europe were reported also in the middle ages, when people believed that flying objects were coming from a sky kingdom called Magonia and inhabited by mysterious and powerful wizards. In a chronicle of the year 840, Agobard the arch-bishop of Lyons speaks of a mob-lynching of three men and one woman, who had landed in the area and admitted (probably under "adequate pressure") of being wizards. It seems that the *Capitularia* by Pipin Le Bref, Charlemagne and Louis I of France contained instructions on the procedures in such cases.

Indian sources still remain one of the major sources for ufologists and alienists, also because in fact they contain many interesting references, although people often quote them with little accuracy; for example not many people have understood that the various *parvas* are sections of the *Mahabharata* and not separate books, not to speak of those who classify Nagas, Rakshasas and Yakshas as "castes" or identify the Asvinis (who are two twin brothers sons of Surya) with the entire population of Atlantis. In one article we have found "according to the Hyndu Yogis" quoted as if it was the title of a literary work; in another article yet, the "technological" meaning of the word *deva*, connected to the root *div* ("splendid, luminous"), is explained claiming that the Devas got their name "because they used laser swords as weapons".

Technology in Vedic India

Many descriptions that were considered mere mythology until a few decade ago have become suddenly realistic with the nuclear experiments of fusion and fission, sub-atomic and quanta physics, the unified field theory, the theory of parallel universes, nano-technologies, computers and artificial intelligence and so on. The truly updated scientific resarchers in the field of physics and mathematics live in a world that the mass of people could consider unrealistical science fiction, and they cannot really communicate effectively with the public or with researchers in the fields of "social sciences" such as anthropology, archeology and history.

Unfortunately scientists and scholars are handicapped by the excessive fragmentation of specializations and the absence of a fundamental science of awareness - we are not talking of simple epistemology (the discussion on the validity of opinions) or psychology (the study of mental mechanisms), but something much deeper, that has not been defined or explored yet by western conventional academics. The gap can be filled by studying the original Vedic knowledge, as it has been suggested by many science pioneers such as Julius Robert Oppenheimer (1904-1967), Niels Bohr (1885-1962), John Archibald Wheeler (1911-2008), David Bohm (1917-1992), Carl Sagan (1934-1996), Werner Heisenberg (1901-1976), Andrew Thomas (1906-2001) and Fritjof Capra (born in 1939).

Regarding the level of scientific knowledge of ancient India, one of the items often mentioned is the *Tables of Varahamira* (an existing manuscript is dated 500 CE) that contain mathematical data on atomic structure and the *Brihat Sathaka*, that speaks about the measurement of time from the *kastha* (1/0.00000003rd of a second) to the *kalpa* (4.32 billion years); modern commentators have noted that the *kastha* has a duration similar to the existence of some mesons and iperions (sub-atomic particles) while the *kalpa* is similar to the time of disintegration of radio isotopes such as uranium 238 (4.1 billion years).

The decimal system and the concept of zero and infinite were already present in the Vedic texts, as well as geometry, algebra, quadratic equations, square root and cube root, trigonometry, algorithm, the so-called Fibonacci sequence, binary numbering - all contained in manuscripts that trace back at least to the early centuries of this era. The decimal system already appears in the measuring sets found at Mohenjo Daro and Harappa; the Indian origin of the decimal system and of the understanding of zero/ infinity has been recognized by many mathematicians, starting with Pierre Simon Laplace (1749-1827).

The most famous names of Indo-Vedic authors of mathematical treatises are Brahmagupta, Apastamba, Baudhayana, Pingala, Hiranyakesin, Virahanka, Gopala, Hemachandra, Manava, Varaha, Vadhula, Mahavira, Bhaskara, Sripati, Mahendra Suri, Madhava from Sangama-grama and Nilakantha Somayaji. Between 1911 and 1918 Bharati Krishna Tirtha wrote the treatise entitled *Vedic mathematics* (published in 1965), presenting an ancient integrated system, particularly suitable for mental calculations. The *Sulba sutras* are an ancient classical text that connects advanced mathematics with astronomy and the science of building (not just architecture); it enabled the precise calculation of the movements of planets, stars and constellations, including the clear concept of precession of the equinoxes. Among the most famous texts still existing there are *Surya siddhanta* (in slightly different versions), *Vedanga jyotisha* (Lagadha's version still existing), *Siddhanta tilaka* and *Sisya-dhi-vriddhi-da* by Lalla (without any mention of *vimanas* or space travel), *Siddhanta siromani* by Bhaskara, and *Jyotir mimamsa* by Nilakantha Somayaji.

It is important to understand that Vedic knowledge, by its very declaration, has been expressed and codified originally by extraordinary personalities in extremely ancient times and the subsequent texts are based on the original authorities, simply as copies or as commentaries, therefore it is easy to be confused when trying to assign a date or a time frame to a document. Different works, compiled by different authors or scribes, can also have the same title or very similar titles because they deal with the same subject and often quote previous works that may have the same title. *Surya siddhanta* is one of the most famous examples, because its original compilation is attributed to Maya Danava.

German scholar Hans Torwesten (born in 1944) author of *Vedanta - heart of Hinduism*, wrote, "A fair number of leading physicists and biologists have found parallels between modern science and Hindu ideas. In America, many writers such as JD Salinger (*An Adventure in Vedanta: JD Salinger's the Glass Family*), Henry Miller, Aldous Huxley, Gerald Heard, and Christopher Isherwood, were in contact with the Vedanta. Most of them came from elevated intellectual circles which rejected the dogmatism of the Christian Churches yet longed for spirituality and satisfactory answers to the fundamental questions of existence. In Vedanta, they found a wide-open, universal, and philosophically oriented religion where even the penetrating scientific mind could find something to its taste."

Welsh scholar Brian David Josephson (born in 1940), pioneer of super-conductivity and the study of magnetic fields, supporter of the possibility of parapsychological phenomena, head of the project of Mind-Matter Unification and Nobel Prize 1973 for physics, wrote, "The Vedanta and the Sankhya hold the key to the laws of mind and thought process which are co-related to the Quantum Field, i.e. the operation and distribution of particles at atomic and molecular levels."

Austrialian physicist and astronomer Andrew Thomas (1906-2001), author of *We are not the first - Riddles of ancient science*, wrote: "The atomic structure of matter is mentioned in the Hindu treatises Vaisesika and Nyaya. The Yoga Vasistha says - there are vast worlds within the hollows of each atom, multifarious as the specks in a sunbeam which we have assumed now as true... In ancient times the day was divided into 60 kala, each equal to 24 minuts, subdivided into 60 vikala, each equal to 24 seconds. Then followed a further sixty-fold subdivision of time into para, tatpara, vitatpara, ima and finally, kastha or 1/300,000,000 of a second. Is this reckoning of time a folk memory from a highly technological civilization? Without sensitive instruments the kastha would be absolutely meaningless. This fact supports the bold hypothesis that the science of nuclear physics is not new."

On the other hand, there is no substance to the story of the "Nine Illuminati" or the "Secret Society of the Nine Unknown Men" that is supposed to have been created by emperor Ashoka with the purpose of classifying and preserving "all the sciences" of ancient times, mentioned as physiology, microbiology, cosmology, gravity, light, alchemy, sociology, communications and propaganda. The story started from a novel written in 1923 by one Talbot Mundy and published in episodes on *Adventure Magazine*; the quality of the work is more or less on the level of the famous novel *The Celestine Prophecy*, especially considering the character of Father Ciprian, who finds the secret books but wants to destroy them because they are "against Christian doctrine".

In the story we find quite a considerable amount of catastrophism and contempt for human nature, because the motivation for such secrecy is explained by Mundy with the idea that Ashoka was afraid that allowing the work of these scientists to be made known would cause it certainly to be used "for the evil purpose of war". But if we were to accept this hypothesis as historically founded, it ensues that secrecy must have been excessive, because such books have actually been lost altogether, or they ended precisely in the hands of the worst and most power-hungry people, that used every small crumb of knowledge for the most evil purposes, and with considerable success, considering the constant increase of violence and aggressions in the last centuries, precisely from Ashoka's times.

It is true that in the course of history much knowledge has been lost, but not because the books have gone secret, but rather because invasions destroyed the books that were normally known and slaughtered the expert teachers that handed them down, as we can see it happened even more radically in the Mediterranean region. It is difficult to make people forget the destruction of the library of Alexandria, although the Establishment propaganda has succeeded in muddying up the waters in regard to its modalities (who, when, why, how), but the west (and in a certain measure, India too) has practically no information about the destruction of the huge university libraries of ancient India, starting from Nalanda and Taxila (Takshasila).

Nalanda (near Bodhgaya, in Bihar), already famous at the time of the historical Buddha as a great center of learning, had about 10,000 teachers and several thousands of students in 642 CE at the time of the visit by Hiuen Tsang (also written Xuanzang). The students arrived regularly from China, Indonesia, Greece, Turkey and other countries that are still more distant, and Ashoka himself, in the 3rd century BCE, had several buildings erected and installed the famous Nagarjuna, who left in charge of the institution his main disciple Aryadeva. In 673 CE Yijing (also written as I Tsing) wrote that the university had 300 apartments and 8 main halls.

The library of Nalanda occupied a 9 storey building and contained so many books that the islamist raiders under Bakhtiyar Khiliji (hopefully nobody will try to squeeze some crypto-etymological derivation from *bhakti*) took months to burn them all (in the year 1200). Other famous universities were in Sirpur (near Rajpur, Chattisgarh, about 150,000 students), Takshashila (Punjab), Vikrama-shila (Bihar), Ratnagiri and Lalitagiri (Orissa), Odantapuri (Bihar), Mithila (Bihar), Somapura (Bengal), Vallabhi (Gujarat), Manyakheta (Karnataka), Vidisha and Namisha (unfortunately the site has been lost among the many ruins of the region), but also in the still existing cities of Varanasi/ Benares (Uttar Pradesh), Kanchipuram (Tamil Nadu), and Srinagar (Kashmir), although the corresponding libraries and universities have been destroyed in the islamist invasions, that according to the chronicles written by the invaders themselves had killed at least 800 million people and enslaved innumerable others, both women (many of the *harems* of the conquerors had thousands of them for each man) and valuable men especially craftsmen and artists and probably scientists as well.

The idea of hiding knowledge at the risk of losing it demonstrates a fundamental lack of wisdom, and this does not certainly encourage us to think that such secret books were particularly valid, if ever they really existed. The Vedic system does not hide knowledge in books to be buried in some crypt (where any idiot with a spade could find them if even by chance, as done by the priest in Talbot's story), but it rather entrusts it to a system of disciplic transmission by which the teacher chooses the disciple that is most qualified ethically and instructs him in the best possible way so that he will in turn become able to transmit the deepest knowledge.

Of course this method is not perfect either, because it depends on favorable circumstances where society produces qualified individuals and protects them physically from violent aggressions and other calamities such famines, diseases, natural catastrophes etc. In the course of history there have been several difficult situations that required some intervention to re-establish the transmission of knowledge in human society, implemented by extraordinary personalities with a particularly wide and clear vision of reality.

The problem of the bad use of knowledge is not due to knowledge itself, that can be used just as easily for beneficial purposes: the fundamental factor consists in the *individual* qualifications of the person who possesses the knowledge - teachers, kings or government officers, warriors, physicians, or any other professional. When such ethical qualifications are actually present at individual and collective levels, in the scientists expert in knowledge and in the ruler who supports and protects them, the distribution of the knowledge to the public promotes a higher quality of life, especially in the field of medicine (that also includes physiology and microbiology) but also in the study of the laws of nature such as gravity, light, cosmology and so on.

If the science books hidden by Ashoka had really been so valuable, they should have been preserved openly, possibly in some well-defended temple, and used to protect the people from wars, because in order to avoid the damage of war it is not sufficient to disarm one's people thus making them more vulnerable to external aggressions and unable to defend themselves - a handicap that obviously affected also (and especially) those who were institutionally charged with protecting the kingdom. In Vedic times the *kshatriyas* utilized very powerful weapons but were bound by a strict ethical or honor code and were therefore able to easily fight back the aggressions of more primitive invaders, who had less effective weapons. Vedic tradition however informs us that also the more powerful dynasties of Asuras had terrible weapons, and then the *kshatriyas* had to work harder in fighting, using the most appropriate weapons, without which they would have to succumb to the evil aggressors.

About the specific identification of the sciences offered by Talbot Mundy, it is certainly a baseless speculation. The most absurd in the list is "propaganda", because the Vedic system was built on principles totally opposed to that concept; the same applies to the "science of communications" that had no reason to exist. Propaganda and communications become "sciences" when there is a need to convince the mass of people to support a government that does not deserve to be supported, winning votes for the drama of general elections and controlling the mass media to condition public opinion, but in the Vedic system there were no mass media or political elections. What actually existed was diplomacy and *intelligence services*, amply used by the government to deal with foreign nations and to collect information and opinions circulating among the public or among the government officers or courtiers. In this field, what most resembles the modern concept of "propaganda and communications" consists in counter-intelligence activities, which means implanting distorted information among enemy spies, but in ancient times this action was never directed towards people in general because it would not have been useful or feasible, considering the social and government structure we already mentioned.

In order of improbability microbiology follows, because Vedic medicine did not consider "microbes" as the most important threat to health, and although it insisted on hygiene especially in the daily routine and inter-personal contacts, on cleanliness and freshness for foods water and living spaces, on the disinfection of instruments especially in surgery, and even using the technique of inoculation, priority was given to the creation of a favorable environment, to the control of food intake and to psycho-physical strengthening in order to keep the immune system in good conditions. Two other unlikely branches are "gravity" and "light", because such fields did not exist separately but were integral part of a wider study of physics and cosmology, or the natural laws of the universe. Finally, considering that ancient peoples and especially Indians gave much greater importance to the science of sound, its complete absence in Talbot's list makes it even more suspicious.

As it often happens, the imaginative speculations by Talbot take inspiration from a grain of truth, and specifically from the Navaratna ("nine jewels") at the court of the ancient king Janaka of Mithila: nine great sages who assisted him as advisors and experts in Vedic knowledge, but that do not correspond at all to the data offered by Talbot and his followers. These sages were not "unknown" or secret at all, because everybody knew them very well; one of the "jewels" was a woman, the famous Rishika Gargi, so also the idea of the "nine *men*" does not apply. Later the tradition was taken up by the famous king Vikramaditya, whose "nine jewels" were Kalidasa (the famous poet), Amarasimha, Dhanvantari, Ghatakapara, Kshapanaka, Shanku, Varahamihira, Vararuchi and Vetala bhatta. In even later times two kings of Nadia in Bengal - Raja Lakshmana Sena (1178-1206) and Raja Krishnachandra (1727-1772) - found a smaller number of candidates and had to content themselves each with a group of Pancharatna ("five jewels"), among which the most famous was the poet Jayadeva, author of *Gita Govinda*; among the other "jewels" are mentioned Gopal Bhara, Bharatachandra Raya and Ramprasad Sena.

Regarding the science of medicine, we can mention the *Susruta samhita*, of which there is still a manuscript dated 600 BCE but with much more ancient references: it contains the details of over 300 types of surgical operations, from cesarian birth to cosmetic surgery (using skin from the cheeks to reconstruct nose, ears and lips) and brain surgery, to the use of probes (*eshya*) and the extraction of fluids (*visravya*), the implant of artificial limbs and removal of stones and cataract. The list of the instruments includes 125 varieties of scalpels, lancets, needles, catheters and so on; also non-invasive techniques were used by means of light and heat. The *Bhoja Prabandha* describes a surgery performed in 927 CE on king Bhoja to remove a brain tumor: the operation was successful and the patient recovered. In the treatises that carry their names, Srusruta and Charaka speak about metabolism, genetics, immune system, general anestesy and other branches of medicine.

Some of the traditional physicians expert in the *Ayur Veda* ("the science of life") still today are able to make a correct and complex diagnosis simply by examining the pulse of the patient. The science of acupuncture and acupressure, transplanted to China with great success, originated in India from the science of *yoga*, that precisely details the 72,000 *nadis* (meridians) and the many *marmas* (nodes) besides the famous *chakras*, that we could compare to "electrical plugs" of the pranic energy. The knowledge of these aspects of the subtle energy physiology of the human body was used not only in medicine, but also in the study of hand to hand combat, as we still see today in the tradition of *kung fu* and other similar martial arts that survived in the far east.

And speaking of *prana*, we can spend a few lines also to remember Nikola Tesla (1856-1943) who adopted this definition as well as the word *akasha* ("space" in Sanskrit), to describe the universe as a cinetic system full of energy that one can tap from any place. According to Leland Anderson, founder of Tesla Society, and to the information collected in the files of the Nikola Tesla Musem, Tesla met Swami Vivekananda (1863-1902) traveling in the west, starting from a speech at the Parliament of Religions that was held in Chicago, USA, in 1893, where Vivekananda met several scientists. However, there is not even a slightest mention of Tesla ever coming in contact with any extraterrestrials.

Nikola Tesla was deeply impressed by his discussions with Vivekananda especially in regard to Sankhya, so much that he started to use Sanskrit words in his studies on physics and became vegetarian. Because Tesla is one of the great geniuses pushed into oblivion by the dominant academic and political system, it is worth to present a few lines to present his work. After studying at the universities of Graz in Austria and Prague in Czechoslovakia, he moved to Strasburg where in 1883 he built the first induction electric motor on a design he had been working at for years. In 1886 the invented arc lighting, in 1888 he made the first electric generator; in the same year he sold to George Westinghouse, of the Westinghouse Electric and Manufacturing Company, his patent for alternating current electrical systems. In 1889 Tesla constructed the first system of electrical conversion and distribution by oscillatory discharges, and in 1890 a high frequency current generator. In 1900, in Long Island (USA), he started to build a tower for wireless radio transmission to freely circulate message, news, images, weather bulletins and so on, with a financement of 150,000 dollars supplied by the American J Pierpont Morgan; for some unspecified reason, at some point Morgan stopped the flow of money and the project was abandoned.

In 1903 Tesla registered patents numbers 723,188 and 725,605 on the fundamental principles of logical systems and computer circuits; in 1927 he registered patent number 223,915 for an airplane with electrical engine. In 1931 at Buffalo, New York, Tesla successfully experimented a system of electrical power for a Pierce Arrow automobile; the engine of 80 horse power and 1,800 rounds per minute, size about 100 cm x 76 cm, was connected to a mysterious box made by Tesla himself; its size was 60x30x15, with two small bars about 8 cm long jutting out. Without any fuel or external power supply, the car reached 144 km/h (90 miles per hour) and continued to run for one week. In 1943 the Supreme Court of the United States (case 369 of 21st June 1943) recognized Tesla full property rights for the invention of the radio, rejecting the claims of Guglielmo Marconi.

Among the other inventions attributed to Tesla we may mention the first hydro-electric plant (experimented at the Niagara waterfalls), the system of fluorescent lighting based on neon, the rotating magnetic field (that was later developed as gyroscope), and the system for refrigeration and cryogenics. At his death, FBI confiscated all his papers, therefore our work of research and verification must necessarily be limited to the examination of the many crumbs that were left around, including a famous article published on 13th July 1930 on the *Milwaukee Sentinel* and entitled *Man's Greatest Achievement*. Here is a brief extract: "Long ago he (man) recognized that all perceptible matter comes from a primary substance, of a tenuity beyond conception and filling all space - the Akasha or luminiferous ether - which is acted upon by the life-giving Prana or creative force, calling into existence, in never ending cycles, all things and phenomena."

The discussion on the intimate nature of matter at the subtle level and nuclear physics is not within the reach of the masses, therefore the two subjects that are most interesting for the public in regard to ancient Indian technology are usually the weapons (*astra*) and the airplanes or space ships (*vimana*). But even these two fields of study are very difficult to analyze for westerners who are still firmly rooted in mechanistic science, because Vedic technology is based on a totally different perspective on the laws of nature. For this reason many alienists fall in the classic *techno-babble* trying to "explain the legends" according to a terminology that is more familiar for them, speaking of radar, cameras, laser, plasma, atomic bombs, radiations, anti-gravity devices, microwaves and so on, just as the "experts" speak of Yoga as a gymnastic technique combined with breating exercises, that is supposed to increase physical well-being and mental relaxation. Unfortunately this reductive mechanistic mentality has also penetrated in India, obstructing really serious and important research and deviating the interest of the public and the government towards a grossly materialistic direction, from which it is impossible to understand the true meaning of Vedic civilization and apply it in practice.

The technology described in the Vedic texts is in fact based on the scientific development of human potential and requires the conscious control of vibrational frequencies (called respectively *vaikhari*, *madhyama*, *pasyanti* and *para*, meaning gross sound, subtle or etheric sound, sub-sound and super-sound) and electro-magnetic fields (which Tesla called *prana*) that we could superficially call "biological" (but do not depend on the functions of the gross material body) capable of altering the status of matter at atomic and sub-atomic levels (Tesla's *akhasa*), while mechanistic science of the western model proceeds in the exactly opposite direction, trying to "improve" the human being with means that are artificial, mechanical, cybernetic, genetic and so on.

This pushes research and empirical experimentation towards an increasing dependence of the human being on the machines, while the Vedic system considers machines (*yantra*) as simply vehicles and instruments. Without understanding this fundamental point it is impossible to understand the technology of ancient India, even when its interpretation tries to use the idea of the very mysterious and elusive "aliens" or puttering around with the so-called *reverse engineering* of concepts and descriptions offered by the Sanskrit texts.

It is true that a serious study of the ancient texts can help us find useful ideas, as demonstrated in the last decades by several Indian scientists (and maybe not just Indian ones), but it is essential to keep the widest possible vision, instead of blindly following the recipes of the "witch potions" circulated by some authors in the field, as we will see later when speaking of the famous *Vimanika shastra*. The required approach is identical to the alchemic science, that is largely symbolic and utilizes elements that are presently unknown or non-existent; a superficial simpleton that fools around with the wrong ingredients and procedures because of confusing literal interpretations can still stumble upon some useful invention (such trementine or *aqua regia*, discovered by chance by an amateur alchimist) but he can also poison or degrade himself by committing abominable actions.

For the same reason it is silly to claim that there cannot have been a technologically advanced civilization thousands of years ago because we have not found heaps of non-degradable garbage such as broken computer keyboards, cement rubble, mountains of plastic packagings and other waste from a non-sustainable industrial system based on consumerism and programmed obsolescence like the present one. If the amount of non-biodegradable waste is to be considered as an evidence of civilization, we are really in trouble.

The first plastic product, bachelite, was "invented" only in 1907 (by Leo Hendrik Baekeland, apparently), yet even our retarded contemporaries have already realized that it is better to recycle and reuse plastic (and not only) rather than accumulating it as waste in garbage dumps or scatter it in the environment. The preservation and recycling-repurposing of resources and materials is certainly a much more sensible and civilized way of living: this is how ancient peoples were able to prosper for many thousands of years without spoiling the planet. What to speak of the damaged devices that cannot be repaired... even human corpses were burned and recycled as ashes into nature without filling up vast areas as graveyards.

To understand Vedic science, that is more similar to the quanta perspective than to the mechanistic perspective (although it goes even beyond quanta physics), it is not enough to manufacture devices and machines and fuels according to the logic of the 20th century, but we need to deeply understand the science of Yoga that enables human beings to develop the amazing *siddhis* ("perfections"), such as the famous *laghima*, that is the power of levitation. Here, too, it is important to understand that such *siddhis* are accessible through divine awareness, but they can also be utilized at a practical level by human beings and even by particularly powerful and intelligent Asuras.

We understand that a simplistic mentality can feel confused and perplexed by this concept especially if it finds it for the first time, starting from a vision of the world that is grossly material and "skeptical", where the concept of deity grossly defines a power that is higher than man - one of the fundamental points that perpetuate the misconception of the Aliens (especially those who are potentially malevolent) as Gods.

The intimate and deep knowledge of the material laws is an objective science, detached from personal motivations, and as such it can be studied and utilized not only by human beings but by Asuras as well, even if the ethical code of the *aryas* requires that only morally qualified students should be admitted to learn to use the most dangerous weapons. We want to highlight the fact that the weapons called "divine" (*daiva*) take such name because they are associated with the specific energy of the ontological categories of the connected Devas, and not because they were exclusively used or owned by the respective Devas. In fact we see that in many circumstances such divine weapons are used by human beings, who have intimate knowledge of the elements.

In a previous chapter we have already elaborated on the meaning of the concept of Deva as ontological category of reality that concerns every thing and every being in the universe. Because the elements exist in all bodies, and from the human position upwards it becomes physically possible to manipulate them at the subtle level, the weapons that are based on the control of the elements through awareness can be utilized also by beings that are not Devas, but they have received an adequate training. However, such training does not transform them into Devas, as unintelligent people might think.

It is at least excessive to pontificate that "the greatest part of scientific discoveries have always been designed for aggression war": it would be like saying that because some criminals use knives to attack their victims, the invention of the knife was motivated by the homicidal desire for violence, or that because there are irresponsible or stupid drivers (about 2 millions deaths each year still at present, without counting the wounded), automobiles have been specifically designed as war instrument or for mass slaughter.

The clear message of Vedic evidence indicates that scientific knowledge has always been traditionally available to human beings, whose main mission in life consists in rising to the level of *divine* knowledge and consciousness in all fields, not just for vehicles and weapons, but also for personal development and social relationships. The original system of *yajna* or rituals for the Devas has the purpose to enable human beings to *associate and cooperate* with the Devas and thus imbibe their manner of thinking: this approach is radically different from the superstitious worship offered to a more powerful being in the attempt of propitiating him or obtaining some special material advantages.

The Vedic treatises on the subject of spaceships do not specifically contain diagrams and technical descriptions of procedures for building or flying them - these things were rather demonstrated practically in a lab during apprenticeship; some alienists claim otherwise, but their theories are unfounded and simply made up from speculations and fantasies. The genuine texts, however, contain the elaboration of the theory that explains the principles of their functioning, just like we could find in university books on nuclear physics, and the special feature that makes them difficult to understand for our contemporary alienists and ufologists is the fact that Vedic science makes no distinction between physics and metaphysics - an idea that only at present is beginning to be considered valid by the general public.

For example Virabahu, the lieutenant of Kartikeya, is said to have authored a treatise on *Mahendrajala*, that some have called "the science of magic", which explains how to walk on water, fly in the air (without vehicles) and so on; this knowledge that we could define as "parapsychological" could be applied to levitation not just of one's body but also of objects (so-called telekinesis), as we find described in the texts on *vimanas*. Another mystical-practical text, compiled by Agastya Rishi, is the *Shakti tantra*, consisting of 8 chapters elaborating on the 64 *shaktis* or *yoginis* of natural elements (air, fire, sun, moon, etc) and how their knowledge enables us to modify the structure of matter.

Matanga Rishi is the author of the treatise entitled *Soudamini kala*, that explains the subtle connection between thoughts or ideas and the etheric blueprint of their tangible manifestation, that some ufologists/ alienists simplistically describe as "the science of electronics". The text also includes an elaboration on how it is possible to use the perception of the subtle level to see inside mountains or in subterranean layers, but we can say already that it is very unlikely about X Rays. Many authors have reported the idea that the "pilots" of the *vimanas* needed "to know the secrets of *mantrika* and *tantrika*", but then go about attempting (or talking about attempting) the mechanical *reverse engineering* of *vimanas* without having the least understanding of these subjects.

Regarding the correct perspective of reading of the Vedic texts, we can quote Sadaputa Das (Richard Thompson), who has explained the traditional descriptions of puranic cosmology as stereographic projections, that is a sort of flattened map of the "region" of Earth, with a diameter corresponding to the orbit of the outermost planet of the solar system (Uranus). Therefore Bhumandala is not a continent or a single planet but a vast region of space, inscribing the orbits of other planets and even the movements of the stars. An important correspondence is the famous astrolabe, or its much more complex version consisting in the Antikytera device (found in 1900 in the Aegean sea at 70 meters depth, inside a ship foundered about 65 BCE), based on a stereographic polar projection of the Earth globe, with the eclictic orbit of the Sun (the zodiac) correctly off-centered, and that enables to calculate a great number of movements of planets and stars. This device has been compared to a computer.

Weapons in Vedic India

In our contemporary society, research and experimentation of the weapons described in Vedic literature is impractical, because military technology is strictly controlled by armies and governments, and many laws prohibit or discourage the possession or utilization of weapons by the public. We are not interested in elaborating on the logic and the implications of this subject, but we want to stress that it is an important factor in the orientation of many researchers, so that ancient technology is very summarily and imprecisely explained with technologies known by the vast public (laser, plasma, atomic bombs etc) or even with the alienist perspective of the "superhuman powers of aliens". As we have already mentioned, this type of simplistic interpretation is totally off the mark.

There is no confirmation either on the claims by some authors saying that in the Indian subcontinent and especially in the Indus valley some areas are still radioactive after thousands of years from the famous wars that are supposed to have destroyed that civilization.

First of all, since the first discoveries about 100 years ago, excavations have brought to light over 1400 cities belonging to the culture that is now called "Indus-Sarasvati" because its documented extension was about 12 times greater than the entire region of ancient Egyptian and Mesopotamian cultures; alienists however continue to insist on Mohenjo Daro only, mostly because it was the most famous site at the time of Davenport and company.

Many authors and bloggers speak of an "ancient destroyed city that is still radioactive" in Rajastan, near Jodhpur - a thriving city with an old history, along which there have never been problems due to radiations of any kind. Another mysterious "ancient city" in the present Thar desert (west of Jodhpur) that according to alienists had about half a million inhabitants before being destroyed by a nuclear war, has never existed: there is absolutely no trace of such type of event, not even a vetrified pebble, and no remains of any building.

Another case often mentioned by alienists is the crater near Bombay (Mumbai), but it has been geologically dated with quite some precision at 50,000 years ago, and has all the characteristics of a meteorite crater, and no radiations.

Let us go back to the famous Mohenjo Daro. According to the alienists, the horrifying stories on the ancient atomic destruction reported by the local people say: "the lords of the sky... annihilated the city with a light resplending like one thousand suns and sounding like the roar of ten thousand thunders. From that time, anyone who ventures into the destroyed places is attacked by evil spirits (radiations) that will make him die".

Considering that Hiroshima and Nagasaki have already been reconstructed, and 70 years after the bombs they already have over one and a half million inhabitants (and no residual radioactivity), we do not find it very likely that any unfortunate person that goes near the ruins of Mohenjo Daro will instantly die after thousands of years from the supposed explosion. However, we are not told exactly which are the sources of this tale, because there is no mention of names, and if we just stop a minute to think, if really the area was seriously radioactive, there could be no "local people" in the radius of dozens or even hundreds of kilometers away. If really any local Pakistani has given this type of declarations to the ufologists, probably the villagers are still laughing about those foolish and gullible tourists.

Furthermore, in almost 100 years none of the many archeologists who have carried excavations and studies on location, and none of the heroic researchers who believe in the "ancient atomic wars" have ever suffered health damages of any kind after staying in the place long enough to conduct their studies (days, weeks, months). We remember that the first excavations at Mohenjo Daro started in 1922, under the direction of RD Banerji of the Archaeological Survey of India, 2 years after the beginning of the excavations at Harappa. During all the 1930s there has been a lot of interest, with several teams of archeologists crowding the place, under the direction of John Marshall, KN Dikshit, Ernest Mackay and many others, but nobody ever reported any radiation sickness or similar health problem. Many other expeditions continued to work assiduously for long periods until 1965, when the intensity of the digging has decreased, but only because the exposure to the weather (especially monsoon rains) of the excavated structures was starting to compromise their stability.

Nonetheless, archeologists have continued to work on site with frequent inspections, conservative interventions and salvaging, exploration with probes, mapping and other documentation work. Still in the 1980s two important projects of archeological exploration have been conducted by the teams directed respectively by German Michael Jansen (RWTH) and Italian Maurizio Tosi (IsMEO). Not even one member of all these teams has reported radiation-connected problems.

Another baseless story is about the many skeletons of ancient inhabitants that were taken by surprise by the nuclear attack and died in the street at the same time. The archeological site of Mohenjo Daro is an open place and many "non-conventional researchers" have visited it, but they did not bring back accurate and verifiable photos, while "conventional" archeologists have documented 37 skeletons (the only ones found in the area) that do not show any sign of sudden death and were not abandoned in the street but had been carefully buried at different times even at a distance of several centuries. And not even one of them shows any sign of abnormal radioactivity.

On the same alienist web pages emphatically declaring that "everything was carbonized or melted" and that "huge masses of walls and foundations have been literally vitrified", we see photos of the remains of the buildings, but these do not show any trace of carbonization or melting or vitrification, not even in a supposed epicenter of an explosion. The internet sites made by teams of professional archeologists publish a greater number of photos that have become practically of public domain, showing the excellent state of preservation of all the buildings, with long tracts of boundary walls and even brick towers up to 5 meters tall. The bricks are seen very clearly in the pictures, quite well aligned and ordered and a nice light cream color, and in fact it seems that before the excavation site was given some kind of archeological protection, the local government had amply availed itself of the ancient bricks to build the nearby railway road - and in this case, too, there were no mysterious deaths of workers or pillagers. Apart from the bricks, in the archeological site there were several terracotta figurines in a perfect state of preservation: not even one of them is vitrified or shows any signs of damage from excessive heat, as we can see from the vast collection in the museum. The constructions still had traces of door frames in painted wood, and the large swimming pool (12x7 meters) still had the layer of bitumen used to waterproof the bottom.

Some "non-conventional researchers" claim they personally had "samples examined in the laboratory at the Institute of Mineralogy at the University of Rome" and that according to the analysis the temperature to which the materials had been exposed had been "extremely high, more than 1500 degrees, which can only be explained with thermonuclear fusion".

Let us skip the fact that there are no documents proving that such laboratory exams have actually been performed. However, it will suffice to check the normal temperatures of artisan pottery ovens compared to the temperatures of nuclear explosions to understand the lack of authoritativeness and competence of those researchers. A pottery oven normally reaches 1400 degrees, and the ovens used for the delicate Sèvres handicrafts are set for 1240 degrees, while a nuclear explosion goes from a minimum of 10 MILLION degrees to 1.2 BILLIONS degrees. If the lab exames have given the claimed results, it only means that at Mohenjo Daro potters had more efficient ovens and produced handicrafts that were slightly more heat-resistant than the ones typical of our present industries.

In his book *Ancient atom bombs: Fact, fraud, and the myth of prehistoric nuclear warfare* (2011), Jason Colavito quotes the excellent and authoritative translation of the *Mahabharata* by Kisari Mohan Ganguli (*The Mahabharata of Krishna-Dwaipayana Vyasa translated into English prose*, published in Calcutta in 1888) to refute the distorted versions presented by Pauwels and Bergier, Davenport, von Däniken, David Hatcher Childress and other authors of the same stream.

Colavito brings the example of the passage quoted by Childress speaking about the destruction of the Vrishnis and Andhakas in which one unidentified Gurkha, flying on a *vimana*, throws a bomb charged with the entire power of the universe and that explodes with the radiance of 10,000 suns, in the form of an incandescent pillar of smoke and flame, that turned the entire race of the Vrishnis and Andhakas into ashes, carbonizing their bodies so that they became unrecognizable and making hair and nails fall (presumably, from the non-carbonized bodies). To escape from such terrible fire, the soldiers had thrown themselves into water to wash their own bodies and equipment. The effects of the weapon had also calcinated the birds (presumably while they were flying), cracked the pots in the kitchens and infected all the food within a few hours.

Colavito correctly remarks that this passage is not found anywhere in the *Mahabharata* and it probably was totally fabricated. The episode of the destruction of the Andhakas and Vrishnis truly is in the *Mahabharata* (Mausala parva, where *mausala* literally means "club") but it has nothing to do with *vimanas* or airships of any kind, or with nuclear weapons or bombs of any kind, with smoke or flames or radiations, and not even with a battle: it describes an episode in Dvaraka (hundreds of kilometers from Kurukshetra) many years after the end of the war. In that story, also narrated in the *Bhagavata Purana*, we see that the descendents of Krishna (who were the above mentioned dynasty or "race" of the Vrishnis and Andakas) are stricken with a curse, the *omen* (sign or symptom) of which was the appearance of a club (*mausala*) of ordinary iron, that had absolutely nothing nuclear or explosive, and that was pulverized (patiently grinding it) on the order of king Ugrasena.

The size of that club seems to have been modest, because it was "given birth" by one member of the dynasty, and its destruction does not seem to have been particularly difficult or dangerous; the ground powder and the last small bit of iron were thrown into the ocean and did not cause any apparent effect, apart from the fact that a fish ate the piece of iron but remained hale and hearty without any sign of damage until it was caught by a fisherman.

The death of the members of the dynasty of Krishna was caused, a short time later, by an angry quarrel among the men of the family, who started to beat one another to death with bamboo canes grown on the beach, but without using any atomic weapon or clubs, either special or normal. And above all, the mysterious Gurkha is never mentioned even slightly in the genuine text of the *Mahabharata*: the complete version is available on internet in pdf format, and anyone can verify directly.

Another passage incorrectly quoted as evidence of "wars among Gods with atomic weapons and spaceships" by many books and blogs on "ancient astronauts" says: "After defeating his enemy, Krishna unscathed and armed, accompanied by the kings, left Girivraja on his divine chariot". The only compatible episode is the killing of Jarasandha, narrated in *Mahabharata* (Sabha parva, chapters 20-24) as well as in the *Bhagavata Purana* (10.72.1-46); on that occasion Krishna went with his friends (and cousins) Arjuna and Bhimasena to Girivraja, the capital of the Magadha kingdom, to defeat the evil Jarasandha, who had imprisoned a great number of *kshatriyas* of royal rank and used them for human sacrifices.

In the original episode there are no spaceships or airplanes or divine weapons of any sort, because although the chariot is called "divine" (and probably it was a beautiful chariot indeed) this does not mean that it was flying: in fact the three friends arrive inconspicuously and incognito dressed as ordinary *brahmanas* and approach Jarasandha to ask him for a donation. If they had arrived in grand style as Gods/gods, flying in the sky and loaded with amazing (or even non-amazing) weapons, they would certainly not have gone unnoticed as we see from the text. Jarasandha agrees to grant their request and Krishna asks for a wrestling combat: only at that moment the tyrant recognizes his visitors and chooses to fight with Bhima, who is the biggest of the three. Then we see a wrestling match, *mano a mano* and without any weapon, and finally Bhima kills his opponent merely with brute force: with one foot he pins down the foot of his opponent to the ground and tears his body into half. At that point, without any further fighting, the three friends go to release the 95 surviving prisoners and leave the city in good terms with the new king, Jarasandha's son.

Vedic literature offers a list of "divine weapons" based on the subtle manipulation of matter at the atomic and sub-atomic levels as we have already mentioned: the *chakras* ("discs") of Dharma, Kala and Vishnu, the *trishula* ("trident", of Shiva and also of Durga and many others), the Brahma sira ("head of Brahma"), the Vajra (of Indra, with an effect described as "thunderbolt"), the Indrajala (a "water" weapon), the Narayana astra and Pasupata astra (one of Vishnu and the other of Shiva, with effects respectively of extreme heat and extreme cold), the Daruna (of Bhaga), the Vayavya (of Vayu, that stops vibrations and wind), the Salila and Saila (that neutralize the illusions of fire and wind), the Haya sira ("horse head"), the Krauncha ("heron"), the Aishika ("grass blade") and the Brahmastra ("the arrow of Brahma"), the two Shaktis ("potencies") of Vishnu and Shiva respectively, the *pasa* ("nooses") called Dharma, Kala and Varuna presided respectively by Yamaraja, Bhairava and the Deva of the ocean, the *ashani* ("missiles") called Suksha ("disseccator") and Ardra ("drencher"), the *astra* ("arrows") of Pinaka (Shiva) and Narayana, the one of Agni (called Shikari, "the tower") and the one of Vayu (called Prathama, "main").

Other extremely powerful weapons were the "clubs" called Kankala Musala ("beater"), Kapalasaka ("skull", of Yama) and Kankana ("golden"), the weapon of the Vidyadharas, the one of the Pisachas, those of Gandharvas called Mohana ("that confuses"), Prasvapana ("that creates sleep") and Prasamana ("that pacifies anger"), and the *astra* ("arrows") called Varshana ("that brings rain"), Soshana ("that dries up"), Santapana ("that enflames"), Vilapana ("that dissolves"), Tamasa ("that brings darkness"), Mayamaya ("that dissipates the effects of illusions"), Tejaprabha ("that radiates"), Sisira ("that freezes"). The Naga pasa causes the loss of consciousness, and the Nadana and Murchadhana create confusion and loss of psycho-physical control. A Sabda-veditva seems to be capable of hitting a hidden target by utilizing sound.

What is not found in the actual literature is the Kamaruchi, that several ufologists quote copying one another as the "intelligent arrow" that goes where one wants. Actually the word *kamaruci* or *kamaruchi* literally means "taste for amorous attraction" and is mentioned in Sanskrit texts as the arrow of Smara (also called Kamadeva or Manmatha, a sort of Indian Cupid) by which the person struck with the arrow is overwhelmed by love lust. It is never mentioned in reference to battles. Specifically, the Kamaruci is mentioned in the *Ramacharita manasa* by Tulsidas, in verse 204: *aratha na dharama na **kama ruci** gati na cahati nirabana, janama janama rati rama pada yaha baradanu na ana*, "I have no liking for wealth nor for religious merits nor for sensuous enjoyment nor again do I seek the state of perfect and perpetual calm. Birth after birth let me have devotion to Sri Rama's feet: this is the only boon I ask and nought else" (Gitapress, Gorakhpur, India).

The Brahmastra is sometimes described as a nuclear weapon, but in fact it is radically different from the bombs of modern western science: first of all it is much more controllable and can be withdrawn or concentrated into a very small area. The action on the nucleus and the sub-atomic particles is very subtle and precise, with temporary and very limited effects, because it does not produce radiations of a nuclear type or pollution of the water sources, harvests or plants. The example of *brahmastra* launched by Asvatthama against Parikshit (at the end of the Kurukshetra war, as described in *Mahabharata*, Sauptika parva, chapter 15, and in *Bhagavata Purana*, 1.8.8-17) was aimed at hitting the fetus still in the womb without causing damage to the mother, and in fact the mother, Uttara, offers to sacrifice her own life in exchange for the life of the unborn child, asking the weapon to strike her instead of the child. A nuclear bomb or missile like those from the 20th or 21st century western technology would not make any difference between a fetus or its mother, and indeed it would annihilate everyone in the radius of many kilometers, so Uttara's prayer would have made no sense at all.

The properties and power of the *astra* (divine weapons) can seem legendary to those who do not know the precise and deep explanations on atomic and sub-atomic reality of matter offered by the science of Yoga, that enable those "paranormal powers" that modern western science is still unable to explain and that reside in the considerable portion of the brain that the vast majority of today's population never utilizes (from 70 to 85% depending on the individuals).

At the level called *cittakasha*, the vibrational space on which human awareness can operate, the sound (*mantra*) can be modulated and applied with a logic similar to the laser instruments, that concentrate simple light beams into a truly terrible weapon. Already ordinary sound is more powerful than ordinary light, so much that certain tones are able to break glass and move objects even at a considerable distance; let us imagine what could be produced by scientific modulation applied with the required knowledge and practice to the modification of the simpler and more primary elements.

Thus we have the Agneyastra that produces the phenomenon of self-combustion (presently acknowledged as possible even spontaneously, albeit in very rare cases) and the Varunastra that condensates atmospheric humidity causing sudden precipitations in the absence of clouds. The descriptions of the Vayuvastra seem to suggest a telekinetic manifestation where a sort of "wind" is created to knock opponents down; however we must understand that such "wind" is not necessarily the ordinary physical manifestation that moves sails, but could also be a sort of kinetic energy (*chi*) of which the martial arts in the far east still have some notion. Obviously the use of such techniques requires extreme preparation with tireless practice in the course of several years. The *mantras* of the *astras* require a minimum of 50 billion repetitions to attain perfection.

We will not elaborate on detailed lists of the different weapons, because apart from enriching our vocabulary, it would not be very useful to better understand the issue we are talking about. Furthermore, it would be impossible to give a detailed explanation of all the "conventional" weapons such as swords, spears, maces, nooses of various sorts, that according to the descriptions do not seem primitive at all, so we will just make a short elaboration. For example, we can mention that traditional texts list 43 varieties of throwing or shooting weapons, 53 types of weapons that can be retrieved after throwing, and in this context, 11 ways to throw the *pasa*, described as a lethal noose with a triangular shape. The length of the typical sword is described as 180 cm or 4 *hasta* - the Indian cubit, corresponding to 45 cm or 18 inches, or 24 *angula* or Indian "fingers", measured approximatively from the elbow to the tip of the medium finger.

It is also important to notice here that the bows mentioned in Vedic texts are described as hugely powerful instruments, massive and extremely heavy, capable of shooting a great variety and often a considerable simultaneous number of projectiles with a speed and a penetration force greater than our contemporary fire arms. The iron used for the conventional weapons could be of various qualities, listed as black (from Anupa), white (from Sataharana), golden (from Kalinga), blue (from Gujarat), grey (from Maharastra), pinkish (from

Karnataka) and "oily" (from Kambhoja); the knowledge of these metals has been lost, but we can imagine that such differences could refer to the quality of the mineral and also to its processing, as for example in the production of steel. We remember that still in the 16th century of the present era the Indian steel produced with traditional methods at Konasamudram, Gatihosahalli and Kodumanal in Tamil Nadu was exported to China, Arab countries and even Europe. For blades and tips, brass and bronze were also used, while for hilts various metals including gold as well as bamboo, horn and so on. Some weapons also used gems such as diamonds, that also had a functional logic and were not just decorative.

The *Ayur Veda* explains that surgical instruments were in carbon-treated steel, to make them more resistant and sharper; naturally the same process was used to temper and sharpen conventional weapons, that acquired a legendary quality and value and became practically indestructible. The process is described in *Loha shastra* by Patanjali Rishi and *Brihat samhita* by Varahamihira. Evidence of this very ancient science is still surviving in some extraordinary artefacts, such as the famous iron pillar of Delhi that we have already mentioned (with reference to von Däniken), but also others such as the pillar of Ashoka at Mehrauli (pure iron of electrolythic quality), the pillar at Kodachadri in Karnataka, the pillar at Dhar in Madhya Pradesh, and the beams of the Sun temple at Konark in Orissa: they are all made of iron and all are extraordinarily rust-free, in spite of several centuries of exposure to the elements - in the case of Konark particularly destructive because of the high percentage of salt and humidity in the air near the ocean, that in the period of a few days seriously damages normal iron and over a few months even steel and stainless steel (produced in modern western industry), as we have seen personally.

Various texts lists also 27 types of war machines, both mobile and fixed, some to shoot arrows, stones and different types of projectiles, others to demolish the war machines of the opposite army, and even a fire extinguisher on wheels. Foot soldiers were armed with shields and bows as tall as men, and used equally long arrows. The war chariots were often huge, 15 meters high and 10 to 16 meters wide, and carried a complete weapon arsenal. The *Harivamsa* mentions the chariot of Tata Danava, saying that it had 8 wheels. Besides the chariot warriors (classified according to their level as *eka rathi, maha rathi* etc), there were foot soldiers, horsemen and elephant-mounted divisions. The elephants carried 6 warriors each, were protected by a group of horsemen, and their training included *upasthana* (jumping over raised obstacles), *samvartana* (avoiding pits and trenches), *samyana* (marching straight or in zig-zag fashion), *vadavadha* (attacking horsemen and foot soldiers), *hastiyuddha* (fighting against other elephants), *nagarayana* (demolishing buildings), *samgramika* (keeping formation in battle).

Another category includes the chemical and mechanical weapons and explosives, called *agnibana* ("fire projectiles"), that were of 3 types, as described by Ramachandra Dikshitar in his *War in ancient India* (1944), compiled from a series of lectures at the Annamalai University; according to his research the *agni dharana* was an incendiary projectile, while the *visvasaghati* was an explosive projectile of the *shrapnel* type. Dikshitar quotes *Atharva Veda* (1.16.4) mentioning fire arms with lead projectiles, *Matsya Purana* (149.8) speaking of lead bullets (called *ayoguda*), and especially more technical texts such as *Vasistha Dhanur Veda* and *Sukra niti sara*, from which we can make a list of fire arms in the categories called Naracha, Nalika and Sataghni. The Nalika was a hand gun used by foot soldiers and horsemen, while the Sataghni ("killer of 100") was a cannon on wheels that shot iron balls. The *agnichurna* ("fire powder") was gun powder: the composition was 4-6 parts of saltpeter, 1 of sulphur and 1 of coal powder made from special trees (such as *arka* or *sruhi*). In the *Mahabharata* (Vana parva, 42.5) fire arms are called *aurva*; in *Niti Cintamani* the gun powder (of which effects and composition are described) is called *aurvagni* ("fire of Aurva") from the name of Aurva Rishi (the *guru* of the emperor Sagara, an ancestor of *avatara* Rama) who was considered an expert in the field.

Vimanas

About the *vimanas*, the space ships or airplanes, or "flying chariots" of which the literature of ancient India offers many examples, many authors have caused quite some confusion, presenting as genuine quotes their personal elaborations motivated by the intention of proving their theories, often in open contradiction with the authentic texts, as we have already seen also with reference to the weapons and the identities of the characters of the stories and their motivations.

The famous *2000 a.C.: Distruzione atomica* ("2000 BC: Atomic destruction") by David Davenport and Ettore Vincenti, published in Italy in 1979, claims that the description of the *brahmastra* weapon in the *Mahabharata* refers to an atomic war unleashed by the *vimanas* of the Devas and that destroyed Lanka, identified as Mohenjo Daro: quite some hodgepodge, considering that the *Mahabharata* speaks about the battle of Kurukshetra, and that site is only a few kilometers from Delhi, ancient Hastinapura the capital of the Kauravas - a battle in which not even one single Deva took part. On the other hand, the battle of Lanka is described in the *Ramayana* and was beyond the ocean after the southern point of India, in the island of Lanka, that after a brief colonial period as Ceylon returned to its ancient name. We know from sure from the *Ramayana* (in all its various versions) that Rama and the Vanaras reached Lanka walking on a bridge of stones on the ocean (the remains of the bridge still exist and can be seen even in the satellite images of NASA), while Mohenjo Daro is in present-day Pakistan, where nobody could honestly place an island or see an ocean, not even during the stormiest and wettest rainy seasons.

As we have already noted, another problem consists in the frequent equivalence proposed by the alienists that identifies the entire civilization of the Indus valley with the single site of Mohenjo Daro, concluding that the atomic destruction of that place (something that has certainly not been demonstrated) brought about the same result, possibly simultaneous, of all the other cities of the same culture. That is a totally unfounded imaginative projection as we can see from the great number of other sites excavated after the discovery of Mohenjo Daro; many archeologists have also started to think that similar evidence could be also under the cities that are still inhabited, such as Benares (Varanasi/ Kasi), Allahabad (Prayaga), Mathura, Delhi (Hastinapura), Ayodhya (under the notorious Babri mosque the remains of a very ancient temple have already been excavated) and still more, named in the scriptures of Vedic times.

In his imaginative elaborations, Davenport mentions the "aryans", that according to his ideas in 2000 BCE were at war against the Mongols (not the Dravidians) original inhabitants of the Indus valley: because the aliens wanted to exploit the gold mines of the region, they made an alliance with the "aryans" and helped them by destroying their enemies of the Mongolian fort at Mohenjo Daro/Lanka. We remember here that the only point that has been historically verified and free from any controversy and doubt, is that the Mongols have always been nomadic and their presence was characteristic of the Caucasus region: the alienist interpretation by Davenport does not even make sense according to the famous Aryan Invasion Theory created by colonial indologists, by which the nomads coming from the Caucasus were the invader "aryans" that destroyed the civilization of Mohenjo Daro.

But let us return to the *vimana* subject: Davenport declares that the word *vimana* literally means "inhabited artificial bird", but while actually the word *vi* as a noun that can be used for "a bird" (although in various texts it is also applied to horses, arrows and wind as we can see from the dictionary, and is connected to *vyoma*, "space"), it is more often used as adverbial prefix with the primary meanings of "separating, distancing" or even in the sense of "distinction by excellence" to intensify the accompanying concept, and appears in many popular words such as *vimala* ("without impurities"), *visuddha* ("perfectly pure"), *vijnana* ("beyond theoretical knowledge"), *visesha* ("special") and *videsha* ("foreign country"), just to make some examples. On the other hand, *man* or *mana* means "measure", and also "respect", and can also be used in computer language to indicate a basis for measuring or programming. It is however certain that nothing in the etymological derivation contains the meaning of "artificial" or "inhabited".

Sanskrit dictionaries give an etymology of "*vimana*" connected to the meaning of "measuring" and "crossing over" and no mention of the meaning of *vi* as "bird": if we want to make imaginative projections of meaning, we could theorize that the literal meaning of "measured" refers to the precise measuring required for the construction and functioning of these vehicles, or/and to the idea of a vehicle that can measure or cover a space through a journey. In the course of centuries, the word *vimana* has come to be applied to the main tower of the Indian temples, considered the airplane of the Deity residing in the temple, especially because the *vimanas* of Vedic literature are often described as veritable flying palaces of many storeys, where travelers could live for long periods. This concept seems to confirm the alienists' theories, but as we have already said, such wonderful airships were not used only by Devas: depicting them in religious architecture was an act of devotional offering of something that was considered very valuable, and not strictly divine. According to the same logic, the images of the Deities in the temples are decorated with jewels and flower garlands, they are presented with offerings of food, lamps, scents and other pleasurale things produced or grown by terrestrials on our planet. This interpretation of the *vimanas* as objects of great value (but not extraterrestrial) is confirmed by the popular use of the word to indicate a terrestrial palace for regular emperors not of divine descent. If we want to be more precise, we should use another Sanskrit word that is much more specific: *gaganauka*, that in the dictionary is translated simply as "space ship". Same for the concept of "astronaut", that in Sanskrit is translated as *vyomachara* ("one who travels in the sky space").

Many space ships are described in various passages of *Puranas* and *Itihasa* in connection with Asuras such as Maya Danava, Drona-mukha, Sumbha and others, and not only about human beings and Devas. Two stories that sound like the modern *alien abductions* are those respectively of Aniruddha and Duryodhana, and no Deva is involved in either.

Aniruddha was a terrestrial human being, the grandson of Krishna, who was carried to the kingdom of the Asura Bana by Citralekha, friend and confidante of Usha, the daughter of Bana, who wanted to meet the very handsome Aniruddha. Immersed in a deep sleep, Aniruddha was taken into the private apartment of Usha, a non-violent abduction that started a wonderful love affair and ended with an official wedding in spite of the understandable perplexity of the concerned relatives. The story is rather different from the *cliché* circulated by the alienists, by which the lusty male Devas kidnap terrestrial women.

Duryodhana, another terrestrial human being, was born with the special "technical" assistence of grand uncle Vyasa but had no divine

DNA; when Duryodhana's wife Gandhari was having a miscarriage, Vyasa (son of Satyavati grandmother of Dhritarastra the husband of Gandhari) had collected the damaged fetus (that was one only) and used its cells (not the mother's ova) to clone 100 brothers, each of them carried to term *in vitro* - exactly the opposite of what happens in artificial insemination. Duryodhana was considered the eldest of the 100 clones, and dedicated his life to try to eliminate the Pandavas (Arjuna, Yudhisthira, Bhima, Nakula, Sahadeva) who were the legitimate heirs to the throne. After a particularly humiliating defeat, Duryodhana had decided to commit suicide in his depression, but a Danava spaceship driven by a Rakshasi named Kritya came to pick him up and took him to Patala for a meeting, where the Asuras proposed an alliance for world conquest (even then).

The famous *pushpaka vimana* of Ravana is described not only in *Ramayana* but in many other texts about the story of prince Rama. In the *Ramayana* we find *vimanas* mentioned as airships in the *kandas* (sections) Ayodhya chapters 5, 7, 15, 17, 27, 88, Aranya 32, 35, 42, 48, 50, Kiskindha 50, 51, Sundara 7, 8, 11, 12, Yuddha 8, 20, 123, 125, 127, 130, and Uttara 6, 41, 82. Besides the mentions in the descriptions of Lanka, in the battle between Rama and Ravana, in the return of Rama to the city of Ayodhya and in Ravana kidnapping Sita, we also find them in a battle between Lava (one of the two sons of Rama, born several years after his return to Ayodhya) and Chandraketu, that is stopped by Rama's intervention.

Various types of flying vehicles are mentioned: the *pushpaka* was very big (it required a landing field) and fast (Vibhisana suggests departing from Lanka after the midday lunch so that they could reach Ayodhya before night, so we can estimate a speed of about 2,500 km/hour) and produced a loud roar, while the vehicle used to kidnap Sita was obviously small and silent because its arrival went completely unnoticed. Also Indrajit the son of Ravana had a personal airplane, and other Rakshasas in the city claim they are capable of air combat. Lanka is described as "studded with space ships" (Yuddha kanda, 20) and still today there are several localities in Lanka (the island known as Ceylon, not Mohenjo Daro) that carry ancient names connected to the concept of spaceships and airports: Weragantota ("landing place" in Sinhalese language), Mahiyangana, Usangoda on the south coast, Gurulupotha at Mahiyangana, one Wariyapola ("a place to land and take off") at Kurunegala and another at Mattale, and Thotupola Kanda (literally "harbor" and "rock") at Hoton Plains that is a flat high land on a mountain range, almost 200 meters above sea level (it seems quite unlikely that sea boats were involved). The modern airport in Colombo is named Videsha Bandaranayake Guwan Thotupola, in a parallel similar to the use of the word *vimana* ("Bengalized" into *biman*) to refer to airplanes and even for the name of Bangladesh national air carrier, Biman Airlines.

After the Pushpaka vimana, the most famous airship in Vedic scriptures is the Tripura vimana taken down by Shiva. The story tells that the Asura Taraka had three sons, named Vidyunmali, Tarakasha and Viryavana (later called collectively Tripurasura), who had a triple space ship built by the famous Maya Danava. It was a mother ship carrying many smaller aircrafts, and the three parts of the huge ship were respectively made of gold, silver and iron, and each was as big as a city. In this case, too, there is no basis to speak of an "aerial battle between Devas" because in a first stage the three Asuras roamed around the universe causing destruction and terror on various planets without getting any opposition to their aggression. In the second stage the Devas, afflicted by that intolerable situation, approached Shiva to ask for his help, and he did not even need to get on an airplane to execute his mission, because from land he shot one single arrow that instantly destroyed the entire structure. In order of popularity of the quotes we have Salva's airplane, with which a terrestrial man attacks Dvaraka, the city of Krishna (*Bhagavata Purana* 10.72.21-22, 10.76), as we have already analyzed in previous chapters.

King Citraketu (human and terrestrial) travels around the universe with his space ship (*Bhagavata Purana* 8.10.16-17), from which, flying low over the Kailasa, he sees Shiva and Parvati sitting together in affectionate attitude, in the company of many sages. Always in the *Bhagavata Purana* we see Kardama Muni creating a beautiful flying palace on which he goes on a cruise to visit various planets in the company of his wife Devahuti for a late honeymoon (*Bhagavata Purana* 3.21.41); still with reference to Devahuti, it seems that a Gandharva traveling on his space ship saw the beautiful Devahuti on a terrace and was so overwhelmed that he fell from his aircraft. A space ship driven by Vishnudutas (literally "servants/ messengers of Vishnu") arrives on Earth to pick up Dhruva to take him to the polar star, where he is given a new residence (*Bhagavata Purana* 4.12.19, 4.12.26) and in another episode Maharaja Nriga boards a space ship going to the heavenly planets (*Bhagavata Purana* 10.64.30). Vishnudutas on a space ship also come to get Ajamila (*Bhagavata Purana* 6.1.44) to take him to Vaikuntha, which in our universe is identified as Svetadvipa or Dhruvaloka. The description of the Vaikuntha planets (*Bhagavata Purana* 2.9.13) includes many beautiful space ships roaming around in the universe.

The use of space ships appears implicit on other occasions, especially in regard to the descriptions of Daityas conquering the various planetary systems, specifically Hiranyakasipu (*Bhagavata Purana* 7.4.5-7) and Bali Maharaja (*Bhagavata Purana* 8.15). A similar implication refers to the battle between Devas and Asuras in which Indra fights against Vritra (*Bhagavata Purana* 6.10.24-28) with weapons thrown from the sky.

The *Mahabharata* speaks of *vimanas*, but not particularly about the battle of Kurukshetra, where the only instance is the fight between Karna and one Rakshasa (Drona parva, 176.59-86). Another episode, with more details and more extended, shows Arjuna who, in preparation for the war, goes to the heavenly planets where he will help his father Indra to destroy Hiranyapura ("city of gold"), a space settlement of Asuras of the clans of Nivatakavachas, Kalakeyas and Paulomas (Vana parva, chapters 168, 169, 172, 173); on that occasion Matali the pilot of Indra's ship comes down to Earth to pick up Arjuna and take him to Indraloka. Several texts tell the story of king Harischandra (also spelled Harishchandra) and his son Trishanku; for example in the *Mahabharata* (Sabha parva, chapter 12) Narada explains to Yudhisthira that Harischandra, who lived in Treta yuga (thousands of years earlier) and was Rama's ancestor, was the only terrestrial accepted as an official member of Indra's assembly (*sabha*) on the heavenly planets. Harischandra's son Trishanku is famous for having tried to access the planets of the Devas without their permission - he was blocked half way (we could say, at the border) and his mentor Visvamitra intervened to have him allowed through, but unsuccessfully.

Various texts speak of the personal spacecraft of the Asura Maya Danava, described in chapter 43 of *Harivamsa* as a ship with a circumference of 12,000 cubits (540 meters); in a subsequent chapter (56) of the same text we see the space ship in action during a battle between Devas and Asuras. Many passages of the *Puranas* tell these stories, and it would be impractical to give all quotes; furthermore, many other passages speak of persons, not only Devas but also Asuras, particularly powerful human beings and Vanaras, who "fly" even without any mention of vehicles (but also *not* specifying that no vehicles were used): because we know for certain from other passages that such vehicles existed as a category, we can presume that the "flight" happened in this way, unless the contrary is specified. The separation between physics and metaphysics is very subtle, because so many other passages speak of *siddhis* or mystic powers obtained through methods that seem to be "metaphysical", without forgetting the fact that even the texts speaking of mechanical vehicles state that the pilot needs to know "the secrets" of *mantra* and *tantra*. Up to which point can we separate the personal qualifications of the driver from the functioning of the vehicle? It is already very difficult for the complex technology of present-day industrialized west, but for Vedic tradition such separation is totally impossible.

Up to which historical period this branch of Vedic knowledge remained vital?

In the 3rd century BCE Kautilya (also called Chanakya and Vishnugupta), the *brahmana* advisor of Chandragupta (321-228 BCE) of the Maurya dynasty, wrote a famous treatise entitled *Artha shastra*, speaking of much more ancient teachings, with reference to the administration of society to attain *artha*, the "acquisition of valuables", which according to the Vedic system constitutes one of the four fundamental purposes of human life. Among the categories of professionals in the various fields, the text mentions the *saubhikas*, described as *akasa yodhinah*, "pilots trained in air/ space combat".

The *Panchatantra* by Vishnu Sharma, from the same period (3rd century BCE) tells a fable about a weaver from the city of Pundravardhanam who had received a gift, an aircraft in the form of Garuda (not "same as Garuda"), which he used to impersonate Vishnu for the purpose of winning the heart of a beautiful princess. The story in itself has a purely allegorical value because it aims at conveying a moral teaching and does not claim to be an historical account, but the aircraft is not presented as a magical object but a truly physical machine - and the concept must have come from some real experience.

Kalidasa, probably the most famous Indian poet, lived at the court of king Vikramaditya in Ujjain around the 1st century BCE; for mainstream academics the dates are controversial because other kings took the title of Vikramaditya, such as Chandragupta II (380-415 CE) and Yasodharman (6th century CE) and ancient Indians did not concern themselves much with historical dates or archeological evidence, because they calculated time in *yugas* and dynasty lines (by birth or by adoption). In any case, it is an historical period that preceded the "historical" middle ages.

Among the Sanskrit works by Kalidasa we can remember especially the *Abhijnanasakuntala* ("Sakuntala's memory"), the *Vikramorvasiyam* ("Urvasi and the hero"), the *Raghuvamsa* ("Raghu's dynasty") and the *Kumarasambhava* ("the appearance of Kumara", also known as Skanda or Kartikeya) and a shorter poem entitled *Meghaduta* ("the messenger cloud"). The *Vikramorvasiyam* tells the story of the Apsara Urvasi and the terrestrial king Pururava, who was a great hero: the two met when Pururava intervened to save the girl, who had been kidnapped by the Asura Kesi. The text says that Pururava jumped aboard his aircraft to pursue Kesi, defeated him and rescued Urvasi. In the *Raghuvamsa* we see Matali, Indra's charioteer or driver, observing the sights below during landing and saying, *aho udagra ramaniya prithvi*, "how beautiful Earth is, seen from up here"; even if we want to consider that Matali was simply "driving Indra's chariot", the observation could not have been made by a person who had never left the ground.

The story of Pururava and Urvasi is also found in other texts and especially in *Rig Veda* 10.95 (*Samvada sukta*), in the form of a dialogue between the two, but according to the *Mahabharata* (Adi parva, chapter 75), in spite of the biographic details, the story is considered highly symbolic and full of meanings about the balance of male and female energies. Also the *Kathasaritasagara* by Somadeva (from Kashmir, 11th century CE) tells the story of Urvasi and Pururava, presenting the earthling king who goes (apparently the concept of flying is implicit) to Indra's planet to ask him permission to marry Urvasi, who is an Apsara dancer at his court. In another story from the collection (the title literally means "flowing ocean of tales") we see two skilled craftsmen, Rajyadhara and Pranadhara; one built amphibious vehicles that could also cross the ocean, the other built an airplane that could carry 1,000 passengers. The *Kathasaritasagara* also speaks of a more ancient story (from one *Brihat katha* that is now lost) where king Padmavata of Avanti has an airplane built in the form of Garuda (the eagle that carries Vishnu); however there is not even one single verse anywhere that suggests that the actual original Garuda was a mechanical ship. There are also several ancient artistic depictions, such as the famous one in Mahabalipuram, in which we can recognize a *vimana* with faces peering from round windows.

Regarding the *Samhitas* (*Rig, Sama, Yajur, Atharva*), the quotes given by ufologists are not very precise, therefore we have decided to verify directly with the version considered most authoritative available, produced by Swami Dayananda (Arya Samaj) with the *devanagari* text and transliteration. Considering that the *Samhitas* are not technical manuals for the construction of spaceships but only contain hymns for the meditation on the Devas as ontological archetypes of the universe, we have found a good number of very interesting verses.

The word *vimana* is only found 2 times, but the word *ratha* ("chariot") is often referred to flying vehicles that go through the sky and over the oceans, travel into space, move without horses by electric energy and/or the energy of light, sun rays or "wind" (someone could say "jet propulsion"), are equipped with engines and turbines (often 6 for each chariot), vocal commands and automatic systems, use liquid fuel and carry various weapons including "fire" missiles. One hymn to Agni (Fire) speaks about its function as fuel for the production of energy and high speed movement (2.10.1). Many verses explicitly state that such wonderful vehicles are sometimes used also by human beings or that human beings express the desire to get some as gift or to use them, as we see in *Rig* 1.9.8, 1.30.17, 1.46.7, 1.52.1, 1.120.10, 11, 1.139.4, 1.140.12, 1.182.2, 4, 2.18.1, 3, 2.31.2, 4, 3.33.9, 5.31.9 11, 8.45.39, *Atharva* 20.71.14, *Sama* 377.

After excluding the references to the "heavenly chariots" of dawn, sun and wind, and the metaphors offering the image of the chariot to describe the human body, the universe, human society, life, time, the kingdom or the nation or the family, there are still dozens of verses that describe the flying vehicles of Devas such as Indra, Pusha, the two Asvins, Agni, the Ribhus and others. Even if we chose to interpret such descriptions in a purely symbolic manner without any "scientific" application, the fact remains that the comparison is clearly expressed in technological language: someone who speaks of engines, fuel, electric energy and the like, must at least have seen something of the kind somewhere, otherwise they could not use such images as a symbolic term of comparison.

We have found some imprecision in the quotes of some alienist researchers, and we would like to present the correct version:

* Tritala, as "3 storeyed vehicle" supposedly mentioned in *Rig Veda* 3.14.1. Actually the verse does not contain any mention of "*tritala*", but like several other verses it speaks of electricity (*vidyut*) as the moving force of the vehicle (*a hota mandro vidathanyasthat satyo yajva kavitamah sa vedhah, **vidyud rathah** sahasasputro agnih sociskesah prithivyam pajo asret*).

* Vidyut Ratha, that some translate as "a vehicle that operates on power"; in fact the definition of *vidyut ratha* is found in *Rig Veda* 3.14.1 (mentioned above), but the translation "on power" is rather poor, because we know that *vidyut* is electricity, and still today in modern Indian languages, the word is used to refer to thunderbolts.

* Trichakra Ratha, mentioned with reference to *Rig Veda* 4.36.1 and translated as "a three-wheeled vehicle designed to operate in the air"; the word *chakra* can have many different meanings, including "engine", which seems to be more appropriate than "wheel" in this case. A much more interesting word in the verse seems to have escaped the alienists: *anasvo* which means "without (the need of) horses", appearing at the beginning of the verse. The fact that it had no horses leads us to suspect that the correct translation of *chakra* in this context may not refer to ordinary wheels.

* The Vayu Ratha is quite correctly mentioned as "wind-powered chariot" as per *Rig Veda* 5.41.6, although the "wind" mentioned in the original verse could refer to many things, including magnetic and gravitational flows; we should remember that in other texts, *avartas* are mentioned as "vortexes of wind or energy".

* Jalayan indeed means "traveling in the water", but the word is not found in *Rig Veda* 6.58.3 as claimed by alienists. The complete verse is *yaste pusannavo antah samudre hiranyayir-antarikse caranti, tabhiryasi dutyam suryasya kamena krita srava icchamanah*; therefore it is a vehicle that moves in the ocean (*antah samudre*) as well as in space (*hiranyayih antarikse caranti*). Of couse, *jalayan* is a valid synonym, but it is not in the verse, and there are other verses that speak of vehicles moving under or above the sea.

* Kara (long first "a"), presented as the name of a machine mentioned in *Rig Veda* 9.14.1 as "a vehicle that operates on ground and in water" is actually a noun predicate meaning "one who does" or "who makes", as for example the author of an action (also *karta*). The expression of the verse is *karam bibhrat*, meaning "the creation of the universe", while the word *kara* could mean "operator" (in the sense "one who operates") while *karayana* means "vehicle carrying the operator".

Vaimanika shastra

The first clarification required to dissipate the most frequent misconceptions is that the definition of *Vaimanika shastra* (in the various spelling forms presently circulating) does not refer to a specific text with some historical date of compilation, but to any book that specifically speaks about airplanes or spaceships, as opposed to the *shastra* of other types that mention them only in passing and with reference to edifying stories or religiously based stories - such as the *shastra* we have mentioned in the previous chapters as *Ramayana, Mahabharata, Puranas* etc.

The definition also applies to the fact that the *Vaimanika shastra* is attributed to Bharadhvaja, because Bharadhvaja (sometimes written as Bharadwaja or similar variations) is one of the great Rishis of Vedic antiquity together with Kasyapa (father of the Adityas and the Daityas), Atri, Vasistha, Visvamitra, Gautama and Jamadagni (father of Parasurama). Bharadhvaja, son of Brihaspati (the priest of the Devas), is one of the authors of the hymns in the *Rig Veda* and one of the characters in the *Ramayana* (Rama and Sita go to visit him in his *ashrama*), and is also mentioned in the *Mahabharata* as the father of Drona (the martial arts teacher of the royal family of the Kauravas-Pandavas). We remember that according to Vedic tradition, several thousands of years passed between the time of Rama and the time of the *Mahabharata*.

In the Vedic system an authority in a specific field can take the name of a previous authority as a sort of honorific title, and therefore there can have been several Bharadhvajas along history, but it is not impossible that one particular person endowed with great knowledge has continued to live for thousands of years - something that Vedic tradition recognizes as within the human potential through the acquisition of the *yoga siddhis*. However, we should not be confused about the qualifying principles in Vedic scriptures, because the authority of Bharadhvaja does not have anything to do with his longevity, his parentage, or with other external circumstances: it is simply based on the value of knowledge in itself. Here it is essential to understand that the perspective of Vedic tradition is radically different from the abrahamic and post-abrahamic perspective of conventional academics: trying to make them fit together at all costs would be, to use a popular expression, like trying to fit a round peg into a square hole. It is always possible to enlarge the hole or to reduce the size of the peg to make them more compatible with each other, but they will never correspond precisely.

Bharadhvaja is also considered the author of the original text of the *Dhanur Veda*, the treatise on weapons and military science, that also speaks about air combat and therefore about airships and pilots (*vaimanika*, literally "of the *vimanas*") and about the knowledge of machines (*yantra sarvasva*). Obviously the science was not invented by Bharadhvaja himself, because Vedic knowledge is eternal and is re-established at the beginning of each age, both on Earth and on other planets, through the introspection of Rishis ("those who see") who are immensely qualified in personal realization. We cannot rule out that other great sages and scientists composed treatises on the subject in different historical periods; among alienists there is also a rumor about one *Agastya samhita* in which Agastya Rishi describes two types of airplanes, but since the *Agastya samhita* has never been available in English, and only a few fragments remain of the original Sanskrit, it is impossible to verify; from the quoted references it seems it was simply a passing mention within some edifying story, and not a technical manual. Unfortunately there is no surviving complete manuscript of Bharadhvaja's *Dhanur Veda* so we need to rely on quotes offered by other authors: this point is particularly important to understand in our verification research on *vimanas*.

The same applies also to other texts speaking about *vimanas* (that are in the general *category* of *vaimanika shastra*) but carry apparently different titles, as for example the *Samarangana sutradhara* written in Sanskrit in "historical" period by king Bhoja Paramara of Dhar (1000-1055 CE), that seems to be the most reliable among the available texts, also because there is an English version by Sanskrit scholar R Cedric Leonard, of which some interesting passages have been presented in the book *Mercury, UFO Messenger of the Gods* by William Clendenon, published in 1990. The *Samarangana sutradhara* consists of 83 chapters, dealing from architecture and planning of cities, temples and houses (*vastu shastra*) to the rules of arts and crafts (*silpa shastra*) and includes a chapter on *yantras*, a definition that in Sanskrit is rather wide and includes machineries and vehicles, and even one type of automaton or mechanical man (verses 101-107) to use as sentry, with great mobility also for fingers and wrists, neck and eyes.

The Sanskrit word *yantra* means "machine" and "vehicle", but could also refer to a geometrical diagram that carries subtle powers, material or spiritual, and that functions according to precise physical and metaphysical laws. The primary elements of the *yantra* are called *bija* ("seeds"), and in this particular context they can refer to a predominance of earth, water, air, fire or space (ether), that constitute the modality of power of the *yantra*. The earth element includes everything solid (such as metals as iron and copper and organic tissues), the water element includes everything liquid (as for example mercury, the *rasa* or the "juice" of all solid substances, solutions of all kinds and organic liquids), the air element includes everything gaseous and also whatever moves spontaneously (not just the wind but also electrical and magnetic currents, radiations, radio waves etc), the fire element includes everything hot or burning (such as acids, metabolic and biochemical processes, thermo-nuclear effects, infrared rays, friction, the heating effect of electricity etc), the ether element includes every space (both empty and full). *Samarangana sutradhara* describes various *yantras*, of which some are called *svayam vahaka*, "self-transported" or "self-moving".

In chapter 31, not less than 230 verses speak about the construction of airships that can also go under water and reach the proximity of the Sun and the stars (*suryamandala* and *nakshatra mandala*), as we see in verses 45 to 79; however there are no specific instructions on how to build or drive them (comparable to the technical manuals of our contemporary pilots) because such information is eminently practical and must be learned in the lab, through direct observation. The treatise explicitly states that such vehicles are very versatile, can take off and land also vertically, can be almost soundless (so much that one can hear the music and theatre plays that are performed on the ground) or produce thunderous roars, and have devices that enable the pilots to hide the ship and "see hidden things".

Verses 95-100 describe one type of mechanical airplane of a small size, that flies "like a bird" and can carry one pilot and one passenger, and one or two tanks of fuel called *para* ("superior"), a word that can also be used to refer to mercury. The propulsion power of the engine is described as produced by the interaction of the fuel with air and fire, but as we have seen, these definitions can also be applied to magnetic currents and to the heat generated by atomic movements, therefore the engineers who are striving to reconstruct the engine cannot count on simplistic and literal interpretations.

The idea of the shape "similar to a bird" is not characteristic of all *vimanas*, because Bhoja also describes air ships that are artistically built in the shape of chariots, elephants or horses, as we can still see in the traditional chariots of the Ratha Yatra in Puri (Orissa, India) and in the boats or floats at the Chandana Yatra in Puri. On the other hand, we see that many temples, as the famous temple of Surya at Konark, are built in the shape of chariot, with many great wheels that seem exactly like those of ordinary chariots but do not perform that function. Therefore it is not strange that actual aircrafts built to look like chariots may have wheels and artistic decorations imitating more ordinary vehicles including artificial "animals"; descriptions clearly say that such vehicle moves by itself, without any need for horses or other animals to pull it. Also engines are mentioned clearly, up to 40 per vehicle, and of 32 types, powered by friction, heat, water pressure, solar energy, or a combination of factors (*samyojaka*).

The smaller models, designed to carry a pilot and one or two passengers, are made with light wood and special alloys of copper, iron and lead. The larger models can be complex constructions, sometimes with more storeys: flying fortresses or palaces with apartments, salons, terraces, stairs and gardens, that can carry hundreds of passengers even for very long journeys. Three types of *vimanas* are mentioned: the simple "mecanical" (*krtitaka*) that function on fuel, those more complex that function on subtle principles we could compare to solar and electro-magnetic energy (*tantrika*), and some that are even more difficult to understand - the *mantrika*, based on the principles of *prana* and *akhasa*. In the first category there is a list of 25 types, in the second 56 types, in the third 32 simple ones and 25 complex. In no case *vimanas* are said to function like propulsion jets as imaginatively speculated by some authors that are totally devoid of qualifications to understand the topic; the descriptions of elephants fleeing in panic and grass uprooted and scattered away by the reactors are totally manufactured.

In 1943 (with a reprint in 1959) the Sarvadeshika Arya Pratinidhi Sabha (Dayanand Bhavan, New Delhi) published a book in Hindi language, entitled *Brihad Vimana Shastra* and compiled by Swami Brahma Muni Parivrajak (Gurukul Kangdi, Hardwar), with the support of the commodore of Indian air force SN Goyal. The material is presented as an extract from the *Yantra sarvasva* that is a part of the *Vaimanika shastra* (literally "knowledge of flying machines") attributed to Bharadhvaja Rishi (one of the great sages of Vedic times back over 5,000 years ago, as we have already seen) but in which compilation? Probably in the one dictated between 1903 and 1923 by Subbaraya Shastry "by *channeling*" and circulated in Sanskrit already from 1919 in an incomplete form, as we will see later, under the title of *Vymanika prakaranam*.

This *Brihad Vimana shastra* illustrates 339 types of land vehicles, 783 types of ships and boats and 101 types of airplanes or space crafts - of which 25 types (including the Pushpaka, famous for being the personal airship of Ravana in *Ramayana*) are *mantrika vimana* (working on sound and bio-magnetic vibrations) and are generally used in Treta yuga, 56 types (including the Bhairava and Nandaka) are *tantrika vimana* (working on what we could call nuclear energy) and are used in Dvapara yuga, and 25 types are *krtitaka vimana* (working on electrical, chemical and mechanical engines) and are used in Kali yuga, in the period when human beings have less ability to understand and manipulate matter at subtle level.

The "simple" aircrafts are elaborated in 8 chapters for a total of 3,000 verses, like in the book by Subbaraya Shastry published by Josyer in 1973, so it could be based on the same book translated in Hindi instead of English, with some added elaboration; it says that one can make vehicles unbreakable (*abhedya*), uninflammable (*adahya*) and invisible, and intercept the conversations from the cabin of other aircrafts (*para sabda graha*). The chapters called *vastra adhikarana* and *ahara adhikarana* explain respectively the type of clothing and food that are suitable for pilots and passengers. There is also mention of 6 previous texts: *Vimana Chandrika* by Narayana Muni, *Vyoma Yana Mantra* by Shaunaka, *Yantra Kalpa* by Garga, *Yana Bindu* by Vachaspati, *Kheta Yana Pradipika* by Chakrayani, and *Vyoma Yanarka Prakasha* by Dundi Natha.

Thus we see already 4 versions of the title: *Vimana shastra, Vymanika shastra, Vymanika prakaranam*, and *Brihad vimana shastra*. As we have already observed, these are probably copies or versions of the same book, that most authors or researchers consider as derived from the one published in 1973 by the International Academy of Sanskrit Research of GR Josyer, under the title *Vymaanika Shaastra Aeronautics of Maharshi Bharadwaaja*, that is also quoted by David Hatcher Childress in his *Vimana Aircraft of Ancient India and Atlantis*, still considered the primary reference source for ufologists and alienists, who often copy and paste its passages.

That book is not the publication of an ancient manuscript, but it has been compiled "by mystic channeling during visions" by Pandit Subbaraya Shastry who dictated it to his friend G Venkatachala Sharma. There are still the 23 notebooks, with the 3,000 verses in 8 chapters, hand written by Venkatachala Sharma between 1st August 1918 and 23rd August 1923, with copies sent to various libraries; it seems verified that one of those copies was sent to the Oriental

Library of Baroda (on 3rd June 1919). The drawings contained in the volume (picturing the models called Rukma, Sundara, Tripura and Sakuna) were not copied from ancient manuscripts either, but were made by one TK Ellappa (who was working in an engineering school) based on the descriptions by Subbaraya Shastry and approved by him on 2nd December 1923, however the participation of Ellappa was recognized only in 1952.

There are different opinions on the work of Subbaraya Shastry. Some accept it as a sacred scripture, compiled by a genuine Rishi and therefore not subject to mistakes, others criticize it heavily, and the situation has worsened because of the inaccurate statements of both parties. For example there are inconsistent quotes about the opinion expressed on *Vaimanika shastra* by professor Dileep Kumar Kanjilal, of Calcutta Sanskrit College: according to some authors he stated that the text had been compiled by Bharadhvaja between the 4th century BCE and the 10th century CE - this particular source even claims that the professor presented this theory at the 6th Congress of the Ancient Astronaut Society in Monaco in 1979. Another source reports instead that professor Kanjilal expressed serious doubts on the antiquity of the text and quotes a declaration as follows: "Since the transcripts of the work date from the early 20th century the authenticity of the Vaimanika Shastra may be pertinently questioned. On careful analysis it has been found that the work retained some antique features pertaining to an old Shastra."

Another scholar who became interested in the issue is one professor MA Lakshmithathachar, presented as director of the Academy of Sanskrit Research of Melkote, who is reported to have declared to journalists that his study on the *Vaimanika shastra* by Bharadhvaja was done on an ancient manuscript, that according to him was "over 1,000 years old", but nobody was able to show it, and many consider it non-existent. Others claim that the "ancient text" was discovered in 1918 (maybe they mean 1919), at the Baroda Royal Sanskrit Library, but it is not difficult to imagine where it could be coming from. Others have stated that the text of the *Vimanika shastra* by Bharadhvaja was "mysteriously found in a temple" in 1875 (apparently until that time nobody had ever noticed its existence!), while other alienists and ufologists state that there were no copies before 1918. The date of 1875 is closer to a meeting in 1885 between

Pandit Subbaraya Shastry and the astrologer B Suryanarain Rao, who in 1911 started to publish in Madras (presently Chennai) a magazine entitled *Bhowthika Kalaa Nidhi* ("the treasure of physical sciences"), of which 6 issues still exist, containing extracts of their conversations on the subject.

The most vicious critics are obviously the mechanistic scientists who shaped their beliefs on the academic dogma of old times: for example in 1974 a study by aereonautical engineers of the Indian Institute of Science in Bangalore has labeled Subbaraya Shastry's work as "*poor concoctions*" showing complete ignorance in the field of aereonautics. A NASA scientist, Ram Prasad Gandhiraman, even organized an on-line petition collecting many signatures to ask the Indian Science Congress to cancel a lecture of captain Anand J Bodas (ex director of a school for air pilots) on the subject "Ancient sciences through Sanskrit" because "it mixes mythology with science".

Some have observed that the publication of the various *Vimanika shastra* happened after the beginning of the history of flight in western countries: in 1848 the Ariel, prototype of monoplane built in England by John Stringfellow (1799-1883) was able to fly for no less than 30 meters, with a steam engine and a wing 3 meters long but without a pilot; immediately with his friend William Samuel Henson (1812-1888) he started to advertise for a future international airline named Aerial Transit Company. Those early models by Stringfellow look very similar to the structure of birds and kites and probably inspired the Sakuna vimana of K Ellappa's drawings. In 1886, France, Clement Ader (1841-1925) built the Eole, a sort of mechanical bat with a 20 horsepower steam engine and a wing span of 14 meters; the test flight was done in 1890 and the prototype rose about 20 cm from the ground, flying for about 50 meters.

In the United States, between 1904 and 1905 the famous brothers Orville and Wilbur Wright built (after many years of experiments with gliders) a "heavy" prototype with engine, that was able to fly for about 800 meters at the height of 10 meters, and in Brazil between 1906 and 1907 Santos Dumont (1873-1932) built and flew an airplane "heavier than air" called 14bis, rising for about 5 meters for a length of 60 meters in a park in Paris; the second experiment was a flight of 220 meters in 21.5 seconds.

The first useful flight was in 1914 in the United States, for 23 miles (37 km) from St Petersburg (Florida) to Tampa (Florida), replacing the ferry between the two harbors. In 1916 the Aircraft Transport and Travel (AT&T) was founded, and later developed into the British Aiways, that in 1919 attempted the first flight over the English Channel and to Paris. The British Royal Air Force was formed in 1918, while the US Air Force had already existed since 1907 but still working with balloons and dirigibles to make signals as they had done since the start of the Union Army Balloon Corps in 1894: they started to use airplanes only in 1915. In 1918 the Société des lignes Latécoère started a service between France and Spain, the Deutsche Luft-Reederei stated working in 1919 for a total of 1000 miles (about 1610 km) per year, while its national flights in Russia were subsequently managed under the name of Aeroflot. The first national airlines were the Dutch KLM (1919), the Colombian Avianca (1919), the Australian Qantas (1921) and the airlines of Czechoslovak Republic (1923); however the dates refer to the foundation and not to the beginning of commercial flights.

The famous transatlantic flight by Charles Augustus Lindbergh was in 1927, on a monoplane named *Spirit of Saint Louis*, but we are not particularly interested here in the history of great air pilots: rather we want to verify the possible impact that western aircraft technology could have had in the cultural perception of Indians about *vimanas*.

The first western airplanes arrived in India in 1929 with regular flights of the British Imperial Airways from London to Cairo, reaching Basra and Karachi (presently in Pakistan but at that time part of India) and in 1936 it was possible to fly to Calcutta when service was extended to Penang and Hong Kong. But already in 1895 Shivakar Bapuji Talpade (born in 1864 in Bombay) and his wife had given a public demonstration on the Chowpatti beach in Mumbai, showing a *vimana* with a mercury engine (allegedly) and a cylindrical bamboo structure (much more visible), that was also temporarily exhibited in the city hall by the Bombay Art Society. The functioning of that engine has been described as "with mercury ions", comparable to the device that was invented in the west by Goddard but not before 1906; obviously it was not perfect, but a rise to 500 meters (1,500 feet) of height easily supersedes the achievements of the pioneers of western aircrafts in those times.

The event, in the presence of the Maharaja of Baroda Sri Satyajirao Gaekwad and the magistrate Mahadeva Govinda Ranade, was reported by the daily newspaper *Kesari* (in the local Marathi language) directed by Lokamanya Bal Gangadhar Tilak, and mentioned in the *Annals* of the Bhandarkar Oriental Research Institute. It is also mentioned by DK Kanjilal in his *Vimana in Ancient India: Aereoplanes or flying machines in ancient India* (1985). The flying machine, that Talpade had named Maruta sakhi ("the girlfriend of the winds"), went up to about 500 meters, to the great costernation of the British and jubilation of the nationalist Indians who attended; later it was sold by Talpade's relatives to the British organization Raley Brothers (information supplied by P Satwelkar, one of Talpade's students).

How did Talpade come to effect that flight test? Talpade was acquainted with a Bombay industrialist named Poonjilal Giridhar, who had been to visit Subbaraya Shastry at least on one occasion for 2 weeks; when he returned, Poonjilal Giridhar spoke with Talpade, who in turn went to see Shastry and invited him to Bombay; however we do not know the dates of these events and their time-line. It seems that before meeting Subbaraya Shastry, Talpade had read the *Rigvedadic Bhasya Bhumika* and *Rigved Yajurved Bashya* by Dayananda Swami, on the suggestion of his school teacher Chiranjilal Verma. In his commentaries, Dayananda clearly spoke of the existence of space ships and other technological wonders of Vedic India.

Some sources say that Talpade had also studied some manuscripts entitled *Vimanachandrika* by Acharya Narayana Muni, *Vimana Bindu* by Acharya Vachaspati, *Vimana yantra* by Maharishi Shownik, and *Yantra Kalpa* by Maharishi Garg Muni; except for Narayana Muni and Vachaspati Acharya (that cannot be identified easily), Maharishi Shownik could be Saunaka Rishi and Garg Muni could be Garga Muni, both mentioned in *Bhagavata Purana* as great ancient scholars. None of these texts however is available, or maybe even existing. In the list of Talpade's readings we also find one *Brihad Vaimanika Shastra* by Maharishi Bharadwaja, but it is not clear whether this refers to an ancient manuscript preceding the compilation by Subbaraya Shastry or to a copy of Shastry's work.

As we have already mentioned, between 1918 and 1923 Subbaraya Shastry, helped by Venkatachala Sharma, wrote down 3,000 Sanskrit verses and sent copies to various centers of learning, including one in 1918 to the Baroda library and in 1944 to a library named Rajakiya Sanskrit Mahavidyalaya but without references to the place, so it could be the one in Ranchi or one in Bangalore - some critics even put it in Baroda probably confusing it with the one that received the manuscript in 1918. In any case the original manuscript remained "forgotten" in Venkatachala Sharma's cupboard, especially after the death of Shastry in 1941 and until 1952, the year when GR Josyer, honorary director of the International Academy of Sanskrit Research, presented the notebooks at an exhibition of ancient works organized by the Academy at Mysore. The English translation was completed in 1973. The text mentions 97 previous authorities and their works, of which at least 20 specifically speak about space ships, but it seems that none of such texts are still existing in the original version, much less in available translations. The names of the authorities mentioned are almost impossible to identify because they are not accompanied by patronimics or geographical indicators, therefore the "Nathas" listed as Shankha, Visvambhara, Bodhananda, Siddhanatha and their companions could even be disincarnated entities, since the entire story openly revolves around *channeling* (see the section on occultism).

Confusion spreads because many popular writers repeat passages of subsequent works written in English (especially by Davenport and Childress) quoting as a source a "*Rahasya-Lahari and other works, by Lalla and other masters*". The association between "master Lalla" and the *Rahasya Lahari* can easily create misunderstandings, because there has really been a famous Lalla (short for Lakshmi Dhara) who can be identified historically, but he has written a commentary to the *Soundarya Lahari*, a famous work by Adi Shankara, that has absolutely nothing to do with *vimanas* because it speaks of the worship on the Mother Goddess (called *sundari*, "beautiful", from which *soundarya*, "of the beautiful"). On the other hand, the commonly known *Rahasya Lahari* is a very successful series of mystery tales (*rahasya* means "mystery" and *lahari* means "waves") written in the early 1900s by the Bengali novelist Dinendra Kumar Ray, who created the character of the British detective Robert Blake, copying it from the series *Sexton Blake* published in England, to the point of being sued for plagiarism. That *Rahasya Lahari* does not contain any mention of *vimanas* or space ships.

The situation becomes even worse because the text by Subbaraya Shastry largely consists of passages that we could call incomprehensible or quite badly translated into English, if not deeply questionable or even contrary to the general principles of Vedic culture: the lists of ingredients seem to come from the Harry Potter's book of magical potions and include donkey urine, ox bile and other nonsense inviting a *slugfest* from the critics belonging to the mainstream academic world. Among the disconcerting statements, we find that the Lalla Acharya mentioned in the text explains that metallurgy knows 12 types of metals: those extracted from mines are only one category, because there are also those "born from minerals" (although we do not understand how these would be different from those extracted from mines), those "born" from salt, mud, plants, water, worms, flesh, hair and eggs, and those that are "corrupted" which belong to still another category (maybe the rusted ones).

The drawings published in the various post-1973 editions are not helping much, to the great dismay of many Indian researchers who are interested in demonstrating the validity of the ancient Hindu culture. We can mention for example Kavya Vaddadi, an Indian girl who is an enthusiast of the *vimana* idea and who studied aerodynamics at school and built some small papier maché models after Ellappa's drawings, to see whether they were "aerodynamic" or not. Vaddadi founded the VEDAS (Vaddadi Engineering Design and Analysis Services) and is a member of SWASTIK (Scientific Works on Advanced Space Technology Investigations for Knowledge); both organizations are full of good will, ready to be interviewed by the self-declared atheist Giorgio Tsoukalos (*Ancient Aliens*, especially in the episode *Voices of the Gods*, on the assumption that all Gods have never existed except as aliens) and to publish articles on any magazine or internet site, and anxious to cooperate with international "organizations" such as the Italian publishing house Enigma Edizioni. Together with the Enigma director (Enrico Baccarini), Vaddadi has written *Vimanas and the Wars of the Gods*, a book that is defined by Vaddadi herself in an interview for the newspaper *The Hindu News* as follows: "*The book has details on vimanas based on the stories told to children*".

This should already make us understand her level of knowledge and understanding of scriptures and Vedic knowledge, but we went ahead to dig deeper. Our Research Center contacted her by email, and Vaddadi immediately and enthusiastically replied "whatever Baccarini said is all true". We have already examined what Baccarini said, and we have seen it is a bunch of offensive nonsense.

However, Vaddadi admitted that the "reverse engineered models of the *vimanas*" she constructed after "almost 6 years of study", were simply "outer shape 3D modeling, a non-flying static prototype which can be 3D printed and visualise aircraft shape in which the ancient people used to fly". In other words, it is merely a projection of the external shape of the objects pictured in K Ellappa's drawings, just like one could make a clay bust from a picture or painting of a person - real or imaginary it does not matter at all, because the clay bust is just a shape without any functions or content. Yet, Vaddadi's second book is entitled precisely *Reverse Engineering Vedic Vimanas*, which she claims is endorsed by scientists such as one Prahlada Rama Rao of NASA and one GM Nair ex director of ISRO (we suppose the acronym stands for Indian Space Research Organisation).

Here are some interesting quotes from her email:

* "I did not yet investigate this in deep. It depends on the way we can understand the facts. The terms used and interpretation of the texts also depends"

* "It depends on the way we can understand the facts. The terms used and interpretation of the texts also depends"

* "That may or may not be true. Because I met an 80 year old man who says that Rama Ravana never existed, and the Ramayana is astronomy. Someone translated or interpreted wrongly and made up stories. This old man says he invented veda bhasha, which is older than Sanskrit. He says There is no rama, no Ravana, no sita."

* "Ravana and Salva also treated as gods"

* "And coming to religion, I believe that some fake baba type of person came and started religions"

Any further comment is superfluous, because such statements are perfectly clear and give a very precise idea about Vaddadi's qualifications in regard to the knowledge of Vedic culture and the contents of Hindu scriptures.

According to the information published by Vaddadi, one AJ Shaka of the University of California, Irvine, has transformed mercury into gold through an alchemic process requiring 23 hours, although the university does not seem to have given any announcement about the extraordinary feat. Other breakthroughs are presented as more technically inclined: in Varanasi a team of researchers who analyzed the Vedic texts are said to have built a sort of spectroscope named Dhvanta pramapaka Yantra. However, a Dhvanta pramapaka Yantra (the same device?) is presented as "a material similar to glass that is not detected by radars" in another paper published by one Dongre of the Benaras Hindu University, based on the ancient text entitled *Amsu bodhini* (published in 1931). Other types of glass (or maybe mirrors, or spectroscopes, it is not clear) are called Vidyutdarpana, Ravishakti Apakarshana Darpana, Ushna Shakti Apakarshana Darpana and Vakra Prasarana Yantra, but none of them has been constructed yet.

The organization named SWASTIK (that we mentioned earlier) has solemnly announced the "startling discovery" that the Rukma vimana could make interstellar travels by *levitating* with "antigravity electromagnets", that is by using "a simple dipole magnet positioned in the magnetic fields of another dipole magnet, oriented with like poles facing each other, so that the force between magnets repels the two magnets", because "all types of magnets have been used to generate lift for magnetic levitation; permanent magnets, electro-magnets, ferromagnetism, diamagnetism" etc. But this "extraordinary discovery of magnetic levitation" could at most make a small magnetic model float in a small magnetic field to distance itself from another magnet, not from Earth itself. How big and powerful should the "ground magnet" be, to send off a ship into external space against the Earth's gravity pull? And after reaching destination, how will it be able to lift off again (without a similarly large magnet) and return to Earth without being kept out by the same magnet that sent it away in the first place?

Seriously, we cannot blame the criticism by mechanistic academics in front of such pathetic intellectual shallowness. We want to clarify that we are not supporters of the extremist skepticism of conventional academia, as often quoted in the exemple of expert Antoine Magnan, who became famous for declaring in 1934 that according to the laws of aereodynamics, bumblebees should not be able to fly. But honestly we cannot support the dreadfully naive enthusiasts that want us to believe that the authoritativeness of the short and vastly non-translatable descriptions offered by Subbaraya Shastry's text has been sufficiently demonstrated by a small "outer shape" model thrown in a "*wind tunnel*" to see if it is "aerodynamic", under the authority of one Travis Taylor whose identity remains unclear - he might be the *Graduate Research Assistant* at the University of New Mexico School of Engineering that applied for *internship* at NASA as per Linkedin profile, or maybe the *scientist and science fiction writer* who worked at NASA for 16 years as per Wikipedia, both coming from Alabama, USA. Or maybe they are the same person, presented in different ways?

Other technologies mentioned by Vaddadi are the Galileo HAA (High Altitude Airship) with solar propulsion, the military aircrafts such as Mig-29 and EFT that have vocal commands, the R-73 missiles controlled from the pilot's helmet, and the devices with liquid mercury vortex in electro-magnetic field, that can be watched on Youtube. All these, however, have nothing to do with the *Vaimanika shastra* because not even one of the technicians that have built them has ever mentioned such a source - and here we begin to suspect that the participation, support or endorsement by the "regular" scientists mentioned by Vaddadi might only refer to this type of information and not to the issue of Vedic *vimanas*.

Vaddadi also speaks extensively about the materials anciently used for the building of *vimanas*, such as special metallic alloys named as Raja loha, Pancha loha, Arara tamra loha, Tamo garbha loha and Badhira loha, that a scientist named as CSR Prabhu is trying to reproduce - or maybe he has already, but there is no actual information about that. What is certain is that the small models advertised by Vaddadi and Enigma are not made with these metals, and they have never moved by themselves, with or without magnets. Considering that the information about the Raja loha is that it has "golden color", is called "manufactured gold" and is used to build the Rukma vimana, the results of the experiments are quite open to many possibilities.

The list of ingredients to make the Raja loha includes lead, iron pyrites, iron, mercury, 3 types of salt, borax, mica, silver, aconite, benzoin, ammonium chloride, chickpea flour, seawater foam, and a mixture of milk, yogurt, clarified butter, sugar and honey. All stuff anyone can get relatively easily, provided the lab is close to the shore of a particularly active ocean (because of the sea foam, that should probably be freshly collected as it sets in seconds into ordinary sea water) and so we should expect any time some flight demonstration in some coastal city of India. In the meantime, we would like to remain moderately skeptical.

At least Vaddadi says that the reconstruction of this ancient technology is a very difficult job, especially because the materials and ingredients of the lists are mostly unknown: the words can have several meanings or even be merely symbolic, the plants mentioned could be extinct, and nobody can be sure that the procedures have been correctly understood until they give the same results described in the texts. The problem is worsened by the fact that Vedic knowledge has been generally forgotten or almost forgotten, and that the translations presently available are rather pathetic. Vaddadi wishes for the creation of "an army of Sanskrit experts" for a decent translation of Subbaraya Shastry's verses, but our opinion is that even just one could be enough, if only he knew what he is doing and understood the genuine Vedic scriptures to the point of being able to recognize when Shastry's text leaves the acceptable area and becomes mere ramblings of a spiritist medium or clairvoiyant, who "sees" things without being able to actually understand his visions.

The size of the gap between the present knowledge and the level to be attained can be somehow evaluated when we think that even just a few decades ago there were still qualified *brahmanas* who could kindle a fire simply with *mantras*, without matches or gas lighters, while today even the traditional ayurvedic doctors send their patients to the allopathic test lab to analyze blood samples and make electro-cardiograms, and then usually prescribe industrial pills or at best a cycle of laxatives and emetics (*pancha karma*) for any health problem and in any physical condition of the patient. What to speak of the building of space ships or the multiple levels of meanings of the Vedic *suktas*, the vast majority of Hindu scholars is even unable to correctly quote ther text of *Bhagavad gita*, that is the shortest, most famous, most valid in itself, and written in very clear and simple language.

For this reason, Indian researchers continue to seek and offer technological references based on western science: for example the ione engine (mercury based) developed in 1959 by Harold Kaufman at the Glenn Research Center of NASA, and that apparently was further developed into a prototype tested for sub-orbital flight with the *Space Electric Rocket Test I* (SERT I) and then with SERT II, for a total of 8 months. A later version has replaced the mercury (that was liquid) and cesius (solid) with xenon, that is already a gas at ordinary temperatures without the need of heating, although the efficiency of the system is reduced. The xenon-ion-engine has been used for example by the Hughes Research Laboratories (now HRL Laboratories, Malibu California) in 1979 for the SCATHA (*Air Force Geophysics Laboratory's Spacecraft Charging at High Altitude*), and then in 1997 in the commercial satellite *PanAmSat 5*. It seems that similar projects have also been implemented in France with the mercury-ion-engine presented at the international Space Congress, Paris 1959, and the "Fetonte project" of a satellite working with a mercury solar furnace in 1966, also built without any references to *vimana* texts. Therefore there is no ground for the equivalence with the engines or motors mentioned in Vedic scriptures: the *vimanas* could have been much more advanced.

This of course does not mean that the *Vaimanika shastra* mentioned by Davenport in his *2000 BC: Atomic Destruction* and by Childress in his *Vimana Aircraft of Ancient India and Atlantis* is devoid of any value. Certainly it contains many useful ideas that deserve our attention, but it is not a manual for building and driving space ships, as claimed by many alienists. Probably the most interesting aspect is about the famous 32 secrets mentioned at the beginning of the text, that are probably summarized from the "stories told to children", which however does not invalidate the possibility of valid foundations.

The first verse (*sutra*) of Shastry's work recites: *vega samyat vimano anda-janam*, "a vimana is defined by its speed of movement, similar to the birds ("those that are born from eggs"). Maybe here is the origin of the connection that alienists make with birds, but the Sanskrit word used in this verse is not *vi*, but *anda-ja*.

The second verse (*sutra*) adds: *rahasya ajna adhikari*, "one who is qualified knows the secrets"), where *rahasya* means "secret", and *ajnadhikari* means "one who is qualified because of knowledge". Maybe here is the origin of the alienist connection with the imaginary *Rahasya lahari*, also because some authors seem to have taken the verse *Rahasyagnyodhikaaree* as the title of a separate book from which they quote "the second verse", and Josyer's bad English translation adds the idea of "pilot" that was absent in the original Sanskrit, thus skipping the crucial preliminary step of construction, that is also based on the "secret" not revealed in the available texts.

Here is the list of the 32 secrets, illustrated in the clearest possible way:

1. *gudha*, or *vayu tattva prakarana*, by which one utilizes *vayu* to hide the vehicle from sight; *vayu* does not simply mean "air" or "wind", but also applies to the "subtle airs" such as the *prana vayu*, that flows both in the human body and in all living beings, and also in moving water, in the sunlight and so on,

2. *drisya*, or *visva kriya darpana*, by which one utilizes mirrors to see outside the vehicle and to project an illusory image of the vehicle itself for defensive purposes,

3. *vimukha*, by which one emits a cloud of poison (*visha*) to neutralize pursuers,

4. *rupa karshana*, by which one can see the images of distant objects, as for example by television or videocamera with enlargement functions,

5. *stabdha*, by which a cloud of dust (*apasmara*) is emitted to confuse pursuers,

6. *chapala*, by which one can make sudden acceleration or change of course,

7. *parasabda grahaka*, by which one can perceive distant sounds and conversations,

8. *adrisya*, to make the vehicle optically invisible,

9. *paroksha*, to hide,

10. *aparoksha*, to reveal hidden things,

11. *sankocha*, to contract or compress parts of the vehicle,

12. *vistrita*, to expand or enlarge parts of the vehicle,

13. *virupa karana*, to project images (that we could call holograms) of the vehicle,

14. *rupantara*, to project terrifying images,

15. *surupa*, to project beautiful and attractive images to attract attention,

16. *jyotirbhaga*, to project light beams,

17. *tamomaya*, to project darkness,

18. *pralaya*, to disintegrate or project destruction scenes,

19. *tara*, to project stars or a starry sky,

20. *mahasabda vimohana*, to produce a very loud roar,

21. *langhana*, to "jump", not to be confused with *laghima siddhi* or levitation,

22. *sarpa gamana*, that programs a zig-zag course,

23. *sarvatomukha*, by which the vehicle can rotate 360 degrees,

24. *kriya grahana*, to "take what needs to be done", probably a reading of a program like in computers where the expression is normally used,

25. *dik pradarshana*, to see the direction or trace a course,

26. *akasha kara*, to tune in or create the illusion of subtle space (*akasha*),

27. *jalada rupa*, to project the optical illusion of a cloud,

28. *karshana*, to drag along,

29. *rodri*, for vertical ascent,

30. *shaktiakarshana*, to attract energy,

31. *sammohana kara*, to project optical illusions by manipulating energy fields.

Conclusion

As we have already declared several times, we believe that Vedic knowledge deserves a much better treatment than what has been done by authors and researchers in these last centuries. Vedic tradition, and Hinduism that is its present heir, leave lots of interpretation space and allow individual experimentation, and certainly do not order the persecution of dissidents or heretics or blasphemers, but they do not fall into the opposite excess of assigning the same value to all opinions, irrespective of their effectiveness or actual basis.

What enabled Vedic tradition to survive better than any other ancient culture is the system of cross-verification between *guru, sadhu, shastra*, that is between the teachings of one's own personal spiritual masters, the teachings and examples of persons who are universally recognized as situated on a level of knowledge and realization of *dharma* and *vidya* (the *sadhus*) and the scriptures that are universally recognized both by *gurus* and *sadhus*. Scriptures themselves are protected by the same cross-verification system, because each verse must be consistent with the fundamental principles of *dharma* (natural universal ethics) and *vidya* (physical and metaphysical knowledge) presented in ALL the other genuine scriptures.

In this way when a teacher, an authority or a scripture appear in open contradiction with the fundamental reference elements, it becomes essential to get deeper into the search to establish whether it is just an apparent contradiction or it is an actual deviation. In the case of deviation, any authority (*guru*, *sadhu*, *shastra*) must be immediately abandoned, irrespective of its position or social or political power. This is the ideal protection against any dogmatic tendency.

Repeated invasions and aggressions, that were brutal, cruel and diabolically clever, have considerably weakened the social and cultural texture of Hinduism, and although genuine knowledge continues to survive in many individuals who personally have the required qualities (*guna* and *karma*), the conditions in which these persons live and work are becoming increasingly difficult because of global degradation and non-sustainable development.

Even the "Hindu Renaissance" advertised by the Hindu religious nationalist organizations has failed to re-establish the correct parameters of ideology and action, and at this point the only option is to write down the knowledge and the indications for the journey that are necessary to attain realization even at individual level, without a solid social and cultural structure to support us.

A book is sent into the world like a message in a bottle thrown into the ocean, and we never know where it will finally reach, even after our disappearance and/ or the disappearance of the conditions of life that we take for granted today.

This publication of ours could be read by someone who may become in the future an important element in the survival and reconstruction of human civilization: this is our great hope.

If you are interested in understanding the existence of Godhead and the existence of entities that are different and superior to ordinary human beings, your perception ability is strong enough to rise above the level of gross and trivial materialism on which the "weapons of mass distraction" try to keep the public in general into the well-known trend towards the so-called cultural idiotization. Disinformation propaganda can and must be overcome.

There are many things that cannot be explained simplistically with the official version of the academic Establishment, and there are many ideas that not even the most evil powers can suppress or hide from the eyes of the public and especially of those who have the intelligence and determination to search for the proper answers. This is a fundamental law of the universe: there must always be a way out from the rats' maze, although it may be difficult to see or to reach, because difficulties are a necessary test for learning, by which we show our value, first of all to ourselves and to the Witness who lives in the hearts of all beings.

Vedic knowledge, that is the focus of our research and our personal practice, contains a treasure of incredible value in physical and metaphysical sciences, and offers an integrated vision of these two fields, that was lost in the west many centuries ago.

The authors who try to trivialize Vedic knowledge by presenting distorted or false information could be simply ignorant and confused, but it is possible that they could be acting on selfish motivations, more or less deliberately or consciously, or even on more sinister plans. In any case, it is important to alert the public so that disinformation will not cause too wide and deep damages, especially in a delicate historic moment such as the present situation at global level, with huge changes made inevitable by the spreading of the non-sustainable development model through globalization.

Whether we choose to "believe in aliens" or to "believe in Gods", a part of the message is certainly true: we must stop destroying our planet and mankind, and switch to a way of life that is more elevated, more conscious, and in better harmony with the rest of the universe.

It is the second part of the message and its practical application that hide the trap where we should not fall. The sentiments that push us into the trap are excessive respect and awe towards the so-called authorities recognized at social level, the habit to passively accept the version imposed by media and governments, the lack of faith in our own fundamental eternal nature, the pressure of public opinion, the desire for belonging or social endorsement, the fear of taking too much personal responsibility.

Actually it does not matter at all whether we believe in Aliens or Gods, because neither Aliens nor Gods can intervene to save us from ourselves. This is not how the universe works: we must stop waiting or following Messiahs or Saviors or Masters that are supposed to automatically solve all our problems in exchange for absolute loyalty, obedience and worship. History has demonstrated that it is not a good solution.

Not even the violent destruction of the present way of life can be helpful with the application of some sort of global reset from which to start again with a better vision, because what will emerge from global destruction is not the best men but the worst ones, and the needs of mere survival in a disaster environment would soon turn even good men in selfish brutes, incapable of any social, ethical or spiritual order, and uninterested in any higher aspiration.

Vedic knowledge offers us the way out, presenting the Gods as ontological archetypal personalities that each human being can and must realize internally, to become able to participate to the universal consciousness and act accordingly. The genuine *vimanika shastra* also have this purpose. We have seen that technical indications are subordinate to inner realization - that in scriptural Sanskrit language is defined as *mantrika* and *tantrika*.

Without this genuine divine realization, the construction of plasma weapons or space ships made invisible with mirrors or even genujine Vedic technology will be of no help to us, just like it has never really been of help to the various Asuras who used them for purposes that are against the benefit of the universe.

The distinction between Devas and Asuras is therefore a fundamental requisite, a basic teaching transmitted by eternal Vedic knowledge for our education, here and now as well, and not for Hindus only, but for people who identify with any other ideology.

We want to repeat once again that it is not necessary to believe in the information presented in Vedic scriptures, but if you choose to mention them as the source of your information, you need to be honest and correct in reporting their contents.

The author and the Research Center

Parama Karuna Devi was born in 1957 in Milano (Italy) as Paola Mosconi, in a family that was deeply attached to its Longobard cultural and historical heritage. She taught herself how to read at an extremely young age, by watching television that in that period had appeared in Italian homes of middle burgeoisie, especially with cultural programs; she was admitted to primary school one year earlier than normal. The experience of the first school classes, among children who practiced simplest pen skills to start learning the alphabet, reinforced the sense of cultural distance she already felt for her birth family, and stimulated her interest for different and wider horizons that can be freely explored through the magic of printed words. Soon she finished to peruse the two encyclopedias that constituted the only literary resource of the family, and on all occasions she tried to get more books, insisting on titles and subjects that her parents found incomprehensible and disconcerting, such as archeology and oriental civilizations.

In the early 1970s she encountered the "alternative" culture revolution, that had been developing in Italy; she became an activist of ethical vegetarianism and a passionate follower of Indian culture, towards which she felt a strong spiritual affinity and that perfectly answered all her existential questions. Unwilling to submit to the dogma, limitations, shortcomings and prejudice of the academic system prevailing in western culture, she abandoned formal studies after successfully completing her college studies by sitting at one time for several years' worth exams. Instead of engaging in a regular university curriculum as expected by her family, she chose to get deeper into foreign languages and to find a professional outlet that would enable her to become independent under all aspects, and still continue her personal research.

In 1978 she came in contact with the Hare Krishnas (International Society for Krishna Consciousness) and moved into their *ashrama*, where in 7 years she completed the Italian translation of the books by

Bhaktivedanta Swami Prabhupada, the founder of the movement. At the same time, she continued her research on the theory and practice of vegetarian culture, learning the secrets of international cookery from devotees coming from all over the world, and even creating new techniques and recipes (especially in the *trompe l'oeil* category - such as eggless omelette, happy tuna spread, etc) that she presented in a successful radio series, named "Radio Cucina", that has been broadcast nationally for decades by the movement radio, RKC (Radio Krishna Centrale), where she also ran a program based on questions and answers on Indian philosophy. Besides, she actively engaged in the personal service of the Deities of Jagannatha and Radha Krishna installed in the temple, especially during the great religious festivals celebrated in the *ashrama*.

In 1984, after an intense *sadhana* period, she underwent an experience of awareness transformation, in which she recovered many memories of various previous lifetimes and especially the knowledge of Sanskrit, that she began to teach very successfully in the Gurukula in Villa Vrindavana. The journey to India in the same year helped the opening of new channels of awareness and the recovery of other memories; she began to travel alone all over the sub-continent, from the Himalayas to the extreme southern tip of India. She visited Vrindavana, Mathura, Dvaraka, Gujarat and Rajasthan, Ranikhet, Haidakhan, Ayodhya, Varanasi, Prayaga, Calcutta, west Bengal, Tripura, Manipur, Orissa and especially Jagannatha Puri, Tirupati, Kanchipuram and Tamil Nadu, Madras, Madurai, Kanyakumari, Trishur, Udupi, Guruvayur, Mangalore, Bangalore and Bombay, mixing with the local people, attending Hindu temples and entering in contact with many extraordinary personalities. Specifically, she received special blessings from Bhakti Vaibhava Puri Gosvami, Bhakti Svarupa Damodara Gosvami and Fakir Mohan Das, who explicitly confirm her realizations and her spiritual mission.

From 1989 to 1993 she spent some periods in Milan, Italy, where she started the Associazione Culturale Vegetariana and Centro Verde, organizing vegetarian cooking courses and writing several books on vegetarianism. She also cooperated to the translation of several texts of the New Age culture and Indian spirituality, with various publishing houses including Gita Nagari Press and Centro Studi Bhaktivedanta.

In 1994 she settled in Jagannatha Puri, Orissa. She wrote and published *Puri, the Home of Lord Jagannatha* (highly appreciated by local people and at global level), *The Power of Kalpa Vriksha*, and *Prasnottara ratna malika* ("The necklace of perfect questions") which is the translation and commentary to the text authored by Adi Shankara, prepared on the direct and personal request of the then *yuva shankaracharya* of Kanchi.

Under the guidance and tutelage of Bhagavan Mishra (*deula purohita* of Sri Jagannatha Puri Mandir), Jagannatha Mahapatra (*mukti mandapa brahmana* of Sri Jagannatha Puri Mandir), Ganeshvara Tripathi, Simanchala Panda and other representatives of the local orthodox Hindu community, she underwent the traditional purification ceremonies known as *suddhi, prayaschitta, vratyastoma* and *diksha*, that officialized her membership to Vedic orthodox Hinduism, sanctioning her *adhikara* to the performance of traditional ritual sacrifices and direct worship to the Deities. She also interacted and cooperated with the Acharya family (*raj guru* of the royal family in Puri) and with the Rathsharma family (Ravi Narayana and Surya Narayana, the sons of the famous Pandita Sadashiva Rathsharma.

In 1996 she was appointed as a member for the organizing committee for the Gopala Utsava at the traditional Hindu temple of Sakshi Gopala and subsequently she was invited to many academic and cultural events - by Bharatiya Itihasa Sankalana Samiti, Indira Gandhi National Centre for the Arts (IGNCA), Academy of Yoga and Oriental Studies, Utkala University, Jagannatha Sanskrit Vidyalaya, Karma Kanda Vedic Gurukula and Rastriya Svayamsevaka Sangha. Later, between 2014 and 2015, on the request by RSS she worked at starting and managing in Hyderabad, India, a center for the training of activists in the movement for Hindu Renaissance.

In 1998 she participated to the Ratha Yatra of Lingaraja at Ekamra, during which she received important instructions; subsequently she entered various internet discussion groups about Vedic-Hindu Resurgence, where she found ample information to continue her studies on Vedic literature and tradition. She also began connecting this knowledge with the exploration and study of other pre-abrahamic cultures at global level, discovering important similarities and significant connections.

Through the global Net she also continued to research the history of the various cultures of the world, as well as archeology and paleontology, connecting and cooperating with the Resurgence movements of Ancient Religions especially in the Greek, Roman and Celtic area.

In 1998 she started the Jagannatha Vallabha Vedic Research Center, with the primary purpose of producing and publishing literary works on Hinduism and Vedic culture, and to interact with governmental and non-governmental agencies working in the same field. The headquarters of the Center were established in the vicinity of the Jagannatha Vallabha village, in the rural area around the city of Puri.

In 2006 she started a charitable primary school for the village children, named Bhaktivedanta Siksha Niketana, and as Honorary President of PAVAN (a local NGO charity engaged in social work) she organized various programs including free distribution of vegetarian food, construction of wells for fresh water, and seminars on sustainable development and preventative medicine.

In the course of several years she has assisted several persons to explore their karmic journey along multiple lifetimes and to use that awareness for their personal progress in the present time. She has a few students of various nationalities, of whom she takes care in a personalized and direct manner, especially through correspondence (emails) and telephone, restricting personal meetings to a minimum. This choice aims at dedicating as much time as possible to literary and spiritual activities, and to discourage the development of material and superficial relationships based on the physical contact and social conventions rather than on a genuine spiritual exchange and true teaching work, that must focus on what each student knows and learns and his/ her personal progress in the development of knowledge and realization.

After completing a detailed *bhasya* (translation and commentary in 18 volumes, plus appendixes) of *Bhagavad gita*, a volume with the translation of all the 108 *Upanishads*, one *Introduction to Vedic Knowledge*, and a comprehensive summary of *Bhagavata Purana*, she is presently engaged in two major multi-volume projects, one on *The Awakening of the Mother Goddess*, and one on *The life and teachings of Krishna Chaitanya*.

Work is also going on for the reprint of her old books on vegetarianism, a Manual for traditional religious ceremonies in orthodox Hinduism (3 volumes), a book on sustainable development, an essay on Vedic social system, and a new edition on the book on Jagannatha and Puri.

To contact Mataji Parama Karuna Devi:

E-mail: jagannathavallabhavedic@gmail.com

+91 94373 00906

www.jagannathavallabha.com

18140177R00155

Printed in Great Britain
by Amazon